Phil Taylor

THE POWER

Phil Taylor
THE POWER
My Autobiography

Phil Taylor with Sid Waddell

CollinsWillow
An Imprint of HarperCollinsPublishers

First published in 2003 by
CollinsWillow
an imprint of HarperCollins*Publishers*
London

© Phil Taylor 2003

1 3 5 7 9 8 6 4 2

A CIP catalogue record for this book is
available from the British Library

ISBN 0 00 716821 7

Set in Meridien with Spectrum MT display
Typeset by Rowland Phototypesetting Ltd,
Bury St Edmunds, Suffolk

Printed and bound in Great Britain by
Clays Ltd, St Ives plc

The HarperCollins website address is
www.harpercollins.co.uk

All photographs courtesy of Phil Taylor with the
exception of the following: **Empics** 16(br);
Getty Images 8(t), 9(b), 10, 11, 12, 13, 14, 15(t, ml & mr);
James Horton/Rex Features 8(b); **Mirror Syndication
International** 6(b); **Neil Tingle/Action Plus** 9(t);
Steve Daszko 4(t), 6(t); **The Sentinel** 5(b), 7(tl & b), 16(bl).

For Yvonne, Lisa, Chris, Kelly and Nathalie,
and grandson Mathew

CONTENTS

Acknowledgements ix

Prologue 1

Chapter 1: Potteries and Poverty 7

Chapter 2: Hard Graft and Soft Knocks 18

Chapter 3: The Generous Crafty Cockney 28

Chapter 4: World Champion 40

Chapter 5: The Greatest Final 53

Chapter 6: Darts in Turmoil 71

Chapter 7: The Haunted Pub 89

Chapter 8: Switch on the Power 100

Chapter 9: Equal with Eric 108

Chapter 10: Joining the Legends 125

Chapter 11: An End to Strife? 137

Chapter 12: Making More History 152

Chapter 13: A Right Barney 169

Chapter 14: On the Shamrock Oche 185

Chapter 15: Danger: Athlete at Work   199

Chapter 16: My Darkest Hour   213

Chapter 17: Showing Them How   224

Chapter 18: The Appliance of Science   242

Chapter 19: The Holy Grail   262

Chapter 20: Have Board, Will Travel   271

Chapter 21: Team Taylor   287

Chapter 22: Part Exchange   295

Chapter 23: Staggers into Saggars   303

Career Highlights   319

Index   325

ACKNOWLEDGEMENTS

A lot of people helped me on this book. In particular I'd like to thank the following: Dick Allix, Eric Bristow's former manager; Tommy Cox, who was my manager for many years; Gayle Farmer, media and communications manager of the Professional Darts Corporation; Olly Seton of the GEM Group; Dave Lewis, landlord of the Saggar Makers pub; Richard Lowy of Unicorn Products; my manager Barry Hearn; Pat Williams, who provided all the statistics; George Sutherland, my right-hand man; Jody Malam, Simon Cole and John Gwynne of Sky Sports; Giles Smith and Kate Battersby; Tony Wood of *Darts World*; and Michael Doggart and Tom Whiting from HarperCollins*Publishers*.

Finally, many thanks to my pal Sid Waddell – and his wife Irene – for labouring long and hard at pulling the various strands of my life together.

Phil Taylor
Bradwell, Stoke-on-Trent
September 2003

History! History! History!

It will not surprise anyone who knows me to learn that my 24 hours of darting destiny in Blackpool in the summer of 2002 started with a Chinese takeaway.

A friend of mine had just made a big order of ribs and chow mein over the phone. My share of the bill was a tenner. I gave him a £20 note, and as he reached for the change I said, 'No, put it on me getting a nine-dart finish against Chris Mason tomorrow.' Talk about tempting fate. Nine darts is the minimum you can go out from in a game of 501 and there was £100,000 for anybody who could do it in the Stan James World Matchplay Championship.

Cut to the Winter Gardens the following night and my quarter-final match. The 2,500-strong crowd at the Winter Gardens is one of the most colourful, knowledgeable and vocal in the world. They come dressed as Vikings and, in the case of 'Tarts for Darts' – secretaries from Essex – in St Trinian's outfits. As Chris and I waited for our theme tunes to ring out I spotted a flag with the logo 'Boss Pie Bashers' and a line of lads in T-shirts reading Dart Vader, Lee Van Dart and even John McEnDart. What is more, even before they could see me hundreds were shouting, 'Come on the Power, give us a nine-dart!' If I could it would bring a lot of pleasure to a lot of people, especially the Taylor family, now sitting expectantly in the front row.

I had heard a whisper that commentators Sid Waddell and Dave Lanning and a syndicate of the Sky crew had a 25–1 bet on my doing the nine-dart. I hoped my mate had got odds as good.

The players' marshal, Bobby Bourn, asked us for the umpteenth time if we needed the toilet. Normally I'm off out the back with a minute to go. But I felt great. Suddenly it was show time. Chris walked to the stage with lights flashing, dry ice swirling and music loud enough to take the roof off. Then 'I've Got the Power' started and the thunder and lightning effects kicked in. I started to walk to the stage and the hair I had spent an hour making look sleek was switched and slapped cock-eyed despite my having a Panzer division of bouncers carving a track through the crowd.

As we threw our practice darts there were more screams for a nine-dart. I was totally and absolutely relaxed. In the first round I had beaten Shayne Burgess

10–0 with an average of 101. Then I took out Kevin Painter 13–6 with a 104 average. I was hot and so was Chris. With Sid bellowing in the commentary box, 'Something in my Geordie water tells me something special will happen tonight!' and Dave agreeing, we got to the end of leg four all square at 2–2. All that was in my mind at that point was putting in a heavy leg so that I would go into the three-minute commercial break at 3–2. But the gods of darts thought otherwise.

My concentration was focused by his first throw of 135. I needed at least 140. I did better: 180. Sid screeched to emphasize the drama, 'You've heard of painting by numbers, well this is darting by numbers!' Chris opened the door for more from the Power with only 41. Again I was thinking of 140 – at least. In went 180. There was now no pressure at all on me. I didn't care what Chris got. You could have heard a flight drop as I stepped up to the oche. I didn't think of the nine-dart, the money or the eight times I have missed it on Sky. Just hit the bloody thing, I thought. The crowd gasped as I hit the 60. Sid was as quiet as if commentating on a royal funeral. 'Oh my goodness, two darts for history . . .' The next one hit the middle of the treble 19. Sid hissed 'History'. Then double 12. Sid was reduced to a mere gasp. 'History!' Sid for once was not exaggerating; it was the first-ever live nine-dart on British television.

I turned to look at a sea of white betting slips being waved in ecstasy. Chris gave me an almighty hug. I ran to the edge of the stage and asked my mate if he'd managed to get the bet on. He gave me the thumbs up and mouthed '10–1'. I'd stuck another daft tenner on myself, even though I thought the odds were rubbish. My poverty-ridden boyhood in the Potteries was coming out; I was thinking about £200 when there was £100,000 waiting for me in a steel cage in the Stan James VIP suite.

It is strange how fate deals you different hands; one minute you are on top of the world and the next facing a black pit of despair.

In the three years before hitting the nine-dart in Blackpool I had played the best darts of my life. But for much of that time I had been carrying a burden that almost led me to sit in my car and let the exhaust fumes do their worst.

My nightmare started at an afternoon darts exhibition in Scotland in October 1999 where I met up with two women darts fans. This began a saga that ended in my being found guilty of indecent assault in March 2001. My face was plastered all over the papers.

Like a fool I had tried to hide the whole business from Yvonne and my family. Their reaction was one of massive shock followed by bitter remonstrations. For a time I thought Yvonne and I would split up. In the dark days after the conviction I sat in our home late at night and seriously considered suicide.

The shame did not end there. At the end of 2000 I had got a letter telling me I was to be awarded the MBE.

But in May 2001 I got another letter; because of my conviction I would not be receiving the honour.

These are the highs and lows in the life of the 10-times World Champion – there were plenty of others in between. What you will read is how those moments drove me to write and rewrite darts history in so many ways.

CHAPTER 1

Potteries and Poverty

I am very proud of the little patch of England in which I was born and raised. I may be one of the only thriving business concerns still going in the Potteries, but there is still plenty to see in the five towns. At the end of March 2003 my wife Yvonne and I took my friend Sid Waddell on a tour of our world. Now the experts say that the Stoke-on-Trent area gets less sunshine than anywhere else in Britain, as little as one day per year. Well, let me tell you, in spring 2003 we had two sunny days and the local sights looked smashing, even the mouldering brickwork of the old bottle kilns.

We started our trip at the palatial Taylor residence in Bradwell, just down the road from the crematorium. My success at darts has meant that we now live in a nice detached house – though I'm not sure what the neighbours think of the Taylormobile, my camper van, being parked outside. The first landmark we point out to Sid is the Cricketers Arms in May Bank where I was the landlord for seven years and where I had one hell of a lot of trouble with a ghost called Charlie.

We then took the winding road to Longton and Sid was almost weeping with nostalgia when we got near the bus station. He jumped out of the car and stood like a pilgrim at a shrine in front of what looked like no more than a disused office block. 'Look at the sign!' Sid yelled. Above him was a bright plastic sign with a jester logo that said 'Jollees'. This was indeed Mecca to Sid and millions of darts fans between 1979 and 1985. The nightclub, which closed down long ago, was the home of the Embassy World Professional Darts Championship where my mentor, Eric Bristow, held court 'poised like a preying mantis, face fit to grace an Etruscan coin', according to Sid. We told Sid we had never been able to afford to go.

Down the bank and under the railway bridge we went to find yet more nostalgia and darts history for Sid. The Crown pub, he told us excitedly, is where the players stayed during the Embassy Championship of 1979. The great Cliff Lazarenko ran the 24-hour bar after being eliminated and David Coleman swapped sports stories with the darters until the early hours of the morning over a whisky or two. Yvonne and I shook our heads; all that had been happening in our home town and us without two pennies to rub together. I told

a window cleaner but a sander. We could not have afforded either. There was no electricity or running water, so we had to wash in the yard.

After I was born my mother had three miscarriages in four years, and following the last of these she had to spend a week in hospital recovering. One neighbour came in to look after me, one to make up my dad's sandwiches for work, one to clean up and another to do the shopping. Dr Beveridge told my parents that they were lucky to have me and advised them to have no more children. As it was, when I was about three they nearly lost me as well. Both my parents went out to work, so they had a woman in to look after me. One day I wandered off to play in Tunstall Park, where there were two lakes, the smaller of which was about six feet deep. I managed to fall into this lake, and splashed around helplessly before somehow doggie-paddling to the bank; I scrambled out and walked home soaking wet. When they got home dad and mum went mad, even though I protested 'I got out by myself'. After that my mum stayed at home for a couple of years until I could look after myself.

My mum had various jobs: on the toffee counter at Woolworths, at Kent's porcelain factory and at another works where they made pottery 'whimsies', birds and animals. My dad was at the sharper, and heavier, end of graft in the Potteries, and I have inherited his work ethic. When he left school he went as apprentice to a builder, but was laid off once he qualified for proper money. So at the age of 18 he went to work for Daniel Platts, who made floor and quarry tiles. Dad's job was back-breaking. Each day he had to shift tons of clay in and out of kilns by hand. He had to lift big wet squares in and then take the dry ones out. This work kept him whippet-thin, but my mother begged him to give it up and get something lighter. After seven years dad took a lighter job with another tile company, H. and R. Johnson's. He would never take a day off work even if the weather was bad or he was ill.

As if this was not enough, when I was four and mum went back to work, he used to get up at 6.30 and take me to my grandma's house two miles away. Our 'transport' was an old black police bike with only one pedal! Thank God the road to granny's was mainly downhill. I would sit on the handlebars and dad would crank away in lopsided fashion. Then I would be deposited in front of the fire and would immediately go back to sleep.

My mother was very clever at making ends meet, but even so the wages coming in only balanced our out-goings for about five days of the week. To get money for the other two she and I would go and collect copper wire from derelict sites and sell it for eight shillings a load. She also took me in an old pushchair to a colliery waste tip to scrabble about for coal to bring home and burn. When that ran out my mates and I would often rip down railings from allotments to use for firewood.

At Christmas I got new things like a rocking horse or a pedal car; this was financed by weekly payments into a club. But mum's biggest coup was to get a television into a house that had no electricity supply! This is how it happened. My mum ran a catalogue and the lady next door was a member, paying five shillings a week. A deal was done. A bloke brought the telly and asked where to plug it in. Mum said, 'Just leave it there in the corner near the wall.' He did this reluctantly, looking around in vain for sockets and leaving the house shaking his head. Then dad and I ran a wire through from next door and we hooked our telly up. In return mum let the neighbour off her payments for a few weeks.

Before I started school I met the first ghost in my life. After the ceilings were fixed I used to play upstairs in the bedrooms at our house in one of two halves of an old wardrobe laid out on the floor. I called it my boat and would dress up as a pirate with a little plastic sword and a captain's hat made out of Stoke's *Evening Sentinel*. Suddenly in the other half of the boat/wardrobe would appear an old man in a suit, smiling at me in a kindly way. I saw the ghost several times, and when my mum mentioned it to the neighbours they said it was probably the previous occupant. Unlike Charlie, our later ghost at the Cricketers, this one did not chuck ornaments around.

When I was nearly five we moved to a semi-detached house at Mill Hill, near my grandparents, where we had the joys of electricity and hot water.

My dad was a keen sportsman. He loved cricket and was a good pace bowler. One of the masters at his school

13

would have him bowling flat out at a wall for ages. And his accuracy with a ball, which I have inherited, came out in a most useful way. When I was about eight, Dad took me to a fair and made a beeline for the coconut shy. He paid his money, got three wooden balls and took off his jacket. He then flexed muscles that Bruce Lee would have been proud of. Next thing I knew dad was marking out a run-up! A small crowd gathered to see this strange person in action, but they were soon applauding. Dad hurtled up to the line and never missed. He toppled three coconuts with three balls. The stallholder came out and took the sand out from under the coconuts, thus making them harder to knock off. This did not put dad off. He struck again, even breaking a ball or two. We had to make him stop, and persuade him to change some of the coconuts for dolls and ornaments or we'd still be eating them yet.

We had the odd day trip on a bus to Blackpool, thanks to a five-shillings-a-week club my mum joined, and once dad got £41 for 23 points on the football pools and we went to Butlins for a week. All this frugality and ingenuity was fine, but just after my seventh birthday mum went over the top. She was a dab hand at cruising round jumble sales and coming back with clothes for me, or woollens she could unravel and reknit. Now at first I thought the white wool thingy with tiny blue flecks that she was knitting was going to be a scarf, but I was wrong. It was a pair of trousers and a waistcoat. Naturally I refused point blank to put them on. She pointed out that it was winter and the white wool was extra warm and durable. Then she looked meaningfully at the clog she often hurled at dad and me if he was grumpy or I hadn't made the tea for them coming home from work. So I wore the white outfit all the way across Abbey Hulton, the roughest estate in England and known to us as 'Comanche Country', to my auntie's house. I was punched and kicked at by a gang of thugs shouting 'Sheepdog, sheepdog!' That's maybe why in Blackpool in 1996 I went on television feeling no qualms about wearing a green spangled cape and looking like Snoop Doggy Dog.

My playing-out clothes were second-hand, but my school clothes were new. When I needed new shoes my mum would go to see Mrs Lawton, the lady who ran the local pay-as-you-go credit club. I got new clothes from Naylor's in Tunstall where you could pay for your stuff weekly.

Just up the road from our house were the clay hills where we would hack out coal with axes. I did this with Fitzroy Ellis, my best mate, the only black lad in my school, who lived with his one-legged granddad, the local cobbler. His family were very poor and Fitzroy had to fill sacks of coal to sell rather than to use. We would try to drag him away for a game of football but he would stick at it. He scrabbled and hacked for coal until he was 14 and had the best physique of any of us. Nobody bullied Fitzroy.

Like Robbie Williams, I went to Mill Hill infants

school, but I didn't make much of a mark at schoolwork or sport. I usually ended up around the middle of the class when we had tests. I liked playing football, but I was inclined to be fat so I always persuaded mum to write me notes to get off PE. I didn't want to go in the showers and be called a little fatty. But all that changed dramatically when I was 13 and at secondary school. In the summer holidays of 1973 I stopped being an ugly duckling and became, if I do say it myself, a bit of a swan. Some of the lads didn't recognize me, and girls who had said 'Piss off, fatso' a few weeks before were giving me the eye.

Seeing that I had trimmed up, my mum said she would give me no more notes to avoid PE so I bit the bullet and hurled myself into football and cricket. Like my dad I could bowl accurately, even if my pace was not as good as his. And at home playing on a crushed-paper board and later on a real board behind the kitchen door, I made the discovery that I was good at darts. My parents often played together and I joined in. Once again, there was an omen. When I was 13 I was chucking darts in the games room of the Ryan Hall Catholic Club, where Robbie Williams did some of his earliest boyhood gigs. An old man came over and watched me play for five minutes. 'One day, son, you will be the best darts player in the world.' Then he just turned and left and I never saw him again.

I have to admit that I only liked one thing at school apart from sport, and that was geography. This was because my uncle Ray had emigrated to Australia a few years before and I liked looking at maps and working out where he might be. Otherwise I thought school was a complete waste of time, and I couldn't wait to get out when I was 15 and earn some money.

CHAPTER 2

Hard Graft and Soft Knocks

My first job after leaving school was delivering meat by bicycle for a butcher. I didn't last very long since I have to admit I was not very conscientious. The people at the shop would wrap the meat in brown paper and carefully put the address on. But by the time I had made a few deliveries the blood would have soaked through all the parcels and made the next few addresses unreadable, so I sometimes took the meat home and we had it for dinner. Not surprisingly there were complaints, and I left.

My next job was as a trainee electrician at Wolstanton Colliery. This was not very convenient because it involved taking two bus rides from home. But it wasn't long before a brighter prospect came up. The husband of a lady my mum worked with was in the sheet metal business at a nearby works and he got me a start as an apprentice. At first I was little more than a fitter's mate. I would go out with an experienced worker and we would install metal dust-extraction ducts into factories. There was a lot of dirty air in pottery factories so there was a big demand for ducts. We also installed machine guards. It was hard work and it involved being outside in all weathers. But the one accident I had was all my own fault. I was up on this roof wearing bell-bottoms when I tripped on them, fell through the roof and only saved myself from a nasty fall by grabbing a bracket and swinging like a monkey. All this for £12 a week. But the good thing was that the job had perks or – if you like – scams. We worked a lot at the weekend when some of the factories had only skeleton staffs, so when we working in cake or biscuit factories we went in with empty tool boxes and loaded up. I remember once getting a haul of 100 Penguin biscuits. Now this was not just devilment or because we were poor; mum had been losing weight and dad and I were worried. So we made her pick up a Penguin every time she had a cup of tea and she began putting the beef back on.

About this time I had my first experience of serious darts. Though he was a quiet, hard-working fellow, my dad Doug went out to the pub more or less every night. He could not bear sitting around in the house. Our son Chris is exactly the same; after a hard day's work he'll smarten up and go down the Saggar Makers pub – another landmark in the Taylor family story – for a couple of pints and a game of pool. Dad didn't really go down to the Riley Arms in Tunstall for the drink; a couple of pints would last him all night. He went for the dominoes and a game of cards called 'high and low jacks', but most of all for the darts.

When I was 17 I joined him. Dad was a good-standard pub player and possibly would have made super league, and take it from me you had to be good to win a game at the Riley. The A team was always top of the Smallthorne League and there was intense competition to get into their two lesser teams. There was always a tense atmosphere round the board even on non-match nights. Whenever I went to try to chalk a game there would be a list of 20 people waiting to play, so you could sometimes wait over an hour before you touched the chalk, never mind your arrows. Then, when you did get on, you were shaking with nerves. The winner stayed on, so if you lost you were at the back of the queue again. From the start I rarely lost, even when I played A team players. And I was full of myself. I used to shout, 'I don't know how you lot are top of the league when a kid like me can beat you!' But I was too young to play in their teams, even if they had asked me.

I was so keen I used to go to another pub round the corner where the board was less used and practise before going to the Riley. My dedication paid off and before long I was playing darts for money. One of the stars at the Riley was Kenny Massey, a Staffordshire county player. He was a superb player but a very bad loser; if he lost he would jam his darts in his pocket and storm out. But on a good night he would fling a dart at a double and turn to shake your hand before it plopped in. His mates told tales of Kenny playing at home on three practice boards at the same time and doing all kinds of fancy shots. He and I teamed up to play money matches and he did well out of it; I didn't do so well. Kenny would put up a £50 stake and we'd play a couple of lads at singles. If we won, Kenny would pocket £45 from our opponents and slip me a fiver. But I never thought it was unfair. A fiver was a lot of money to me then. I took quite a lot of stick at that time as a 'cocky little git', which I suppose I was, but the experience was priceless. In fact if I had stuck to serious darts at 17 instead of waiting until I was 25, I would have been a millionaire years ago. What stopped me? Easy answer – girls.

My puppy fat was gone now and I decided to get in shape. I was a big fan of the Incredible Hulk on television and I wanted to acquire the physique. So I went to a gym regularly and worked hard on the weights. I got up to a good standard, bench-pressing 300lbs and doing curls with 400. I would look round at others at the gym and always try to work harder. I set myself challenges. I didn't want to put on weight but I did want to look like a macho man.

It just about worked. The main stomping ground for me, and half the kids in Tunstall, was the Sneyd Arms which had a disco on most nights. The music was Slade, Mud and the Bay City Rollers and the place was always packed. The police used to raid the pub often, knowing that a lot of the clientele were under age. My friends and I would rush into the ladies' because the coppers wouldn't come in there. I was very proud of what I called my 'pulling suit' – a gleaming white three-piece with flares, just like the one John Travolta wore in 'Saturday Night Fever'. I reckon it was the only one in Stoke-on-Trent!

Then one night I saw a vision in an expensive black velvet jacket and I walked nonchalantly over to her, employed no chat-up whatever, and kissed her on the cheek. Her name was Yvonne Rawlinson, she was 15, and she lived a couple of miles away. Later on I drove her home in my battered Hillman Imp, which, she admitted afterwards, made a bigger impact on her than my pulling suit.

We began to go steady.

A few months before I met Yvonne I had changed jobs. I had left the sheet metal job and begun an apprentice-ship with a firm called Vanroy. This involved work on lathes and milling machines and, though it was boring, paid well; I got about £40 a week. And, just like my last job, there were perks. I would hide a plastic bag under my machine to catch brass or bronze filings, then I'd sell them on to a dealer. I would have been sacked on the spot if I'd been caught.

The firm sent me to college to learn the theoretical side of the job and I had trouble from the start. I joined a course that had already been running for three months, so it took a bit of catching up. I suppose I asked one or two daft questions in my first couple of days and some of the class, who were a rowdy lot, and a few of the teachers thought I was having them on. My first fight was actually with one of the teachers! It happened in my first week as we were about to watch a film show. Some of the class were larking about as usual and I was eating crisps when the teacher came in. He ignored the others, made straight for me and told me to stop eating the crisps. He grabbed me by the throat and pushed me up against the wall. I saw red, had a go at him and pushed him down some steps. Then I was picked on by two gobby lads, but I soon shut them up. I threatened one with a mallet and gave the other a good hiding. Not bad going for a bloke supposed to be studying the finer points of health and safety in the workplace! At the end of the course I passed all the exams.

I stayed at Vanroy for two-and-a-half years, then in 1980, when the firm were making people redundant, I got an opportunity to move. My uncle Ray had come back from Australia and was working as a ceramic turner. He had worked for Wedgwood, making candlesticks and vases. Now he got me a job – my third apprenticeship – as a turner with A. G. Hackney. The job involved making bedposts, beer-pump handles, toilet-chain handles, furniture castors and insulators for electricity pylons. This was my working world for eight-and-a-half years before I took the plunge as a professional darts player.

*

Yvonne and I had been courting steadily since our meeting at the Sneyd Arms in 1977. She left school at 15 and went to work in a pottery factory as a fettler, trimming the rough edges off clay and sticking handles on teacups. At the time she was making more than me so she usually bought the drinks. We went to pubs and the discos at the Sneyd. I got on well with her parents, Alf and Dorothy, even though Alf's obsession with motorbikes could prove a bit of a problem on occasions. Once he insisted on stripping his bike down in the kitchen and a spark flew off and set the place on fire. The Rawlinsons, just like the Taylors, had a dartboard in their house and we had many happy hours on it. Yvonne was quite a good player – a fact that would come in very handy later on. In the early 1980s we used to watch darts on television and I have to say that I did not like Eric Bristow; he was far too cocky and arrogant. My favourite was Dave Whitcombe: good-natured, lovely thrower, equable temperament. I also liked the style and gentlemanly bearing of John Lowe. Another favourite was Cliff Lazarenko, though I wished he could be more consistent.

With the help of my parents, Yvonne and I got the odd caravan holiday. It often cost no more than £50 for the pair of us and dad and mum to have a week away. And it was due to a cock-up on our holiday to Devon in 1981 that I had my second stab at darts. We got lost down some leafy lanes and couldn't find the caravan our friend was loaning us. So in desperation we saw a sign for a holiday flat to let. Fate stepped in again. Over the road was a small holiday camp where we went for a drink. In the bar was a poster saying that Peter Locke, built like a brick wall and a top Welsh international, would be coming along to play all-comers in a day or two. He would give challengers a 500-point start in a game of 1001.

'I'm going to have a bit of that,' I said to Yvonne.

'But you're not a proper player,' she said.

I winked but did not let on about the money games at the Riley Arms. Dad and I practised like mad and we were in the front row of an audience of only about 10 waiting for Peter on the night. Suddenly a bloke got on stage, welcomed us, and said that Peter had been forced to cry off, but another Welsh star, the diminutive Chris Johns, would stand in. There was no mention of any 500-point start. It didn't make any difference because I got up and wiped the floor with Chris. I beat him three or four times and got a bottle of wine each go. He took it very well, even buying me and dad a pint. A week later another member of the Welsh international team walked in, Dap Cairns, all black beard and twinkling eyes. I beat him in the first game, then we had to have a break because Dap said he had been playing in the wrong shoes! He went out to his car and came back wearing his famous 'daps' – white plimsolls painted black, stuck together with ancient pieces of tape. These were what he wore to play for Wales when the regulations forbade white shoes. They obviously helped him.

Out of the next four games I won only one. But taking six bottles of plonk from two stars I had seen playing darts on telly was not a bad feat. Destiny must have been driving me somewhere.

Pretty soon I had other things on my mind, as Yvonne was pregnant. Six weeks before the baby was due we decided to have a short holiday in Blackpool. I had bought a cheap Volkswagen Beetle with a dodgy starter motor, and I often had to bump start it. We hadn't booked anywhere, so we just pitched up at a guesthouse and settled in. At about 5 o'clock in the morning Yvonne's waters broke and she was having really bad pains. I ran down the stairs shouting 'Hello!' and trying to find a light. I felt my way in a panic through the pitch darkness to reception and managed to grab a phone. I dialled 999 and they asked, 'Where are you?' I had no idea of the guesthouse name or even the street. I told them to wait. Clad only in my underpants I ran outside, clocked the name of the guesthouse, then ran up to the end of the street to see a sign that said Alexandra Road. I raced back and gave the information. The ambulance came and took Yvonne off. I got dressed and found the car wouldn't start. I tried pushing and bumping but it was no good. Eventually a milkman helped me out, and I set off hell for leather to the hospital.

Our daughter Lisa was born that night and she only weighed 4lbs 4oz. Yvonne had to stay in hospital for three weeks and I drove over to visit as often as I could. Eventually Chris came along in 1983, and that was a normal birth; Kelly was born prematurely in 1989; and Nathalie was delivered by Caesarean in 1992. Apparently Yvonne developed gestational diabetes for the duration of her pregnancy when carrying girls. We have always been grateful for all the help we received, so I have made a point of doing several charity exhibitions for the baby-care unit at the North Staffordshire Royal Infirmary.

When Lisa was born in 1982, Yvonne and I lived in separate houses with our respective parents; now we had to get a home to bring up a family. We chose a tiny terraced house at 35 Blake Street in Burslem, mainly because it was only 150 yards from my work. It was nearly a year before we could afford to put the deposit down and move in. We had saved carefully to pay the £800 needed and the £200 solicitors' fees; the price of the house was £8,000. In those days we were so poor I paid 50 pence a week into a club and got pans and crockery from a catalogue.

CHAPTER 3

The Generous Crafty Cockney

I have already mentioned the importance to Stoke and its people of having Jollees as the home of world darts. But you can hardly imagine what it meant to the local darting fraternity when Eric Bristow, the Crafty Cockney, shifted his roots from Stoke Newington in London to the Potteries. It was almost like Jesus relocating from the Holy Land to Milton Keynes.

And the lad did it in style. On arriving in Staffordshire he signed up for the local county darts team. He won the 1985 Embassy World Professional title – his fourth, and the last to be played at Jollees – and together with his partner, local lass and world-class darter Maureen Flowers, opened a darting palace called the Crafty Cockney in a working-men's club in Smallthorne, a couple of miles from our house. Dozens of coaches used to descend on the club regularly and young darters would pour out to play on the excellent boards there. Eric could usually be glimpsed in his palatial private snooker room, surrounded by his glittering trophies. But, always one of the lads, he would mooch out, fag continually on the go, and have a throw with the punters and pull a few pints.

It was on a night in June 1985 that our lifelines crossed.

Yvonne and I were having one of our rare nights out. We were chronically short of money, and so we headed for the Crafty Cockney because it was close and the prices were reasonable. Eric and Maureen were on the stage doing an exhibition. He did nothing up on that stage to alter my opinion, formed from the telly, that he was a bighead. He was showing off all the time and apparently had no respect at all for his opponents.

'I could beat him,' I told Yvonne confidently. She looked at me disbelievingly. She was not convinced even after seeing my exploits against the Welsh stars. But a few weeks later she presented me with a set of darts for my 25th birthday.

The darts were thick 28-gram Leighton Rees style and I tried them out for the first time in a pub in Biddulph. My opponent was a local star who had qualified for a television event. I beat him hollow over two games and he could not believe that I was not a regular league player. He chucked his darts away and slunk out! Boosted by this triumph I started playing on Tuesday nights with my dad. Later on I joined the team at the

Burslem Central working men's club. My captain, Alan Bridge, a Staffordshire county player, advised me to get more match practice by playing more nights a week and to set my sights on the county team.

At this point it will be as well to explain the route to the top in darts as it then was. In 1973 a Londoner called Olly Croft, who ran a successful tile business, decided to try to do for darts what Alf Ramsey had done for English football in 1966. Together with a group of friends he started the British Darts Organisation, at first a non-profit-making body, designed to systematize the game and develop an inter-county competition. By 1986 the BDO had come on in leaps and bounds. They had sponsors for open tournaments and the county system fed international teams whose matches appeared on the BBC. They also organized the Embassy World Professional Championship. My aims were simple – play well enough in super league matches to get into the Staffordshire team. It was going to be a tall order; Eric Bristow, Les Capewell and Lionel Smith spearheaded a very tough outfit. I would have to play out of my socks to get in.

I was determined to reach my full potential as a darts player. A mate of mine who worked in a furniture factory made me a proper oche – in our bedroom! It had lights from a car-boot sale and a wooden mark from an old settee on the floor. It was perfect, except for Yvonne trying to read as darts whizzed past her left ear. And I often stubbed my toe on the mark as I went to the toilet in the middle of the night.

I worked on my game for hours. I'd just have cup of tea after work and haul myself upstairs. I knew I was good enough to be a top player and that practise I must if I wanted to be the best. At the start of matches I used to tense up when 'Game on' was called so I tried to simulate match attitude in the bedroom. I imagined I was playing a tough opponent. I'd do two hours of practice on bulls and high finishes, then take on Eric or Jocky Wilson in the world finals. I would try to do 12-dart legs to beat them. I would pop downstairs, watch a bit of telly, then make myself rattle in four 180s before bed. I cursed and swore at bad shots I made, but I also maintained relaxation. That's the paradox of top darts: you must be tense enough to compete but relaxed enough to play your normal game.

All the practice worked; after a few months with Burslem, Alan Bridge asked me to join the crack team at a local pub called the Huntsman. This was the best super league team in Stoke. We won the merits, the pairs, the lot. Alan would buy me the odd drink on match night because I was skint. And, bless his heart, he went on doing this until I was in the Staffordshire A team and ranked number 10 in the world.

But I had a major problem; I could play great in practice but I couldn't consistently take my form through to match night. My captain told me he couldn't keep playing me and he made me reserve. Then he hit me with another bombshell. He said he might even put my dad in the team instead of me! As it turned out he put a lad called Andrew Bulger in my place. I knew he was nowhere near as good as me. I seethed at the put-down but practised harder. I swore it would never happen to me again, and it didn't. Looking back it seems like just the sort of psychology that Eric Bristow used on me later. It was not long before I got my hands on a trophy, the singles merits in the Smallthorne League. I danced all the way home with it.

Eric Bristow, who was to alter my life completely a few months later, entered my world again, albeit briefly, when I was playing for the Huntsman in the Crafty Cockney. I remember whispers starting as I was poised to throw. 'Brissy's here. Brissy's here.' You'd think Robert Redford had walked in. I felt certain he would watch me and I got butterflies. He had, and still has, a charisma that I have also observed with Ally McCoist. There can be a thousand people in a room and they all stop and stare when Eric swans in.

Throughout the 1986–87 darts season I consolidated my super league form. I regularly took chalks to watch how other players went for certain finishes. For example, if you need 91, is it best to go for treble 17 or bull to start the shot? At first I was completely bamboozled, thinking that there was no way I'd master the shot-outs. But I stuck in and learned all the scoring patterns. It is rather like trying to handle a fast car; after a while it doesn't seem so fast. John Wilkinson, landlord of the Huntsman, was very good to me and not only with the darts. He let me work behind the bar at weekends to make a bit of extra cash to pay my darts subs, and I was allowed to take home pop and crisps for the kids. John also sponsored me for my first big-money tournament, a £1,000 knock-out at Burslem. This happened in the summer of 1987 and John put up my £50 entry fee on the understanding that I would halve my winnings with him. Sad to say I did not win the tournament, but my name did get spread around for two good reasons. Chris Gee, landlord of the Swan pub where the tournament was to be held, had me knocking on his door 10 minutes before opening time, waving my entry money and racing to the practice board. Among the stars who came to play were John Weatherall of Staffordshire and England international John Cosnett. I drew the latter and he got me mad when he sneered at the fact that I was 'not even a county player' and asked who he would be playing next. I showed him just what I was made of; I beat him 3–0 over the best of five legs. Sadly I went out soon after that. The eventual winner was Steve Gittings of Telford.

I was on top of the super league averages by now and thought that surely the county call-up would come soon. I had heard whispers that I still didn't have enough experience. Then, in September 1987, I got the call to play for the Staffordshire B team against London. Yvonne and I were so badly off that we had to do the whole thing on the cheap. It was the first time either of us had ever stayed in a hotel, and we sat around gawping and making sandwiches from the packets of bread, butter, cheese and ham we had brought with us. I didn't socialize in the bar, partly because I couldn't afford it, but mainly because this was a first step in my dream – to play darts for a living. Under the eagle eyes of Eric Bristow, Les Capewell, Harry Augustus and my mate Alan Bridge, all waiting to play for the A team, I won my match 3–0 in style, despite nerves and severe stomach cramps, and took the man-of-the-match award. From that heady moment I would never look back.

They put me in the Staffordshire A team for the next match and I did not let them down all season. In fact Eric and I won the man-of-the-match awards most weeks. For him it was just another bauble to put on a low shelf at the Cockney, but for me it was worthy of the top shelf at Blake Street. Much more important, there was pound-a-man kitty that went to the man of the match, and £12 was a godsend to us Taylors.

I have vivid memories of some of my best county performances and of Eric, now becoming a friend, studying my every shot. I don't honestly know if in the autumn of 1987 he had any plans to act as a mentor or a sponsor, but he was always giving me tips on scoring and the right attitude I would need for top performance: 'Never give a chucker an even chance – bully them every shot.' I think he liked my bubbling aggression and the fact that I cursed myself when I threw a bad shot.

In a county game at the Crafty Cockney against Glamorgan, with Leighton Rees, Ceri Morgan and Peter Locke in their side, I was drawn to play Welsh international Dai Furness. I got the impression he thought a nobody like me would be a walkover. He was wrong. My cocky grin would have done Eric proud, and so would the scoreline of 3–0 in 14, 14 and 16 darts.

Then, as now, I relished really tough matches. Against the West Midlands I drew Steve Beaton, who had not lost a match for several seasons. I beat him 3–0. You had to play well every time out. As well as Glamorgan, one of our big rivals was London, with Dave Lee, a giant with hinges tattooed inside his elbows, and Alan Glazier, one of the first touring professionals, in their ranks. Surrey also had a crack squad that included Bob Anderson, alias the 'Limestone Cowboy', Peter Evison and Richie Gardner, who threw tiny darts the size of builder's nails. I remember playing Peter Taylor of Surrey at Lakeside, Frimley Green, which from 1986 was the home of the Embassy World Professional Championships, despite having tonsillitis. I was going to cry off but Eric advised me to get up and throw. 'The illness will give you that bit of edge, mate.' He was not wrong: I took Taylor apart with four 180s.

Then there began an avalanche of good darts that led to Eric offering to sponsor me on the world professional circuit with his own money. I had heard a whisper that Maureen and Eric were planning big things for me while playing in the British Open just before Christmas 1987. A lad called Roy Emery mentioned it in practice, but mentally I filed it away and thought nothing more about it.

Early in 1988 I won the sub-area finals of the *News of the World* competition at the Crafty Cockney against a field that contained some county players. Then I went to Tamworth for the next stage, but was beaten by Wayne Jones of the West Midlands. It was after this setback that Eric Bristow came up with the offer that would radically change my whole life. He was willing to put up thousands of pounds to sponsor me round the world as a professional. 'Pay me back if you win anything,' was all he said. It would mean taking voluntary redundancy from work and a big step into the wide blue yonder.

My job was very easy, especially with my background in engineering. I would be given a drawing of, say, a beer-pump handle and told to make 1,000. I would order up the clay, then set the sizes required on the lathe. The expertise came in allowing for what would happen when the clay was fired. In my early days I learned a life lesson. I made a bad job of some stuff and Derek Jones, my manager, gave me a right bollocking. 'You've dropped a total codge here, young Taylor. I want no more of it.' I swore to myself there and then that there would be no more mistakes, and I never made any more. It was precise work and I was meticulous. After eight-and-a-half years I was a making about £200 a week. But it did not hold the future that I wanted for myself.

The prospect of being a professional darts player was overwhelmingly attractive. Before I made my big decision to take voluntary redundancy, I looked around at my colleagues. There were six other turners and the youngest was about 50. I'll end up just like them, I thought. I want out. The lads at work thought I was mad. They told me there was no way I was going to beat Eric, Jocky Wilson and John Lowe. 'Just watch me!' I told them. The boss, Geoff Bloor, who had invested a lot of time and money in me, said I was making a big mistake, but he told me I could come back to my old job any time. On the other hand John Wilkinson, who used to play football for Preston, said I was doing the right thing. He had gambled on a sporting career and again on running a pub. When he started at the Huntsman he had no carpets. He was one of my earliest sponsors.

But my biggest vote of confidence came from Yvonne. We talked about the offer for weeks and she told me to go for it. She knew I was a hard worker and, if it all fell to bits, I would get another job locally. But even if she had not believed in me, I don't think she wanted to be the one who held me back from my dream.

At the end of February 1988 I took the big step. I took voluntary redundancy and got about £2,000, half of which we used to pay off our debts. Then I signed on the dole. I got £74 a week right through to winning the Embassy in 1990, because most of my darts earnings were going straight back to Eric!

My first bit of 'professional' action came by pure chance. I went down to Jollees one day to watch a tournament in which my county colleague John Weatherall was playing. He was beaten by a young lad and came off the stage frowning deeply. Maybe I should have kept my distance, but I went over and said 'Unlucky'. He turned very nasty and gave me a mouthful of abuse. Then he challenged me, saying he wanted to play me for big money. I said no problem, even though, as usual, I was scratting around to pay my league subs. He suggested we play for £200 a side. I could not back down so I agreed. 'You haven't got £200,' he snorted. 'Oh yes I have,' I said, then shot off to ring Eric. 'Er, John Weatherall wants a money match and . . .' I got no further. 'How much?' I told him £200. 'Ring him back and tell him you'll play for £500,' said Eric, confidently. I did this, but John wasn't having any of it. So we stuck with the first challenge and agreed to play for £200 a side. We played the first match at John's pub, the Nelson, in Biddulph and the return, for the same money, at the Crafty Cockney. I won each one easily and Eric handed me £200.

Despite now being a professional darts player, I still made extra efforts to earn some money on the side. Since 1985 I had supplemented my wages by buying old Vauxhall Vivas or Princesses for £50 and doing them up. I continued this after I turned pro. In fact this little line of extra work was the reason I spent some of my first prize money on a shower. I never stopped. Work all day on the lathe, shower, work on cars, shower, play darts, shower. I also had a job delivering plant hire for a few weeks.

Yvonne and I took another big step. On 9 April 1988 we got married. It was at 10.30 in the morning at Hanley Registry Office. Dad and mum were there and so was Alfie, Yvonne's dad; her mum, Dorothy, couldn't make it because she had a bad back. And then – at 2 o'clock in the afternoon – I played a county match at the Crafty Cockney while Yvonne stayed at home with the kids. The wedding resumed in the evening with a reception at the Huntsman. The Staffordshire players were there, and I admit that I had my darts in my pocket all the time – but I resisted the urge to pop down to the bar for a throw during the speeches!

CHAPTER 4

World Champion

One of the main reasons Eric Bristow became my mentor and sponsor was because of all the hours of practice I put in with him after he was affected by dartitis in early 1988. Dartitis is like the yips in golf, and means you cannot let go of the dart at the optimum moment. It hit him very suddenly and like a ton of bricks. 'One day I got up, tried a throw and realized I couldn't let go of the bloody thing! I was gutted. I thought the only world I had known since I was 11 was gone,' he said at the time. Maybe he believed that helping, coaxing, cajoling and even humiliating me as his protégé would make him find his own way back into that world. Who knows?

My other way of practice was a little bit less intense. Yvonne was not a bad player. She usually hit one 60 each time to the board. We would play all different games at the oche in our bedroom and the loser would make the tea or wash up. We even played a form of 'strip darts', which usually ended with Yvonne losing all her clothes. Maybe that's why we have four kids!

I celebrated the start of my new career by taking the Burslem knock-out title. Once again there was a top-class field. Paul Reynolds of Yorkshire was coming, along with Brian Cairns of Wales, Ronnie Peel of Lancashire, my old rival John Weatherall, Brian Langworth, a brilliant veteran from Sheffield, and Steve Gittings, the holder. I started by beating Gittings by 4–2, then I beat Ray Battye of Yorkshire 5–2 with a 99.3 average. And in the final I beat John Weatherall – again.

I was on fire on the dartboard at this time. I had moved up to fifth in the national rankings and there was talk of my playing for England. My dad drove me to Skegness for the Lincolnshire Open. We had to leave Burslem at 4.30 in the morning, but it was a success-ful outing. I threw the winning dart and picked up the first prize of £750 at 7 o'clock. The money came in very handy and proved that I was starting my new career well, but what was really making me buzz was the thought of going abroad for the first time; to Finland, Denmark and Canada. This was all thanks to Eric's sponsorship.

The way it worked was simple. For tournaments abroad Eric's agent, Dick Allix, would send me an airline ticket, make the hotel arrangements and pay all my entry fees. These would all be billed to Eric. In return

I would hand over all my winnings from these tournaments to Eric. The system would last until such time as I could pay my own way round the world circuit. It was a great gesture by Eric but, as I soon discovered, he got his pound of flesh in his own pointed way. My domestic winnings such as the Lincolnshire and later Derbyshire Opens, where I won £500 – the first time I ever saw £50 notes and where I upset my mum with some bad language on the oche – were my own. I kept mum sweet by buying her a new coat out of my winnings.

A few days later I was with Eric on a plane to Scandinavia. And what a contrast in the two styles. Eric had the seat back and was sleeping just after take-off; I ran around the cabin like a first-time tourist taking pictures of everything and everybody. I even snapped the wing of the plane! Sad to say my excitement and nerves lasted on to the oche in Finland and Denmark. I got nowhere. But thanks to a bit of top psychology from Dr Bristow I came really good in Canada.

Eric did not like rushing things at major tournaments. He liked to get there early and acclimatize. So we found ourselves in Monkton in Canada with some time to kill before the Canadian Open. We practised all day, then Eric said 'Let's go to the pictures.' So we did. We sat like two kids eating crisps and popcorn watching 'Rambo' one night and Arnold Schwarzenegger the next. I relaxed completely and came of age as a professional.

In the early rounds I beat established professionals Keith Deller, World Champion in 1983, Denis Ovens and

Mike Gregory. Then I disposed of Chris Johns 4–0 in the semi-final. I reminded him of the matches for bottles of wine years before and he laughed. My opponent in the final was Bob Anderson, and I thought he would make a game of it. As it happened, the final was played very late and Bob was looking tired. I won 5–1 and was dis-appointed not to do a whitewash. Eric's work on making me a darting bully was paying off. I was trembling with excitement as I took the cheque for $5,000.

I had it in my hands for all of three minutes. Eric was waiting as I stepped off the stage and he took the cheque away from me. 'Payback, my son, first instalment.' I was happy; the win got me eight world-ranking points and put me on top of the rankings. I had paved my way to the top tournaments on television and that was where the big money was. Over the next 18 months Eric laid out about £8,000 on me and I paid it back from singles, pairs and mixed-pairs matches on the world circuit.

At first I had really disliked Eric's image. He was very cocky and aggressive when he played darts. And away from the board he still says and does things I do not like. But I know that he has been generous with his money to other players as well as me. Overall, he and I became like brothers. And how can you hate a bloke who pockets your winnings and then takes you out for your first taste of lobster! That's what he did in Canada.

But probably the worst aspect of the sponsorship arrangement was yet to come. Eric never let me forget about our deal. I would be sitting at a tournament having the odd drink with the lads and he would shout across the room, 'Get off your arse and get practising, Taylor, you still owe me thousands.' It was very humiliating, but off I would go to practise. If I rang him and said I'd lost in a semi-final, he would tell me to ring back when I'd won a final. In this way he was very like my dad, who used to chide me if I missed a session at the weights in my teens. It was callous but it made me a winner. Eric did not teach me how to play darts, but he certainly did teach me how to win.

On the lighter side, a few days after my win in Canada Yvonne and I went to Lakeside in Surrey along with 64 other darting couples to play in the Hayward's Pickles mixed pairs. We got ninth place and prize money of £150, which as usual we invested in something for the house. This time it was a video player.

Over the next 18 months I consolidated my reputation at county level and on the international scene. I went to the Unipart British Professional tournament in Redcar, where I had a bit of a run but played badly and lost to my early idol Dave Whitcombe. I did well in the Denmark Open, the North American Open and the British Open. The last competition was played only a few days before the Embassy and, despite an attack of tonsillitis and a high temperature, I reached the last 16. I had success in mixed-pairs matches with partner Sharon Colclough, also from Staffordshire. Together we picked up the North American mixed-pairs title in Las Vegas. I had Sharon to thank for pointing out in this period something that had upset my parents for a long time – my occasional bad language while playing. I was definitely being too aggressive, shouting at my darts good or bad, a bit like Eric, and was gaining a bad reputation. Sharon gave me a bit of good advice: 'You don't need to carry on like that, let your darts do the talking.' She was right, and I still cringe at the memory of being a bawler.

Then began, though I didn't know it at the time, the run-up to my wildest fantasy.

I had qualified to play in the 1990 Embassy World Professional Championships at Lakeside. The very name is the stuff of darting legend. At the first championship in Nottingham in 1978 Eric, the favourite, was unceremoniously dumped out in round one by the slow-playing American Conrad Daniels. The mighty Leighton Rees took the title against John Lowe. A year later, at Jollees in Stoke, Lowe reversed the roles and become champion. 'And when Lowe gets home to Clay Cross there'll be a reception as if the Ayatollah Khomeini had walked into town,' was Sid Waddell's immortal punchline. In 1980 Eric showed Bobby George the way to go home and then gave him a kiss. Jocky Wilson was a flamboyant winner in 1982, and in 1983 Eric let in the 100–1 outsider Keith Deller when he decided, for some reason, that the rookie could not get 138 with three darts. He learned his lesson, and Eric wrote his own legend when he took the championship in 1984, 1985 and 1986.

I was twitching to get into this action. I had been to

the famous venue a couple of times and hoped that I would not be overcome by the unique atmosphere. In fact I wrote down my impossible dream. Just below the section on the official biography where it asked for occupation – 'Unemployed engineer' – there was a space for your ambition. In it I wrote: 'To meet Eric in the final and win 6–5 in the tie-breaker.' You don't have to be Charles Dickens to have great expectations. And amazingly the dream came true, but in two separate parts: in 1990 I met Eric in the Embassy final, and two years later I played a successful 6–5 final to beat Mike Gregory.

For three weeks before the tournament, due to start on 5 January, Eric and I practised together at the Cross Keys pub in Northwood. We even practised on Christmas Day for three hours when the pub was closed to the public. I got on his nerves from the very start. I would often practise in carpet slippers and I would sip nothing stronger than cups of black tea. Eric preferred his fag and a few beers. We played some games with sets and some with just legs, and at one stage I was ahead 17–0 on matches. But this did not worry Eric. He loved it up on the stage with all the cameras and he played better up there. Eric and Maureen were no longer together but she still took a strong interest in my progress. Both of them loaned me videos of my opponents. My friend Dave Gibson drove with me to the Lakeside and I kept telling him I was not going just for fun. I was determined to win.

My first opponent was the very talented Australian Russell Stewart and I beat him 3–1 in sets. I was not sure about Sid dubbing me the 'Crafty Potter' on television, but at least it was better than always being referred to as 'Eric's sidekick'. A lot of players, including Jocky Wilson, didn't like me at first because they thought I would be as arrogant and cheeky as the Cockney. Mind, Eric was always telling people that I would kick their arse on the board, so perhaps it was natural to think I was his clone.

Next I put out Dennis Hickling of Yorkshire 3–0. Then I had a fantastic game against Ronnie 'Pancho' Sharp of Scotland, who had beaten John Lowe earlier. Next I faced literally a giant task in the semi-final. Cliff Lazarenko was an England international and a former winner of the British Open. On the day of our match there was the traditional sponsors' lunch which Cliff and I and all the players attended. I picked at the food and went off to practise at the end of the meal. I noticed Cliff having a pint or two and showing no sign of moving to the practice area. Something told me that he was not going to beat me. This was the era when lads like Cliff, Jocky and Eric had a few beers before the match. They and many others still do. But I feel that era is over and that hungry lads who play without drink are the future of the game.

In 1990 I was very hungry. I hammered Cliff by 5–0 in sets with an average of 100.5. Next stop, my dream, was Eric in the final. There was £24,000 waiting for me and half of Stoke had backed me for the title when my price was a very attractive 125–1.

It certainly wasn't a classic final. Eric played superbly but he was not the force he was in the mid-1980s. He had struggled valiantly with dartitis and his personal life had been in turmoil. Overall I think he was not a hungry player any more. He had a lot of money and a good business going at the Crafty Cockney. On the other hand I wanted it desperately and was very ambitious. You don't hang about for £24,000 when you've been collecting £74 a week on the dole. I also wanted to pay Eric back for the humiliating comments.

We shared the first two sets, then I beat him easily by 6–1. Whenever I saw the 60 bed blocked I went straight and true into the big lower trebles. I knew I had to keep the pressure on Eric as, even with his problems, he never quits. I had played him once before in the British Open and was leading 2–0 but then he hit back like a rattlesnake to win 3–2. My average was 97.5, which became the benchmark for many triumphs since. I also fired in a 12-darter of 136, 136, 180, 49. I scored eight 180s in the match and did a 170 finish. I had played it exactly the way Eric had taught me; like a bully. He shook my hand but did not say a lot at the end – or for six months after. Knowing him he was off practising like mad for the return match.

At exhibitions now I am often asked why Eric became my mentor and sponsor. The answer is that when Eric first saw me play he said it was like watching a mirror image of himself. I shared his arrogant, aggressive approach to the game. He drummed it into me that nobody remembers runners-up, that 'winning is the greatest medicine known to man' and that you had to punish every single mistake. As Dick Allix, Eric's agent, put it, 'Eric nurtured the pup until he saw it was ready to hunt.' But Eric's dad George, who taught Eric to play and count as boy, had a slightly different cast on events. He said to his son, 'Never teach somebody to take your job.' I had now completed my fourth apprenticeship – in winning world titles.

My relationship with Eric Bristow was at times stormy. In the 15 years we have known each other I reckon we have had four or five major fall-outs. These never happened during the thousands of hours we practised together. On those occasions we went at the game hard and then shook hands and went our separate ways. The bust-ups usually came when Eric was at a tournament and lost to a player he did not respect. He would get generally nasty and insult me. I suppose it was due to the pain of losing and I was an easy target because of our player/coach relationship. The result would be several weeks of not speaking to me, then he would sidle up after I'd lost a match and he'd tear strips off me: 'You haven't been practising, you idle git. Get off your fat arse.' He would by now have conveniently forgotten our quarrel.

Eric wanted me to win all the time because he felt his own reputation was on the line. He was my mentor and went round telling everybody I could beat them hollow. In the early years I don't think he thought I would get as good as I did, but at the same time he wanted me to keep going from achievement to achievement. It was as though I was living the legend that he had been robbed of by dartitis.

Eric and I never lived in each others pockets. He was not the type to ring up and suggest a meal or a beer. We were friends through darts. We are also very much alike as people. On the surface he is a brash Londoner and he is definitely much more street-wise than me. I was never an in-your-face person, though I was aggressive when I played. What makes us alike is the fact that we are both only sons. I firmly believe that only children are lonely. You have to make up things to achieve. I used to bowl a cricket ball for hours pretending I was famous. I thought I would be popular if I was famous.

I work hard to do my job right and keep my sponsors happy, but still the shadow of Eric lurks. When I lose I think, 'Hell, I've got to face Brissy', and I avoid him for days.

There was no wild celebrating after my first World Championship win; no champagne or lobsters. We have never been big on merry-making in our family, thanks to years of a very frugal lifestyle. I felt obliged to go to the official meal and I made a short speech. Olly Croft, general secretary of the BDO, who organized the tournament and was England manager, told me that my win was a great incentive to young lads coming on the scene. I didn't say anything to him but I hoped the England call-up was now in the bag. The only sour note came from John Lowe, who told me that I was lucky and would never win the world title again. Maybe it is just jealousy, but John, who I respect for his three World Championship wins, seems reluctant to give me credit.

We had a very quiet night at the hotel and next morning I was flushed with embarrassment. There was a crowd gathered to see me off and I was ashamed for them to see the World Champion's car. It was a battered old Princess I had bought for £30; it even had holes in the doors. I thought, 'Oh shit, wait until they see us rattle off in this lot!'

The next few days were sheer bedlam in Burslem. Blake Street was awash with reporters and newspaper cameramen. Our little house was turned upside down by the television people, taking down curtains and moving the ornaments and furniture for better shots. I got a personal letter from Sir Stanley Matthews congratulating me as another Stoke lad who had made good. I also got a card from Tony Knowles, the snooker player.

But the thing that tickled me most was the reaction of the Stoke public. My win in the £1,000 Burslem tournament six months earlier had received a lot of publicity, so half the town had got a bet on me at 125–1. I remember one little old lady hugging me in the street because she had won over £600. My friend John Wilkinson had lumped heavily on me round by round.

He knocked on my door and showed me a brand new £10,000 car. 'You bought me that, bud,' he said. 'And I'm taking the family to Florida with the change!'

That's the sort of thing that makes you a local hero. Everywhere I went for weeks folks were thanking me for paying for their carpet, washing-machine, even their gas bill. I took the trophy down to Port Vale's ground and paraded it on the pitch.

There was one bloke in Stoke who did not get swept up in euphoria. Alec Hancock, Maureen Flowers' father, asked me to take the Embassy trophy round to the Crafty Cockney to show the customers. I could hear the noise of a massive crowd as I walked down the corridor. I was shaking and the lid on the trophy was rattling. The doorman gave me a dour look – then asked me for the £2 entrance fee! Eventually the Embassy trophy did come to stay at the Crafty Cockney, because Maureen Flowers became my manager and displayed all my trophies there.

CHAPTER 5

The Greatest Final

I was now ready to take the Phil Taylor World Champion show on the road for the first time as an exhibition player. Around 1976 Alan Evans and Alan Glazier had paved the way for this branch of professional darts and there was good money to be made. The mercurial Evans used to knock about in a mauve Daimler and entertain the public for £70 a time. He would get to somewhere like Blackburn or Bristol and play the best 15 players, throwing bull finishes or double doubles to entertain the audience. One Christmas at his home club in the Rhondda valley he threw three bulls to finish on 150. Glazier was called the 'Ton Machine' because of his remarkable consistency on the 100, and his party piece was to hang a Polo mint on a string, let it swing and pin it to the bull. Other players like Cliff Inglis would throw sharpened builder's nails and hit 100-plus shots. At his exhibitions Eric Bristow even used to sell best Stoke dinner plates with his Roman profile on them. Everybody ended the night with a question-and-answer session with the audience. This would usually include a few digs at rivals. Oh yes. And Jocky used to wave his false teeth at the crowd as his final flourish.

You will read later about my attempts to spice up my exhibitions, but I was pretty tame at first. Indeed, in the beginning much of the fun was caused by us getting lost. I remember trying to find a pub in Eastleigh near Portsmouth. My driver and I stopped to ask directions from an old man. He stood up and pointed firmly to his right. For a long minute he puzzled, mumbling to himself. Then he raised his left hand and said 'That way!' We could not stop laughing. On another occasion we asked a man 'Which way is the Gravesend Boat?' He pointed and off we went. After a mile we found ourselves at the dock, looking at a ferry which indeed went to Gravesend.

On the serious side, I changed managers. Maureen Flowers didn't really have the contacts to advance my career, so I turned to Tommy Cox, a genial but extremely shrewd Geordie, who was managing Jocky Wilson and a string of other players. Tommy had been a Northumberland county darts player and was involved in event promotion and sales of darts equipment, as well as management.

Tommy and I first met at Redcar during the British

Professional Championships of 1988. We were all staying at a hotel in Middlesbrough and Tommy gave me a lift back in an extremely fancy Volvo. I was very impressed, and told him that some day I would have a car like his. I think it sparked something in his mind. He must have realized that I was not merely daydreaming.

We had no more contact until the Embassy World Championship of 1990 when Jocky was the defending champion. I remember Tommy wishing me good luck for my semi-final before he left Frimley Green to go home to Whitley Bay.

In April 1990 I decided that Tommy was the right man to manage me. I rang him up at home and he said, 'Phil who?' We still laugh about it. I said that I wanted him to manage me and he was very blunt about his approach. He said that I had to make it clear to him exactly what I wanted from a career as a professional player. He needed to know what I wanted to attain. I think he wanted to know how deeply I yearned for success. He insisted that Yvonne come with me to a meeting because 'she will be the most vital part in whether you succeed or not'. A few days later Yvonne and I met Tommy and talked over the arrangement at the Moat House Hotel at Haydock Park racecourse. We settled on a deal, and Tommy spoke on the phone to Maureen. She was happy to move aside.

Tommy pulled no punches in identifying my big problem. I had won the World Championship at probably the worst time I could. It was in between the good old days of the 1980s and what Tommy and others hoped would be a renaissance of the sport. But for the time being the game was in a deep trough with very little television coverage and we were desperately in need of new sponsors. A few years back an Embassy win was a meal ticket to people like Keith Deller, who had founded a career on a single victory. Tommy Cox told me that building my career would be a long, hard process. He also revealed he was part of a group called the Darts Council who were pressing the British Darts Organisation to buck up their ideas and become more professional. He and other people in the darts business were not prepared to watch the game die. You will read later how this pressure group became the World Darts Council and reformed the entire sport.

I joined a sizeable stable of players. Apart from Jocky, Alan Warriner, Mike Gregory, Jamie Harvey and Peter Evison were all managed at some time by Tommy. For some reason we got a lot of work from cider companies. Tommy used to come on the road with us and we did several multiple exhibitions.

When we were together, sitting in motorway service stations, it became obvious that I was 'the unknown World Champion' and it made me frustrated and upset. People would crowd round Jocky and clamour for his autograph, and ignore me. Tommy was right. I had picked the wrong era to burst on the scene. This went on for three or four years, even after my second dramatic Embassy win.

The point was that now just about all the television

showcase events had vanished from the screen. Throughout the 1980s you could make a name for yourself
on several tournaments on ITV, and the home internationals and the British Professional Championship
were on the BBC. The Embassy was the Blue Riband of
the circuit. It was no wonder that the likes of Alan
Warriner and myself became despondent.

What made it even worse was that the old stagers
were the ones who got on other television shows that
were not actually competitions. Eric, despite dartitis, and
Jocky, because he was an icon, were always popping up.
We considered ourselves 'the nearly men'.

A story from our early days with Sky will illustrate the
problem. In 1994 our first WDC World Championship
had a round-robin format in the early rounds. In fact
the organizers were not even sure that 24 players would
turn up because the BDO was exerting such pressure
against the event. Jocky was down to play on a Thursday
afternoon, and he was a big name. Roger Moody of Sky
rang Tommy Cox saying the producer of the Sky coverage had outlined the schedule to him and they wanted
a change. They wanted Jocky on at night. Tommy told
them he could not make the change. But Roger was
adamant. They wanted Jocky on at night. Tommy was in
a doubly difficult position; he was not only the tournament director but also Jocky's manager. He pointed out
that if he agreed, it would mean some players would
have played two games before Jocky even played one.
Roger's last point was the clincher. 'Look, we've taken

a big chance on darts. Since the year dot Rangers and Celtic have played their derby match on New Year's Day. This year they are playing on Thursday the third – because we want them to!'

This was part of the 'nearly men' syndrome. Although at the time I had twice been World Champion, Jocky was still the bigger draw. Now Tommy and I had to work together to build me a solid professional career.

1990 was a dream year for me. I entered 50 competitions and won 48 of them, and I was capped by England.

But before playing for money or glory I played a very special charity exhibition. It was for the North Staffordshire Royal Infirmary special baby-care unit, because without them we might have lost our first two daughters.

When I got the call to play for England I decided to be big enough to forget the fact that they had not called me up in 1988 or 1989 when I was high in the world rankings. I was invited to join the squad for the home internationals at Lakeside in April. I was really chuffed and wanted not just to represent my country but to be the best player. I decided to splash out on a brand-new white jacket – just the job for sporting an England badge, I thought. It was only the second jacket I had ever had. I also bought some red trousers. I stood on my bedroom oche admiring myself in the mirror. Smashing. Sad to say this was not the regulation gear and did not please Olly Croft, our manager.

The England team was a cracker, full of names guaranteed to bring the fans in: John Lowe, Bob Anderson, Cliff Lazarenko, Steve Beaton, Ronnie Baxter, Peter Evison, Richie Gardner, Dennis Hickling, Ray Battye and Eric as captain. Still, there was a lot of tension in our camp, since we all knew what a ruthless lot the selectors were; one bad game and you could be out. I recall Martin Adams, who was later to become one of my top rivals, burying his head in his hands when he lost. 'They'll never pick me again!' he cried. I had no such worries. I won my games and the man of the match award. I played Peter Masson, the Scottish captain, and I really got to him. Although I had stopped shouting at my darts, when I threw badly I moaned. In my quest for perfection I would mumble away to myself. It would happen if I hit two 60s and then got sloppy with the third dart. It drove Peter to distraction. 'Don't you ever stop moaning?' he asked as he gave me a lukewarm loser's handshake.

Before the great dispute that was to split darts right down the middle, I had a couple of fulfilling years playing for England. Later in 1990 I was chosen for the elite four-man England squad to play in the Europe Cup in Malta. The other members of the team were Eric, John Lowe and Bob Anderson. We were expecting a bit of decent sunshine but it poured with rain and the streets were flooded. The event was held in a gloomy old Second World War prison that had been converted into a sports hall. Again I found my best form. I won the

singles, and the pairs with Bob Anderson. This was just
for honour, but being a professional now I was happy to
win the Malta Open singles against Steve Brown, and
the pairs with Steve Brown. I also dropped in lucky with
a local taxi-driver. I said to this lad that I would need
ferrying around quite a bit and slipped him £10 sterling
the first day. Next morning he was outside my door first
thing and he led the cheering at the darts. Apparently a
tenner a day was good wages.

Playing for England was an honour but, because of all
the travel and buying a uniform, a costly one. There
were some expenses but they didn't cover your outlay.
Some of us were professional players and we did our bit
for England when we could have been playing exhibitions. This is one thing Olly Croft seemed to take insuffi-
cient account of when the schism happened in 1992.

Flying high on confidence and practising religiously,
I was unstoppable on the domestic and foreign fronts.
In Jersey and the Isle of Man I beat Baxter in cracking finals. I won the Finland and the Denmark Opens.
I went to America and, despite the best-of-three-legs
formula, won the North American Open. The British
Pentathlon, a mixture of darts disciplines, fell to me with
a record number of points. At Oxney, near Watford, in
an exhibition I hit 28 180s in 14 legs of 1001. I topped
the year off by taking the World Masters. So why did I
not take the 1991 Embassy title in my stride? Answer:
overconfidence.

I went into the World Championship absolutely smoking. I was in the best form of my life. In practice I was throwing between 30 and 40 180s per session. Eric had a massive bet on my winning the final. Sad to say, once I got on the Lakeside oche, the same nerves set in that had scuppered me in Scandinavia in 1988. I had left my best form on the practice board. The 180s would not go in and my mind started doing somersaults. I had the strong feeling that after my magic year most of the crowd wanted me to lose, to see me knocked off my perch. Also, relaxation at the big moment only comes with experience. I was a hunting dog all right, but at Lakeside my bite was missing.

For the record, I beat Martin Phillips of Wales 3–1 and Tony Payne of America 3–1, before going out to Dennis Priestley 4–3. Mind you, my tournament average was 97.4, compared to 93.5 when I won the year before. So that was some consolation. In the final Dennis beat Eric 6–0, and scored 25 180s in the competition. I liked his style. Like me he preferred cups of tea to pints of beer, and he relaxed by going to his room to catch up on 'Coronation Street'. It was not long before we teamed up and began splitting our winnings. No wonder; we were soulmates.

I was very keen to do well on the exhibition circuit and always got to the venue around 6 o'clock for a start at 7.30. I would set up the gear myself; a free-standing frame, lights and board. Then I would set about entertaining the public the way I thought they wanted to be entertained. Fourteen of the best and the bravest would have assembled to play me, and some had a game plan. Some of the good players wanted to go on early and try to catch me cold. The point was that I was never cold; I had been practising while they were still having their tea. So what the public got from me in my first few years on the exhibition circuit was World Championship final darts, or as Sid Waddell put it at Blackpool years later, 'the nearest thing you will see to public execution this side of Saudi Arabia'. I was planting 20 or so 180s per night. The competitive mood caught on; I would offer lady players a 300-point start in 1001 and they would say 'Not likely!' At the time I reckoned that was what they wanted to see – top pro darts. But later on I realized that it might be impressive, but it was all shade and not enough light. The audience needed a more entertaining display.

But even in the early days, when I was not too self-confident, I would go on the microphone at the end of the night and answer questions. Some were good fun. How much does Jocky drink before a game? What is Eric Bristow really like? What do you think of Bobby George? I'd give a few jokey answers and make some serious points. But if the questions got too personal I would give an answer when I was off stage. Then it would be time for me to join the landlord and his staff to 'socialize'. The image of the darts player in the early 1990s was still that of Fatbelly from the 'Not the Nine O'clock News' sketch, so I was expected to sup pints. When I asked for a cup of tea they thought I was kidding. I was working four or five nights a week, and if I had stayed on the ale till after midnight I'd have been shattered.

I made a deliberate decision to prepare for the 1992 Embassy in such a way as not to peak too early. My exhibition form was great throughout the year. I was runner-up in the Denmark Open but was massively boosted by my form in one early-round match; I hit a 158 check-out to pinch a 3–2 win. I also got to the semi-final in Canada. But one of my best performances was in retaining the North American Open singles title. There was an odd background story to this. At the time I did not go to all the tournaments round the world. I liked being at home and I hated all the travelling. The novelty had well and truly worn off. I especially didn't like being away for nearly three weeks, as the annual American summer trip demanded. So it was with reluctance that I got near the front of the queue at Manchester airport. Suddenly I decided that the trip was not for me and I went home. Yvonne tore me off a strip when I got back, so I went to a travel agent, forked out another £500 and took my daughter Lisa, then aged nine, to the States with me. I landed Friday morning, played Friday night and Saturday morning and, lucky for me, I won. I beat America's Jerry Umberger in the final.

That was not the only time I went home from an airport queue. Sometimes I even made the taxi turn round at the end of the street. I know it let down my pairs partners, but sometimes your responsibility to yourself and your family comes first. As well as working as a professional darts player I was looking round for a pub to run. I was aware of the need to provide for a future beyond the oche.

The American win was the start of my measured build-up to the World Championship. My next big outing was in England colours at the World Cup in Holland, where John Lowe won the singles but I was not at my best.

From the end of October I began consciously to psych myself up for the Embassy. When you are a challenger rather than the holder there is less to think about and you can focus more. I did not practise for seven or eight hours a day like some people do. Sometimes an hour and a half is enough to get your mental mind-set right. It is the same with being overcome with nerves when you walk into an open tournament and see all these good players. Eric told me to have the attitude: 'Well, I'm not going to be playing all these. They are all going home, I'm not.' I would just think it; Eric would say it. Reduce your problems to manageable proportions is the principle. When I was ready I was ratty, twitchy and could not settle to watch television. Yvonne pointed to the stairs, like she still does, and said 'Go away now. You're ready for it.'

Another thing I liked to do then was take a pal from the Potteries along with me to major championships. At Lakeside in 1992 it was Andy Anderson, who ran his own little pottery business. I had played darts with Andy during our lean years, when I went out only once in a blue moon. He was the star at the Pack Horse and had a lovely John Lowe-type style; smooth and rhythmic. He was my room-mate and cheered me on all week.

And what a week it turned out to be. Remember the dream I had written about two years earlier? About winning the title in a 6–5 tie-breaker?

It must have been planned up in darts Valhalla, because I was the number-one seed and Mike Gregory of Bristol, former winner of the British Professional title and an ice-cool player, was number two. Cue fairy tale . . .

I did not look championship material in the first two rounds. In round one I beat the tall, sombre Swede Magnus Caris 3–1 in sets with an average of 93. I was not much better against another Swede, Per Skau, who looked like a young professor. I won, but averaged only 94.5. Then the careful preparation began to pay off. I blitzed Martin Phillips of Wales 4–0 with an average of 98.4. Remember me saying the real Taylor cooks best at 97.5? I did not care who came next.

It was John Lowe, and the match provided a great starter before the main course, the fillet steak and chips, the greatest final the Embassy had ever produced. I raced to a 4–1 lead and was just thinking that Lobo, as Eric called him, was not the best chaser of a game when John had a purple patch and brought the score to 4–4. I had totally lost my concentration while I was so far ahead, and when he pegged me back I was as nervous as my first super league appearance. When I did manage to win 5–4, I sat behind the stage and cried for several minutes. I was absolutely emotionally drained.

Looking back on tapes of the classic 1992 Embassy World Professional Darts Championship final, several small things stand out. I was not as consciously macho as people think. Yes, I had tattoos, but I'd liked them since I was 19; they were just for me. And my Zapata moustache was not trimmed for effect; it would be long, short or non-existent depending on how carefully I wielded the razor. Mind you, the shirt was pure cockiness. It showed a bouncy rat saying 'Not a problem', and was made for me by a friend in Northern Ireland.

Again, the darts I threw then are a long way from the long Power arrows of today. Eric had called my old Leighton Rees darts rubbish and given me a set of his. I didn't like them at first, but they had won me one world title so I persisted with them. They had short barrels, and my angle of entry using them was more like that of Eric's or Dennis Priestley's darts. It was a long time before I realized that these darts were designed to be used by a six-foot man and were unsuitable for someone of my shorter stature; then I lengthened them and began dipping the dart on entry, hence leaving more space for the next ones. I also played much slower then than I do now. Fast means confidence, and that came with experience.

Before the final I was only worried by one thing. Mike had looked deadly on his finishes in matches and in the practice room. My own were going well, but if he got on song . . .

It was a pretty even battle right up to 5–5 in sets, but with Mike looking the likely winner. He was missing no doubles. But then it got to 3–2 in the tie-breaker and this is where he could now have won the game. Luckily it was me to throw first. I composed myself; I had to hold my throw. I started with 95, and continued to lose the plot. Mike wanted 61 for the title. He hit treble 15 to leave double eight. He snatched the next two darts horribly, putting one on the wire and pulling the second inside the wire. I knew that on the darts which would take the bacon he was relying on hope rather than control. I needed double 10 to stay alive. I hit the big 10, leaving an awkward double five to save the match. It went in and I gave myself a little pat on the head. 3–3.

I knew exactly what he was thinking: 'I've had two darts to win the world title and I've missed.' There was now immense pressure on him to hold his throw. He did well, starting with two 140s.

Mike did not start snatching on his doubles again for a while. He slotted 66 to make it 5–4. Once again he was going for glory and I had to save the game. Great start: 26. Surely he would cane me from here. We matched shots: 100, 100, 100. Suddenly he wanted 80 for the title and I wanted 215 to stay alive. He really should have won here. He missed the double top. So he now had thrown three darts for the title – his brain would be reeling. I missed, leaving double eight, but he had three darts at double 20. He hit single 20, then missed double 10 twice. Six shots to win the Embassy and six misses! I knew now that he was completely tied up; if he got another shot at a double he would miss.

Some people say you should play the board and not the man. That is rubbish. I watched my rivals on tape and analysed their weaknesses. In that classic final I watched Gregory as he pushed and pulled the darts through tension. And the knowledge made me relax. Witness the final leg.

We threw for the bull to see who would go first. He hit, I missed; Mike to throw first and he was favourite. I could see by his drawn face that the misses had got to him. I was cool. It was the biggest game of my life but I had prepared perfectly for it. He held on to my coat-tails for a few seconds. I banged in a 13-darter, ending on double top. On commentary Tony Green was hoarse as he rightly extolled 'The greatest Embassy final ever!' The crowd went mad.

Tommy Cox had watched the match from the edge of the stage. He still classes it amongst the best games of all time. I was about to take my family to the official reception, fully expecting to see Tommy there, but sad to say the dispute between the WDC and the BDO had started getting exceedingly personal. I was champion of the world and Olly Croft, whose entire family had tickets, would not give my manager a ticket for the reception. I told them that if Tommy did not get in then I would not be attending either. Tommy got in.

In the months after my win Tommy and I got to know each other well. As you will have gathered, partly due to having no money for much of my adult life, I rarely drink. But Tommy helped me let my hair down on a visit to Rotterdam. We went there for an exhibition, and then I was to play in the Dutch Open the day after. I dutifully did the exhibition, which was a few miles out of the city, and a bunch of reporters who attended gave us a lift back to the middle of Amsterdam. They did an interview with me during the drive. Back in town we went for a drink with them . . . and forgot about the Dutch Open!

Next day, Tommy and I continued our party. We found a pub with a rugby theme and I began to drink vodka and Coke. Now I had never drunk spirits before, and only started on them because my manager liked a short or two now and then. I had no idea that the stuff was so powerful. The bloke behind the bar had a huge moustache, which he kept shaking when I said that my drink had no taste. He also kept topping up my drink with vodka!

By the time we staggered to our hotel the rest of the British lads were back from the Dutch Open and most of them were in bed. We went knocking on doors to find out who had won and, unfortunately for them, Rod Harrington and Steve Beaton, who were sharing, opened their door. We were totally out of order and, for some reason, we pushed Rod and Steve and their mattresses down the stairs. Retribution was swift: I was ill for a week. And Tommy still occasionally wags his finger and says, 'That bloke in Amsterdam must have been putting stuff in your drink.'

Winning my second Embassy should have been the start of a perfect year for me. But from the start there was one nightmare after another, and the seeds were sown for the split that tore the game apart for five bitter years.

CHAPTER 6

Darts in Turmoil

One of the most frequent serious questions at my exhibitions is whether the two sides in darts, the Professional Darts Corporation and the British Darts Organisation, will ever get together. The answer is a definite no; the reasons for the dispute, which still goes on today, were too fundamental. The best way to understand the path to the High Court in mid-1997 and victory for the PDC, or the WDC as it then was, is to consider parallels in tennis and athletics.

The amateur authorities which ran both these sports were anachronisms to players who wanted to make a living out of the sport. And the fact that there was a market for the talents of Hoad and Rosewall and Cram and Coe meant the tide was running with them. The players began to play on a professional circuit.

This is precisely the position that darts was at in early 1992. Quite bluntly, the sport was in crisis. Darts had rapidly become a television stalwart from 1978 and throughout the 1980s, with 8.3 million people tuning in to watch Keith Deller's fairytale victory over Eric Bristow. Then things started to go downhill. From having around 14 events on television a year in 1988, within a couple of years we were down to two. Among the events that disappeared from the screen were the MFI World Matchplay, the MFI World Pairs, the Unipart British Professional Championship, the Butlin's Grand Masters, the Dry Blackthorn Masters, the Autumn Gold Masters, the British Open, the World Masters and the British International Championship.

Part of the reason for the cut-back was policy changes at the BBC and ITV. The BBC, which had led the way, particularly in their extended coverage of the Embassy World Professional Championship, said they were trimming their minority sports, like bowls, rugby league and darts. ITV was much more worrying. Greg Dyke was not interested in attracting the lower-income viewers who he thought made up the darts audience, so it was axed completely.

From the start of this decline, people like Tommy Cox and Dick Allix, Eric Bristow's agent, had tried very hard to do something about the state of the game. Meetings took place with the BDO from 1988 onwards, but the BDO seemed reluctant to face the problems. One serious bone of contention was that, although the players were contracted to agents, the BDO was acting as if they were the agents. Arnold Westlake, a BDO director, argued that Jocky and myself and the others were their players and they did not have to answer to people like Tommy and Dick. Tommy told him bluntly that they certainly had to answer to him since he had written contracts with the players concerned.

The initial name of the pressure group was the Darts Council. At first they had no intention of running events, only raising money to fund events. They always intended that any new events should be run by the BDO. They went as far as electing Olly Croft to their executive committee, but he refused to have anything to do with them.

The World Darts Council, made up of 16 top players and companies involved in darts, was set up in January 1992 to put the sport back on its feet. To get sponsors to come in, the sport had to be on television. The BDO had marked time; the future had to be more professional. As Dick Allix, who would be a key figure in the events of the next few years, put it in a letter to *Darts World* in August 1992: 'If the BDO wants to accept the accolades of success, it must accept the responsibility for failure.' My manager, Tommy Cox, had already told me when I joined him that the WDC was the only hope for the game.

I did not want to fall out with Olly Croft or other friends at the BDO, people like Sam Hawkins and Dave Alderman. I had stayed at Olly's house in Muswell Hill and had been fêted by officials at the Embassy. But even now, 11 years on, the thing that still leaves a nasty taste is how the BDO reacted when our group of professionals decided to take a path that led us to an expensive court case. Swords were immediately drawn. There was no compromise; within a few months of the dispute erupting we were banned from BDO events.

The slippery slope that ended up in court years later began within weeks of my second Embassy win. I found out that the BDO had collaborated on a video of the classic 1992 final between myself and Mike Gregory. It was in the shops, yet no one had said one word about it to either of us. There was no consultation and no money, even though Sid Waddell got a fee for his commentary.

Tommy Cox turned purple with rage when a copy landed on his desk. He was manager of both players and was outraged. The lame excuse from the BDO was that 'the players had signed their rights away'. Tommy asked to see the relevant documents. They did not come. All we had agreed to do was play in the Embassy, not give away commercial rights.

I know the video was good publicity for us and for the game, but I think it was a disgrace to treat us the way they did. We were treated appallingly – as mere players with no rights. And this was the nub of the whole dispute. I think Olly Croft, endorsed by the BDO council, failed to take on board the fact that there was a group of players – myself, Bristow, Lowe and Priestley – who were dedicated professionals, looking to promote events themselves. After this episode relations between the WDC and the BDO went downhill rapidly.

War was declared when the WDC began setting up its own tournaments. In May 1992 all 16 of us 'rebels' attended a pro-am charity darts competition at Doncaster. It was a laugh. Eddie the Eagle was there and a host of 'Coronation Street' stars. I played with comedian Duncan Norvelle, who throws a handy dart, and later I took a fiver off Paul Shane of 'Hi-Di-Hi' at snooker. But the main pointer to the future was the presentation. It was like WWF wrestling. Loud music and a light show greeted the players and spotlights flashed across the arena. On stage was a giant video wall to help the punters follow the action. Sid Waddell was the MC, and he was ebullient even by his standards. We were on a high. We were going to have the first WDC televised tournament on Anglia in October, and Sid was negotiating with Tyne Tees TV to have a tournament in Newcastle in spring 1993.

The debate rumbled on throughout 1992, with the BDO refusing to compromise with the wishes of the WDC to start their own circuit. There were rumours that we would be banned from all BDO events, and later in 1992, because we were getting nowhere, we threatened to boycott the Embassy in January 1993.

As it happened a peace formula was worked out and several WDC players agreed to play in the Embassy of 1993. It had been agreed that the WDC would be recognized in the event programme, and that we could wear

WDC badges when we played. But before play was due to start on day one, there was trouble; Jocky Wilson and Eric Bristow rushed to Tommy Cox, the only WDC official present, and said they had been ordered to take the WDC badges off their playing shirts. Eric was all for walking out there and then. Tommy did not think that was a good thing to do. Things got worse: a hole was cut in Jocky's playing shirt and his badge removed. Tommy was not happy. He went into a side room for a meeting with Keith McKenzie, the BBC executive producer, Peter Dyke of Embassy, Tony Green and Olly Croft. Tommy made the point that, as they had made reference to the WDC in the programme, why ban the badges? McKenzie said it was advertising. Tommy replied that that was ridiculous; it was merely an association badge. McKenzie said the BDO regarded it as advertising. Tommy realized that he was getting nowhere and told them they would never do this to the WDC again. He told Eric and Jocky to play and they did.

On the positive side, we had been making progress with our own events. The Lada UK Masters, played in October 1992 in Norwich, was a great success. We all wore our WDC blazers, and again the game was given a bright, breezy feel. John Gwynne, a schoolteacher turned journalist and an excellent darts caller, shared the up-beat commentary with Dave Lanning. I got to the last eight and then Mike Gregory got revenge for the Embassy match by beating me. He did it in style with a zany 119 shot-out: treble three, treble 20, bull! Mike eventually won the tournament – and the right to drive round in a Lada car all year. He got some stick for this, especially when he won the same honour a year later.

Despite the trouble, John Lowe, Alan Warriner, Bob Anderson and myself, all WDC players, represented England in the four-man Europe Cup in Finland in November 1992. I was in excellent form and won the singles title, beating John Lowe 4–2. And we retained the team title. But I'll never forget John's pep-talk in the final stages. 'Let's win this one, lads, because it is our last!' We did not believe him, but he was proved right. Within six months we were suspended, and then banned.

The poison started for me straight after the Europe Cup. I got a letter saying that I had been dropped down to the Staffordshire B team! Top of the averages in the A team; world champion; twice Europe Cup singles winner. Somebody had leaned heavily on somebody. I phoned Les Capewell, one of the four selectors, and he said he had not voted me out. It was the same with the other three. The hard word must have come from higher.

So, what a superb year as Embassy champion I'd had! It should have been a dream, but it turned out in many ways a nightmare. In fact there was a point when I felt like quitting the game altogether. There had been big problems with Yvonne's third pregnancy. She had been rushed to hospital and diagnosed as having diabetes. I was also hoping to open a club in Stoke and this had been a headache. But what got me down in the main was the horrible atmosphere generated by the dispute. As World Champion I was frequently asked to put the case for the 'rebel' players, and it all got too much for me. But a summer family holiday in the sun and the great atmosphere at the Lada tournament bucked me up.

The build-up to the defence of my Embassy title again involved hours of practice with Eric. At the Lakeside the atmosphere was rotten; people who had treated me like a friend a year ago were different. One little thing summed it all up. In the last three years I had been allowed to do a bit of practice on a board set up in the referees' room. It gave me the focus I got on my oche in Blake Street. In 1993 there was no such facility. I never looked like taking my third title. I struggled through my first-round game against John Joe O'Shea, with a pathetic 91 average, and went out 3–1 to Kevin Spiolek with 89. The cold figures speak for themselves.

Things were, however, coming up to the boil in the dispute. On 4 January 1993, after the fiasco over the WDC badges, 16 of us nailed our colours to the WDC mast. We issued a short policy statement: 'We, the undersigned, members of the World Professional Darts Players Association, mandate the World Darts Council to represent us exclusively on all matters relating to the 1994 World Professional Darts Championship. In particular, we recognize the World Darts Council as the only governing body empowered to commit our participation in any darts tournaments worldwide.' The signatories were John Lowe, Eric Bristow, Cliff Lazarenko, Phil Taylor, Keith Deller, Jamie Harvey, Bob Anderson, Dennis Priestley, Rod Harrington, Kevin Spiolek, Chris Johns, Mike Gregory, Alan Warriner, Jocky Wilson, Peter Evison and Richie Gardner.

The BDO reply was to suspend all 16 of us from all matches under their jurisdiction, from pub to international level. The grounds given were that we were 'bringing the game into disrepute'. This seemed laughable, since the list included half the recently announced England squad. The BDO went on to say that anyone wishing to have the suspension lifted 'may submit a written declaration to the effect that he shall refrain from participation in any boycott threats to BDO darts event and he will also refrain from any involvement in action designed to disrupt the activities of the BDO'.

But this was not all. In April 1993 the BDO asked a WDC delegation to attend a meeting of the full BDO council in Finchley. Tommy Cox, Dick Allix, Bob Anderson, Michael Lowy of Unicorn Products, Marcus Robertson of our PR agency and John Taylor, our sponsorship consultant, walked into a very hostile atmosphere. They were hissed at as they entered the room. Somebody shouted out that the WDC people should be hanged. Tommy Thompson of Lancashire said they should be 'binned'. John Bostock of Yorkshire called our group 'not the kind of people you would like to have living in the same street'. When the WDC party tried to speak they were howled down. There was no agenda. And at one stage BDO chairman Sam Hawkins addressed his troops with the words: 'They are telling porkies, boys.' The 'boys' had their minds made up before our people went in. They wanted the suspension to become an all-out ban.

Phil Jones, a former BDO official who was at the meeting as an impartial observer rather than a BDO delegate, rang Tommy Cox to say that three resolutions proposed by Lancashire and Yorkshire, and amounting to a ban, had been passed. These three resolutions eventually led to the High Court.

- 'Any BDO official or BDO player who is associated with the activities of the World Darts Council shall forfeit the right to organize, attend or participate in any events under the jurisdiction of the British Darts Organization or its members, until a written undertaking is given that they are no longer associated with the World Darts Council.
- All member counties shall refrain from attending or assisting in any exhibitions involving the 16 players named in the WDC statement of 7 January 1993, any players that have affiliated since and any players that may affiliate in future.
- All member counties shall exclude any players that are affiliated to the World Darts Council from darts events under their jurisdiction.'

The ban would not only stop us playing in BDO tournaments, it would stop players and spectators from coming to our exhibitions. Our livelihoods had been placed in jeopardy.

For me and many of the 16, the 'associating' clause was a lot worse than the ban from tournaments. The resolution meant that even people merely attending our exhibitions could be excluded from all BDO darts, and that meant right down to league level. My cousin Jimmy Prince, who played for Staffordshire, was told that he should not even speak to me. A local darts-playing builder was told he must not put a door on my house.

There is no doubt in my mind that the BDO were intent on putting us out of business. I know for certain that landlords connected to Mansfield Brewery were contacted by BDO local officials, and as a result of the phone calls, decided not to have me in exhibitions at their pubs.

The effects on people's lives were dreadful. Freddie Williams, a distinguished referee, was forced to resign from the Essex county committee, and John Raby from Hertfordshire, for involvement with the WDC. The same happened to the long-serving Peter Barron of Northumberland.

But the move that made my blood boil was when the whispering campaign got in the way of my charity work. In August 1993 I was preparing to do my regular exhibition for the special baby-care unit when several super league players rang me to say that they had been told not to take part. As it happens, a number of these players did take part despite the threats.

Despite a plea by John Lowe in his capacity as Players Association secretary to have the ban lifted at the end of 1993, things just got no better. John argued that since the BDO and Embassy had signed a deal for three more years of the World Championship, the WDC could not be seen as a threat to the BDO. But his pleas fell on deaf ears.

A few weeks after the ban was announced a WDC delegation of Tommy Cox, Dick Allix, Marcus Robertson and John Taylor went to see Jonathan Martin, BBC head of sport. He listened, said the BBC would not show darts without the top players and suggested we sit down again and sort things out with the BDO. Two weeks later the BBC put out a statement that the 1994 Embassy would go ahead with players chosen by the BDO.

We had not been sitting around idly hoping for a change of heart. The WDC had now developed a circuit of televised events and we were planning to do our own World Championship with Sky Sports. But there were slight tremors when two of the signatories of our declaration broke ranks. Chris Johns pulled out, and Mike Gregory told Tommy and I that for financial reasons he felt obliged to go back to the BDO. This caused a problem with Sky. Roger Moody said that there must be no more drop-outs. And the BDO were making overtures to Lowe and Warriner; luckily they did not succeed. When we did burst on to Sky at the end of 1993 we had all the

World Champions there had ever been – Lowe, Bristow, Deller, Wilson, Anderson, Priestley and Taylor. The only Embassy champion not with us was Leighton Rees, who was not playing tournament darts at the time.

Away from the dispute the WDC, thanks to the efforts of Tommy Cox, Dick Allix and John Markovic, was making giant strides in setting up televised tournaments. Sid Waddell, while maintaining his role as a BBC commentator, had collaborated with the WDC to stage the Samson Darts Classic in the Tyne Tees studios in Newcastle. A few new nicknames had been dished out by Sid: I was still the Crafty Potter, but Jamie Harvey was the Tartan Tantrum! Still, we were all in show business now. As well as playing darts during our week on Tyneside, we joined the Geordies at work and play. Dennis Priestley and Chris Johns drew the short straw and had to shovel sea coal with waves lapping round them. John Lowe went down to the marina to size up some yachts and Rod Harrington, who used to play junior football with Glenn Hoddle, showed the professionals at Sunderland FC some good ball skills. I practised and took some walks along the sands at Whitley Bay.

In line with WDC policy we played a double to start, a common rule in the north-east and in America. This added a bit of spice to the competition since you ran the risk of being whitewashed. I got to the final, where I was beaten by Bob Anderson. Sid seemed to be everywhere. He was the presenter, producer and commentator. 'Are you sure you don't want to play in the first round?' Dick Allix asked him. There were plans afoot for our own World Championship, and a lot of people thought Sid might leave the BBC and join us.

A few weeks later we had another televised tournament with a difference. It was played at Chesterfield on a Quadro board, with a ring inside the treble ring that gave you quadruple your score. So the immortal cry could ring out, 'Two hundred aaaaand forty!' I actually scored one but did not fare well. Though the rules specified that you should go for the quadruple ring, a lot of players ignored it. Muggins Taylor played on it all the time. But in 1996 I really went to town on the Quadro board. I beat Chris Mason, Shayne Burgess and Alan Warriner, with a 109.3 average, and Dennis Priestley in the final. I put the icing on the cake with a 188 check-out.

All this was great for the professional game, but the real jewel in the WDC crown was not unveiled until 28 December 1993. Our first World Championship was staged over a week at the Circus Tavern in Purfleet, Essex, and Sky Sports covered every dart. More than that, the team led by Martin Turner, and with sensational lighting by Dave Hurley, brought a panache to darts coverage that made the BBC's efforts over the years look Neanderthal.

The club was still hung with Christmas streamers, and when the lights flashed over them and the place filled with dry ice it was a unique, heady atmosphere. Add to that Page Three girls, motorbikes and walk-ons to loud pop music and you have a real show. It was a hit from the minute Jeff Stelling introduced the first two players: 'Please welcome Dennis Priestley and Jocky Brown . . .' OK, Jeff did get a bit excited, but nobody was upset, not even Jocky Wilson. We knew we had backed a winner.

Sid Waddell was preparing to commentate on the Embassy tournament, which was due to start four days after ours. He did not have Sky, so he watched our efforts in a pub near his home in Pudsey. He was gobsmacked: 'I knew that the Sky razzle-dazzle treatment was spot on. Darts needs the wrestling and Super Bowl glitz. The game can become one-dimensional when two great players are rattling up big scores. I knew I would be commentating on some lukewarm stuff at Frimley Green. My heart was with my pals at Purfleet. I wished I had put my mouth there.'

There was, however, one aspect of the WDC plugging of our tournament that I did not like. A few days before we started some of the players went to the Lakeside at Frimley Green and picketed the up-coming Embassy. Jocky and John Lowe had placards saying the real World Championship would be at Purfleet. I know it got us a lot of publicity, but I did not agree with it and did not attend. Bob Potter, the owner of the club, was a personal friend of mine, and I thought there was no need to upset him when our fight was with the BDO.

Thanks to our sponsors Skol there was a £16,000 first prize and the 24 players produced some excellent darts.

The programme boasted rightly that the WDC was taking darts into the 21st century. Phil Jones was brilliant as the gravel-voiced master of ceremonies and John Gwynne and Dave Lanning never let the excitement dip in over 20 hours of live coverage. We all loved the walk-ons with music and girls carrying flags. It made you feel like a real entertainer, and the colourful crowd loved it. They were a different lot to the Lakeside crowd, with local Essex lads and lasses, including the 'Catford Skins', and a lot of students. They mingled quite happily with the out-and-out darts fans.

The only problem with being wall-to-wall live on Sky was the commercial breaks. At our first World Championship, and at the summer tournament in Blackpool in 1994, going off for two-and-a-half minutes every five legs did upset my concentration. My rhythm was affected. With experience I now think the breaks are a good thing. You can sit in the wings and recompose yourself or stay on stage and practise. Players like Eric pull on a fag. Cliff will sup lager. Warriner and Mason have been known to sip a naughty little Chablis from Threshers.

I was not playing at my best but I still managed to get through to the final. I beat Jim Watkins of the USA, Jamie Harvey, Bob Anderson and Steve Brown in the semi-final. In that game I won 5–0 in sets and for the first time all week put my average over 90. In the final I could not up my average and was given a hard time by my friend Dennis Priestley. Dennis went into a 5–0 in sets lead at the interval. I was being walloped. To top it all the sole came away from one of my shoes and was flapping about like a dog's tongue. Dennis was trying to take the one set he needed to win and his family and friends were screaming him on as usual. You can hear everything when you are struggling, and suddenly an urgent throaty voice yelled 'Shake my hand, shake my hand. It will give you inspiration!' I looked down into the animated face of Mike Reid of 'EastEnders'. Like a pillock I actually shook his hand. It must have done me some good because I won the next set! But then Dennis kicked back and became the first WDC World Champion.

The press at last woke up to what we were trying to do: re-establish professional darts with a televised circuit. Simon Barnes of *The Times* got it absolutely right: 'This is no afternoon jolly, no amateur lash-up. For the players, this is not a side-show in life: this is life. It is real, it is serious, it is emphatically not a laughing matter. It is career, reputation, ambition and mortgage: darts is as intense as any other professional sport.' Over the next 10 years that assessment was echoed in all the papers.

Eric Bristow was more colourful and personal when he spoke to the *News of the World*. 'People talk about the two sides getting together. There's no chance of that with Olly [Croft] around. He's only interested in running the whole show. So we'll have our pro circuit and the BDO can run the amateur game.'

As I write this it sounds prophetic. It appears that due to government rulings on tobacco sponsorship the 2003 Embassy World Professional Darts Championship was the last. So whether they like it or not the BDO are back where they started: with the amateur end of our sport.

It makes me sad to see the Embassy go, but you could never base the game on just one championship.

CHAPTER 7

The Haunted Pub

Of all the pubs in Stoke, why did we choose to go and live in one that was haunted? The Saggar Makers, where I go to practise, has a long and interesting history. The Riley Arms and the Huntsman have dark little corners. But there was nothing about the Cricketers Arms in May Bank to suggest music at midnight or spectral figures coming through the walls.

The idea of becoming the landlord of the Cricketers came about by pure accident. I was passing by the pub in the autumn of 1993 when it was all boarded up, taking a video back to a nearby shop. I had been vaguely interested in running a pub from my days at the Huntsman; I knew how to pull pints, and my dad Doug had been made redundant. It seemed just the sort of job my dad would go for, with me backing him up. Just then I bumped into Phil Helms and his brother Steve, who were pals of mine. We got talking about the pub and my ideas about maybe running one, and they suggested that I talk to the brewery about taking over the Cricketers.

It has to be said that the pub did not look like a good bet, but I phoned the brewery anyway and they told me that, although some other people had shown an interest, they would put me at the top of the list. There were, however, and not surprisingly, a couple of problems. The previous licensee was in dispute with the brewery and this took some time to clear up. But the main problem was that the pub was occupied by squatters! Eventually the council got them somewhere else to live and the pub was ours. I cannot say that Yvonne was wholeheartedly in favour of the move. We had just got our house nicely done up and the living quarters in the Cricketers were disgusting. She knew nothing about running a pub and was worried about bringing the kids up in a smoky atmosphere. I persuaded her to give it a go and she felt, like me, that it would be a good opportunity for dad. But the place really was in a terrible state and the first night I sat in the bar in tears wondering what we had taken on. Yvonne started scrubbing at one of the green chairs and discovered it was red underneath. The green was mould!

Over the next six weeks an all-round family effort, with aunts and cousins pitching in, transformed the place. We scrubbed, cleaned and painted the public rooms, the cellar and the living accommodation. We sanded all the wood and varnished the chairs. We also turned a rubble-strewn area at the back into a beer garden. Before we started, dad and I went on a three-day publicans' course in Derbyshire and he had them in hysterics by putting all the answers to the test questions in the wrong boxes. But they passed him anyway.

To our great delight it took off from the first night. It was a pub for working people. I did not want jukeboxes or piped music; I wanted a traditional pub. We had coal fires and I got the John Smith's beer just right. Our prices were cheaper than anywhere else. At first we only opened in the evenings through the week and our clientele came from a broad spectrum. We had business-men and even MPs in our lounge, since it was quiet and comfortable enough for a chat. I acted as DJ at discos on occasions: I would play party music by Mud and the punters never tired of 'Agadoo'. My aunt Pat did the catering for weddings.

We had, of course, several darts teams. I played in them and Yvonne served up the pies and sandwiches. On Tuesdays we played in the local league and I rarely lost a match. Not surprisingly everyone wanted to take me on. I reckon there was more than one fixed draw to try and take my scalp. It was a pleasure to play darts in this atmosphere. All the problems with the BDO were getting me down and suddenly playing darts for a living had become a chore. I had no enthusiasm for travelling or competing. And if you don't go to open tournaments you are not match fit. The opening months of my career as a publican helped me handle things.

My dad Doug was the mainstay of the pub in the first couple of years. He was mine host for at least five days a week. But this was not a role he really enjoyed. We had a great bunch of regulars and they would want to chat about allotments or sport, but dad was never a chatter. Nor did he like it when somebody started moaning about life in general. He hated feeling duty bound to listen, and much preferred the punters' side of the bar to the landlord's.

So he eased off the workload a bit. He would come in on a morning, do the cleaning, sort out the stock and do the cellar work. It was a full day and he enjoyed it. Then he'd go home, have his tea and go for a pint or two at the club. Even there he would not be that talkative; he was a private bloke who didn't stick his nose into other people's business. Mind, after a few pints you could not shut him up. He'd get a bee in his bonnet and bend mum's ear. She would pretend to listen.

My dad was very straight in all his dealings; he would never fiddle. On buses he would hand back change to the conductor if he got too much, and he would never park on double yellow lines. But at the pub, I reckon he took it too far. Occasionally I would borrow a fiver out of the till, and if I hadn't replaced it within the hour he would send one the kids upstairs to get it back from me. It drove me mad. 'It's my money, my till and my bloody beer!' I'd shout. He would shake his head and say things must be done right.

The only time I saw my dad lose his temper with my mother was when I was about 10. My mum and her cousin Susan used to play about with an old ouija board. They would put their fingers on the glass and it would go berserk. The board gave them a solemn warning. It said they were in fact in touch with a good spirit, but if they kept on playing they would encounter a bad spirit, a really evil piece of work.

Soon after my mum and Susan went to a spiritualist church and were very surprised to be approached by the lady who had addressed the gathering. 'You two have had a warning from the other side,' she said. They were shocked. And there was more to come. 'I can see red velvet curtains in your house . . .' They nodded, enrapt. 'Under no circumstances ever play on that ouija board again!'

They ran home and couldn't wait to tell the neighbours. Dad overheard them. He went ballistic; he chucked the ouija board in the bin and for a moment I thought he was going to clout my mother.

Which brings us neatly to Charlie, the china-chucking ghost. He entered our lives about a year after we took over the Cricketers. I first saw him one hectic Friday night. The darts and crib were in full swing when the lager and the beer went off at the same time. I raced down into the cellar and began changing the barrels. Suddenly I was aware of a figure watching me from a few feet away. He was nicely dressed in 1920s' style; bowler hat, pinstriped suit, stiff collar and a thick knotted tie. He did not frighten me – in fact I used to have a joke with him. 'Don't just stand there, Charlie, get that posh jacket off and help me with these bloody barrels!' I'd shout. He never did.

I was not the only one who saw him. Yvonne described him in the same clothes and so did the barmaids. And there was no doubt that Cassy, our German shepherd, was scared of him. She was a working guard dog and we bought her because people were always trying to break in. But she would not go anywhere near the cellar. I would call her down but she would stand at the top of the stairs snuffling. In a way I don't blame her, because Charlie was a bad lot when he got angry.

I would be arranging the china ornaments in the lounge and suddenly one would 'float' off across the room and shatter. I put this down to Charlie being in a bad mood. And one night I got to the end of my tether. About 2 o'clock in the morning all the alarms rang. I jumped out of bed, picked up a samurai sword and a baseball bat, and went downstairs. First I checked under all the barrels in the cellar. Nothing. Then I went into the lounge and was horrified to see my favourite piece of pottery lying in shards. It was a shire horse with full brasses and harness. That was it.

I opened the cellar door, sat on a stool and gave Charlie a piece of my mind: 'Right, Charlie boy, I have had enough of you. If you smash one more ornament round here, I'm going to get the vicar in and exorcize you. I pay the gas, electricity and the mortgage and you just bugger about. If you want to live here you'll have to behave your bloody self!'

This happened in 1996, and in the next five years he never smashed another ornament. I got glimpses of him occasionally and he always looked quite bashful.

If Sky Sports' brilliant live coverage of the first WDC World Championship had been a glimmer of light in the darkness, then the Proton Cars World Matchplay at Blackpool in August 1994 was a flaming beacon.

The usual suspects – Eric, Jocky, Jamie Harvey and company – rolled up to a very posh hotel near Stanley Park in Blackpool for a festival of darting entertainment. It was sweltering hot, so leisurely morning walks around the hotel's golf course were the order of the day. I was happily sauntering past the seventh hole one morning when I heard a swishing and cursing coming from behind a bush. It was comedian Chubby Brown, with a state-of-the-art set of clubs but very little natural ability. 'Do you want a couple of lessons, Phil?' offered Chubby. I thanked him but politely declined.

Chubby was not the only star at our hotel. The Grumbleweeds joined in the odd late-night singsong and Duncan Norvelle, my occasional doubles partner, invited me and my family to the Royal box at his show. I sat there thinking that this was a lot better than turning out handles for toilet chains. Joe Longthorne had been one of my favourites since the days of our £50-a-week budget holidays, and he invited us along to his show as well.

Throughout the week the show-business stars were featured on Sky's coverage of the event. Frank Carson and the Nolan sisters took part in a version of 'Bullseye', but it was the Bachelors who got the short straw. They thought that all they had to do was have a bit of fun, but Sky had different ideas. They asked the boys to coach the Sky commentary team to perform 'Charmaine' live on air! Now this was a bit like asking Jocky to join a Trappist order or Eric to go 24 hours without a fag. John Gwynne is a natural performer and a good singer, but Dave Lanning is no Robbie Williams and Sid Waddell, recently persuaded by Sky executive Roger Moody to join the team, is tone deaf. Still, they managed to pull it off without too many viewer complaints.

Oh yes, in the middle of this mayhem we played darts.

The Winter Gardens had been turned into darts' own Shangri-La by producers Martin Turner, Tony Baines and Rory Hopkins. They had given lighting wizard Dave Hurley *carte blanche* to 'design' the event. I reckon that over the years the BBC at the Embassy at Lakeside had missed the boat. Look at a tape of the 1986 final and compare it to the 2003, and you will see the same flat lighting and the same mundane presentation. Sky had actually not rested on their laurels after Purfleet. They had exploited a unique sporting venue to the hilt. The arena looks like the Milan Opera House with a bit of

Lenin's tomb chucked in for good measure. The balconies disappear into a rococo roof that would have taken Leonardo da Vinci and his lads a year to paint. It is dappled in a changing rainbow of colour. When 2,500 excited fans start yelling and the strains of 'I've Got the Power' by KLM ring out, the atmosphere is unbelievable. The players walk through a crowd of excited, fancy-dressed folk who treat the darts as part of their Blackpool holiday. Lager is at pub prices, hot dogs and chips are available, and you can take the kids in for free. Lovely jubbly.

I love the Circus Tavern in World Championship week, but Blackpool takes the cake for the world's best darting venue.

Going back to that first dazzling week, I had an easy passage through the first round, beating Tom Kirby, who looks like a dapper man of the cloth, 8–2 in legs. Then I had a real ding-dong with Bob Anderson. Bob was chasing me all the way to the 19th leg, and then nicked the match 11–9. I didn't like being out of the competition, but there was plenty to take in.

The commentary team invited me to have a look at their 'eyrie'. Somebody must have heard that Sid sometimes 'screams like a banshee with piles', because Sky had put the commentary position in a shed on the roof! I'm not kidding: we walked along a metal gantry to get to it and we were shooing away seagulls. Inside I brewed up and sat back to watch the lads at work. I noticed straight away that they sometimes had to look away from their monitors to check statistics. This almost caused a disaster. Sid was off duty and was supping tea with his back to the screen. Dave went for a pee and John didn't notice his absence. Then John, thinking Dave would pick up, pulled out a bottle and began to gargle, which is one thing you cannot do on air. 'He wants double aaaaargh aaaaargh . . .' The viewers must have thought he was having a heart attack. Sid grabbed the microphone but could hardly speak for laughing. Mind, on a later occasion when I was commentating with him, Sid did GBH to my toes.

The players' walk-ons were even more spectacular than they had been at Purfleet. The crowd lined the central aisle and applauded, and girls with flags led the players on. Even the bouncers were dressed up for some entries – and they earned their money. Some people do more than applaud; they want to press the flesh. The undoubted walk-on star was Jocky Wilson. He was played on to a folk-rock version of 'You Take the High Road' by Runrig, and it took over two plays of the track – seven minutes – for the wee man to parade 60 yards. It was magic. Jocky also starred in one of Sky's cameo films that are designed to give a breather from wall-to-wall tops and tons. They stuck him in the waxworks down on the promenade between Frank Bruno and Nigel Mansell. Jocky waited until some kids poked their nose near, then made a grab at them. They jumped a mile!

The final was a cracker. Dennis Priestley was the

favourite and was playing some of the best darts of his life. But his opponent was a bit of a dark horse. Larry Butler, nicknamed the 'Bald Eagle' for obvious reasons, was an experienced American, and he had missed a nine-dart finish by only the double earlier in the tournament. He also completed his practice routine by sitting on his bed in the lotus position and meditating. I can just imagine doing that in the Saggar Makers in Burslem – they'd cart me off to the loony bin! Anyway, it worked for Larry; despite an early five-legs lead for Dennis, Larry swooped to a 16–12 victory.

'So there we have it, the so-cool American wins, and we have snow in Blackpool in August . . .' John's words did the wind-up as glitter confetti smothered the two players. And as I went to bed I could hear John leading the Sky team in 'We're All Going Up On Sunshine Mountain' in the bar. It was an apt sentiment at the end of a historic week for Sky, the WDC and for televised darts.

CHAPTER 8

Switch on the Power

In the opening years of the PDC/Sky alliance most big tournaments came down to a struggle between Dennis the Menace and Phil the Power.

Before I tell you the story of how I got my nickname, I have to explain the very special place of Dennis Priestley in my career. Dennis and I are soulmates. We are both proud family men whose wives and kids are always near the front when we play. Jenny Priestley is premier league when it comes to urging on her man if he gets his 'sloppy head' on. He certainly did not have it on for the three years after he won the Embassy world title in 1991. In 1992 Dennis took the Dallas Open, the Welsh Open, the Pacific Masters, the British Pentathlon and the Los Angeles Open. So, not surprisingly, with both of us cherry-picking most tournaments – and with the dispute with the BDO still putting a damper on the exhibition scene – from 1994 to around 2000 Dennis and I pooled our tournament winnings. It was not done religiously, because for a period I missed tournaments, even though – good-hearted lad that he is – Dennis offered to split even when I was not there.

We operated like a small business; we roomed together and played pairs together. It made sound financial sense. Being a darts pro travelling the land playing a sport you loved might seem bliss to some, but the profit margin was narrow. Around 1994 the average exhibition fee was about £300. After £50 to your manager, £40 for petrol, £50 for a caller and £50 for a hotel, it didn't leave a lot. So to cut costs I got a camper van. It was cost-effective, but once in Ireland it got me and my mate into a spot of bother. At about 3 o'clock one morning, exhausted, we parked in what we thought was the car-park of a church. Next morning we were awakened by the bells of early mass. We tried to drive off the 'car-park', only to sink ever deeper into the turf of what was in fact the church green. The locals looked on in horror as we struggled to get away. We were still there when mass finished and the priest came out: he must have had bad eyesight, since he chatted for five minutes and never noticed the gouges in his turf. We had to hire a wagon to pull us out.

So to that famous nickname. I wish that I had thought it up myself, or that Sid, John or Dave had flung it out during some impassioned patch of play. Sad to say, the story is one of everyday humdrum telly life. Just about the hardest worker on the Sky team was Peter Judge, affectionately known as 'Judgey' – always in a smart suit, voice of a crusty magistrate – who was the boss of floor operations. One of his jobs was to get us on our marks for the walk-on. At the 1995 WDC Proton World Matchplay I was waiting in the wings with Gerald Verrier when Judgey asked me what my nickname was. I shrugged. For a second he spoke into his walkie-talkie. 'Right, Phil,' his blue eyes twinkled. 'They are going to play the Power song, so you are now the Power.' Simple as that. Cue thunder, lightning and hair-ruffling. It's a good job they hadn't got 'Pretty Flamingo' cued up in sound!

Thanks to the Sky team the glitz at the 1995 WDC World Championship at the Circus Tavern was as bright and brash as ever. But for once the team went just a little too far.

The walk-ons were becoming ever more elaborate. We had bouncers dressed as Mafia men in fedoras and shades with Dennis Priestley, models dressed as Pearly Queens and a wee man in a kilt belting away on the bagpipes. Rod Harrington arrived at the club in a chauffeur-driven white Rolls Royce. Then someone in the Sky scanner had a brainwave for a Bob Anderson cowboy-style entry that would eclipse Gary Cooper in 'High Noon', Wyatt Earp at the OK Corral and Yul Brynner and the rest of 'The Magnificent Seven'. At least that was the big idea.

Before Bob's match with Jerry Umberger, a horsebox pulled up outside the Circus Tavern and Boz, a fully saddled and bridled veteran show jumper, was led into reception. Boz looked a bit bewildered as he was ushered through to the main arena. For a while he pawed the plush carpet, then, not at all happy with the unfamiliar surroundings, he stood stock still near the bar. He absolutely refused to move an inch further.

That was more than could be said for the 'Limestone Cowboy'. One look at Boz and Bob turned white. He ran to the far end of the club in a muck sweat. 'Don't let that thing come near me,' he cried. 'For some reason horses don't like me. And the feeling is mutual; I've never ridden one in my life and I once had a pony rear up on me, kicking and biting.'

So poor old Boz never got to star on Sky. He was given a bucket of water and taken home to his Essex ranch. Did that stop the Sky team coming up with more wheezes? What do you think?

The atmosphere got better and better as the week proceeded, and so did the darts. John Lowe prepared to take on the holder, Dennis Priestley, and made a portentous remark before the match: 'If the old champion can't beat the new champion, the game is dead.' That was the whole point of the WDC: having tournaments where the old stagers could be challenged by hungry young guns with the old stagers being forced to raise their game. The BDO were always claiming that the WDC was no more than a club for has-beens. But what John showed against Dennis and later against me was the very essence of competitive sport.

John took Dennis to the cleaners at the start of the match. He went two sets clear, then almost got a nine-dart at the start of set three. By the time he sank the sixth 60, Sid was in palpitating form in the commentary box. 'This has got to be the cruellest game in the world. You can forget bull-fighting, this is vicious. John Lowe is walking that oche like a zombie, like one of the undead. Dennis is like Custer at the last stand. The Iroquois one way, the Shoshone the other, and the Apaches behind him . . .' Dennis could only put on a brave face and watch as John went for treble 17 with his seventh dart. It missed. The nine-dart was not on, but John coasted the match. He and I would meet in the semi-final.

The national press were now beginning to realize that our new circuit was flourishing, and the *Daily Express* and the *Independent* wrote approving pieces. Greg Wood in the latter wrote that after a match like the Lowe/ Priestley clash 'the game is in excellent health'. My match against John was to have the Sky commentary team reaching for the thesaurus; it still stands out as one of the greatest ever played.

When I talk to John Gwynne, Dave Lanning and Sid Waddell about the great matches, some favourites leap out: Evans versus Rees at the very first Embassy, when Rees pulled out a magic 10-darter to turn the tide; Bristow against Deller and Eric's fatal decision not to go for the bull to save the game; Jocky snarling at himself and sweating as Bristow pegged back in the 1989 final; myself against Gregory in 1992. They were all great memories. But not, apparently, to the BDO when they took the names of all the WDC players out of the 1995 Embassy programme. It's nice to know that Stalinization is not confined to Russia!

It was on the cards that my clash with John would be good because we had warmed up for it. We had played two head-to-heads, one at his pub, the Unicorn in Chesterfield, and one at the Cricketers. There was very little sparring. At the end of set two we began a series of nine legs that have gone down in darting history. Sid Waddell and John Gwynne were quick to see the drama: 'Lowe swaggering up there and Taylor like a Mafia hitman,' said Sid. 'Make no mistake, folks, you are witnessing a marvellous darts match,' said John. The legs were unbelievable: remember 16 or 17 darts per leg are very good at any level, and they went 15, 14, 15, 15, 14, 12, 13, 13, 12. Sid put it into stratospherical context: 'As the song says, we're heading for Venus, we're way beyond Mars.' John underpinned exactly how well I was playing by reminding viewers that I had just pushed my 180 scoring up to 24. Sid asked, 'Which jouster will have last flick of the lance?'

From about set three I started to enjoy myself. John Lowe is the game's supreme stylist. He was coached by the great Barry Twomlow, winner of the *News of the World* Championship in 1968. John aims to keep all his body, except the arm, as still as possible. Lock the front leg; use the back leg as a rudder; arm through as though oiled. John also never seemed to blink – some people talked about the possibility of him doing an advert for eyedrops.

My tactic was simple: bully every shot. I didn't let the fact that 80 per cent of the Circus crowd were on John's side affect me. In the end he could not match my scoring power or my finishing. I won 5–4 in sets with an average of 96.2. I did a 107 shot-out – treble 19, single 10, double top – to take the match. Sky were very happy. But John had to put a damper on proceedings. When I commented on how entertaining it had been, he countered by saying he had found it boring. Try telling that to hoarse-throated Sid and gasping John in the commentary box. They told me they needed oxygen.

Twenty-four hours later I had an even more partisan crowd against me. Rod Harrington was my opponent in the final, and he comes from Chelmsford. The Essex locals came out in full force to support him, and I think the great expectations of his supporters got to Rod. I won 6–2 in sets. I had matched John Lowe's three World Championships and was now setting my sights on Eric's five.

I wanted to beat Eric's record so much because I was getting fed up with being dubbed 'the World Champ you would pass in the street'. On 'A Question of Sport' a couple of years earlier the teams had not been able to identify me as World Champion. But I knew they would hear about me soon. My tournament average at the World Championship of 1995 was a miserable 90. I knew I had plenty more in the tank. Eric Bristow never usually praised me to my face; he did it behind my back and in the faces of my rivals. But after my third win, Eric was glowing: 'You can win the World Championship as many times as you like, mate.' As they said in Rome, 'praise from Caesar is praise indeed'.

CHAPTER 9

Equal with Eric

If some people had trouble recognizing me as a World Darts Champion in the early 1990s, John Thomas Wilson was a sports star who everybody knew. Since his Embassy victory over John Lowe in 1982 Jocky had hit the headlines on a regular basis. He once described himself as 'fat, boozy and toothless' and was rarely out of the newspapers. ITV spent £2,000 on state-of-the-art dentures for him. He was frequently in trouble with the darts authorities. He lost a court case against his first manager which cost him around £80,000. He sometimes played in top competitions the worse for drink. And in the early 1980s he even appeared on 'Top of the Pops'.

This was a truly bizarre saga and was recently voted one of the biggest TV cock-ups of all time. The production team was trying to illustrate the song 'Jackie Wilson Said' by Dexy's Midnight Runners. A researcher used some misguided initiative and for three minutes Jocky's beaming face stared out at the pop fans. Even in 1995 he was a national icon.

Before I joined him in Tommy Cox's stable I had heard all the stories and played Jocky a time or two when he'd obviously been supping. But I had always found him very friendly and he usually made me laugh. I remember once at the Embassy he had forgotten his shoes. He was wearing old trainers and would not have been allowed to play in them. As it happened Yvonne had bought me some very nice size-nine Hush Puppies for Christmas. So Jocky tried them on and they fitted perfectly. He played in them – and I'm still waiting to get them back!

Around 1994 when he was living in the pretty rough Battle Hill area of Tyneside he needed a new car and I told him not to get one that was too flash. It would cost a fortune to insure, and would probably get stolen. He would not listen and went ahead and bought a very glamorous Mercedes. As it happens, it was not stolen. When Jocky upped sticks and went back to Scotland he left the car in the driveway of his house and the hire-purchase company repossessed it.

Even with diabetes and ulcers Jocky was a star. By the summer of 1995 and the World Matchplay in Blackpool he was off the drink totally, but he would buy rounds for the lads. He balked at paying for designer water so he kept running to the pub toilet to fill his glass with tap water. He stole the show at the Winter Gardens that year, in what was one of his last appearances in the darts big time.

The temperature in Blackpool was in the 90s and Jocky, white hankie acting as a sun hat, posed on a Webster's Yorkshire Bitter dray with Eric Bristow and Cliff Lazarenko. All three held cans of the product, but Jocky did not touch a drop. At the Winter Gardens Jocky again took well over five minutes to get through the crowd to the stage for his encounter with number-one seed Rod Harrington. I watched this match closely, since it was on the cards that Jocky and I would be partners in the upcoming World Team Championships at Ayr.

The Blackpool Corporation water must have suited the wee man down to the ground. With hundreds of Scots holidaymakers cheering him on, Jocky was his old bouncy self and won 8–4. He got an eight-minute standing ovation that brought tears to more eyes than his. He went out next round to Nigel Justice, but it was great to see the old flair in action.

I had a successful, if unspectacular by my later standards, tournament in Blackpool. The highlight of my progress to the final was a 101.5 average in beating Paul Lim 11–4 in legs. In the final I played Dennis Priestley and, despite some of the loudest-ever support for him by the 'Mexborough Mafia', led by wife Jenny and son Adam, I won comfortably 16–11. I was grateful for the £10,000 prize and I got a most unusual bonus. I had hit

19 180s in the week, and the sponsors gave me 19 cases – 456 cans – of their best bitter.

It gave me something to talk about in my interview with Sky. Yes, I said, there would be a party at the Cricketers Arms in May Bank when I got home with the cans. But meanwhile for the next hour beer there would be only £1 a pint. I often stuck in this plug after a win, and it never failed to fill our pub.

Two months later the WDC roadshow moved on to Butlin's at Ayr for the World Pairs Championships. Again the place was heaving with Scots and again, fuelled by water, John Thomas Wilson, my partner, was the star of the show. He was run down and had boils under his arms; I told him to see a doctor when he got back home to Newcastle, but he was reluctant. His granny had told him horrendous tales of English quacks and he believed them. We were drawn against the very handy pairing of Rod Harrington and Peter Evison and in leg four the fun started. Rod needed 81 for the leg. He hit single 15, realized that we needed 170, and so decided against going for 16 and bull. It was a fair bet against an average darter. But not against Jocky. He did not hang about. He went 60, 60, bull. The place erupted. He hugged me. It was my second-last memory of Jocky on the oche.

We lost that game and went to the bar. I asked Jocky what he wanted, thinking that the answer would be water. 'I'll have a double brandy, Phil,' he whispered. 'Anything in it?' I asked. 'Aye, another one.' I laughed, handed him the quadruple brandy and went off. I don't know if he drank it – he was a sick man – but I hope he did. It would have been an apt farewell to world darts.

A few days before Christmas 1995 Jocky and Malvina did a moonlight flit from their house in Wallsend. They moved back 'home', to Kirkcaldy on the coast of Fife. A combination of illness and financial problems meant that Jocky had had enough. I have visited him several times since then in his one-bedroom council flat. One of my early visits was in the summer of 1998. Malvina came to the door, looked very surprised, then went inside. She returned shaking her head. 'Thanks for the visit,' was the message, 'but I don't want any company.' Eventually Jocky came out to look at my camper. He was in a tracksuit, smoking a fag and looked content with his lot in life. He told me he rarely went out, only going to the hospital for treatment for diabetes and depression, or to walk his dog. People were pointing at him. He had been living on the estate for over two years and nobody realized. I got the impression that this was exactly the way he wanted things.

As the end of 1995 approached I had, as usual, a very clear target. If I could retain the World Championship I would match another of Eric Bristow's achievements. Nobody else had ever done back-to-back wins. Dave Lanning had once remarked significantly in commentary: 'Eric was a burglar; Taylor is a mugger.' That sums up the difference between us. Eric would not psych out the lads of today like Wayne Mardle and Kevin Painter. They are more consistent than a lot of the old guard were. They are very heavy scorers, so I prepare accordingly.

For several weeks I did a bit of practice with lads at the pub, and went for sessions on my old oche in Blake Street. On Christmas Day, as usual, I didn't open my presents until I had done an hour's practice. This should not be too much of a surprise – the World Championships always start a couple of days after the holiday, and you can bet that Evison, Priestley and Lowe take their turn on the oche before the turkey and pudding. I had heard that Evison in particular was doing four-hour practice sessions. I thought Rod Harrington would be in with a shout for the title too, but perhaps he had been working too hard on the exhibition circuit. The dispute with the BDO looked certain now to go to the High Court, but I had kept out of it as much as possible. Mind, I did fancy a head-to-head on television with whoever won their championship at Lakeside.

I had now been 'the Power' for 12 months and had done everything to live up to the image. I had certainly livened up my exhibitions. I'd realized early on that the public did not just want good darts; they wanted entertainment. So I told my sponsors, Mansfield Brewery, that I wanted to bring along a singer every night. The lad in question was Alan Dutton, who sang in Hedgehoppers Anonymous in the 1960s and had a hit with

'Good News Week.' The brewery didn't think it was a good idea, but I forced them to let me try it.

It was a sensation. Alan sang selections from Doctor Hook and the Eagles after I'd played darts. Then I would play a few more games and he'd come on again at the end of the night. It was so much fun the brewery reps came every night! We'd all end up dancing and singing.

I also introduced a version of 'Bullseye', the Jim Bowen show, with lads and lasses throwing darts and trying to answer questions. I didn't have the capital to invest in plates with my picture on like Eric, so I used to give my photographs away. This really annoyed some of the other players. People use to say, 'Pay for photos? Phil Taylor gives them away.'

I also started working extra hard on my image. I had a chat with Paul Durrant, managing director of Durro Darts, and he made a good point. He said I should look smart and businesslike on stage; a World Champion should stand out among the other players. So I got some fancy spangled shirts with lightning flashes from a man in Mexborough. And, specially for the 1996 World Championship, I got a green glitter cape with 'Power' lettered on the back in gold. I got the idea from watching the American wrestler Randy 'Macho Man' Savage. Eat your heart out, Bobby George! The press went overboard about my cape, and if you go up dressed like Snoop Doggy Dog (I added glitter shades and a baseball cap that I'd bought in Atlantic City) you have to play well. Fortunately, I did.

On my way to the final I dropped only one set and had a 101 average against Shayne Burgess. Then it was head-to-head with my old mucker Dennis Priestley for the title. I must have played well because Dennis hit 15 180s and averaged 102 – but I still won. The tension really got to me when I needed 166 to take my fourth title. It is a bogey number – you can't get it with three darts – so I went 60, 60 and aimed at single 14 to leave double 16. I missed and hit a single 16. Nobody likes double 15, which is what I had left. When I then hit the double 15, I was too busy cursing my stupid mistake to appreciate the fact that I had become World Champion for the fourth time!

What did we have to do to get the game recognized as a top sport? OK, we had all the papers, posh and red-top, covering our event. But the standard of darts should have produced better headlines than 'Hype takes flight for tawdry glory' and 'Darts, tarts and tungsten tipplers'. Still, I was only one step away from equalling Eric's five world titles. Maybe the press would change tack then.

Oh yes, the cape. What Eric called my 'frog outfit'. People still ask about it at my exhibitions. 'Where is the cloak?' they want to know. Answer: it is not in the darts Hall of Fame, it's in a cardboard box in a charity shop in the Stoke area. I have moved on to better things. Look out for a new white-leather Elvis-inspired outfit, complete with fringes.

During my quarter-final match against Keith Deller,

Sid Waddell and John Gwynne waxed lyrical about my efforts, trying their utmost to stress the skill of darts to a wider audience. 'Sky bring you the very cream of the milk' was how Sid kicked off. 'Darts of outrageous proportions,' John agreed. Then Sid really got cranked up. 'Taylor is into that treble-18 cover like a fox on speed . . . When William Tell was playing in the Swiss super league, he was hitting the apple. Taylor is hitting the middle of the apple . . . He is nicknamed the Power – and one of his mates has just put 50p in the meter.'

Some people find this patter a bit of a nuisance, but an overwhelming proportion of viewers love it. I think it fits in beautifully with Sky's razzmatazz. Darts at the highest level can get one-dimensional as ton follows ton, so the commentator cannot afford to be passive or just plain boring. I don't think Tony Green of the BBC adds anything to the viewers' pleasure or understanding.

Moreover, on this occasion Sid and John were psychic. Sid pondered poetically: 'Maybe, John, there's a darts Valhalla, so we'll all end up in the sky sometime, sitting sipping mead and watching the great ghosts.' John had a wish 'to see the Power take on the Crafty Cockney in his heyday'. Twelve months later the wish was granted.

The road to my classic match with my mentor Eric Bristow, and my equalling his five World Championships, was no smooth progression.

In the Webster's World Matchplay at Blackpool in the

summer of 1996 we all got a reminder of the class lurk-
ing in the WDC ranks. Peter Evison, alias the 'Fen Tiger',
did not always shine brightly, but at the Winter Gardens
he was on fire. We all knew Peter could play – he had
won the World Masters in 1989 and the Samson Classic
in 1994 – but I had no idea of the pasting he was to dish
out to me. In our second-round match I was 5–0 down
in a race to eight in no time at all. And in the sixth leg
he burst a 140 finish! The final score was 8–1 to him and
his average was 105. I never got a look in, and Peter
went on to win the title.

I had more luck a few weeks later at the Willows
Variety Centre in Salford in the World Pairs Championships. My new partner was Bob Anderson and, since
there were no horses to worry about, the Limestone
Cowboy was at home on this range. We battled successfully through the field to set up a final with two young
guns, Steve Raw and Chris Mason. Steve is built as solid
as a rock and Mace the Ace is a thoroughbred. The final
was a cracker and had Sid in commentary asking 'What
is the melting point of tungsten?' (He was actually sent
the answer by a fan who is a metal worker; apparently it
is 3,700 degrees Fahrenheit.)

After a ding-dong final Bob and I just shaded it 18–15.
And I ended the game in tears: I was relieved, and a
little bit ashamed that Bob had carried me through the
middle 10 legs. But that was a stream compared to the
torrents of tears that were to flow at Purfleet as I went
for my fifth world title.

I didn't go to Purfleet full of big ideas about records. In fact I had a small technical problem that could easily become a big one. At Blackpool and Salford I hadn't been happy with my grip on the dart. I had recently signed with sponsors Unicorn Products and I got their expert, Alex Ross, to help me figure out the problem. Alex added extra rings to the grip and that did the trick; in the 1997 World Championships I threw with the best set of darts I have ever had.

I had been practising hard and sailed through the round-robin stages with comfortable victories over Chris Mason and Gerald Verrier. Then in the quarter finals I beat Keith Deller 5–1 in sets with a 98.4 average.

Meanwhile, there was a sensation occurring in the tournament; Eric had reeled back the years and was out to show everybody, including me, that there was still life in the old Cockney. Sid Waddell and Dave Lanning charted his resurgence vividly. 'You can trust darts players with best porcelain, as long as you put the right stuff in it,' said Sid, as Eric banged in the 60s in a group-stage match against Bob Anderson. Eric won, and Sid proclaimed it 'a historic day for darts'. And Eric was by no means finished. He came through the group stage and took on Alan Warriner; the winner would play me in the semi-final. Surely Eric would stumble.

Sid did not think so. 'They made Dick Whittington mayor of London, maybe Eric is on some secret list.' Dave Lanning was also convinced we were seeing the old Eric. 'It takes your breath away to see this resuscita-

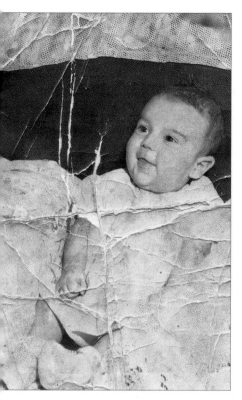

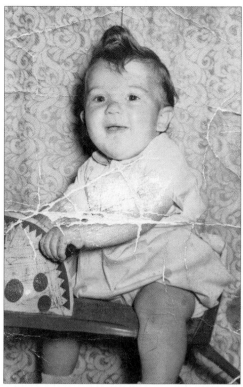

My mum was proud of producing a big baby of good fighting stock. I'm told I look just like my great grandfather Boag Harvey, a famous bare-knuckle fighter.

We had no money to spare when I was little. I played in a boat created from a clothes drawer, or this rocking horse made by one of my uncles.

My very first home – we had no electricity and half the windows were missing. No wonder I went walkabout to the park and fell in the lake.

Aged four, and probably having just seen the ghost of the old man upstairs; or was mum telling me off for bashing the paintwork with my toy car?

I was a lonely but imaginative boy. At the age of eight I played cricket in the yard for England and learned to fight when mum made me wear white wool trousers.

With my dad and a friend on holiday. You can see the puppy fat that still bother me – now it's doggy fat.

I'm in my late teens here and I've dabbled in darts, but girls and discos are now top of my list.

Mills and Boon eat your heart out. With a 15-year-old Yvonne, my wife-to-be, whom I'd just met at the Sneyd Arms Disco where I was the local John Travolta.

My parents Doug and Liz (on the right) get cosy on a rare night out. Dad deserved a pint now and then because he worked like a Trojan.

A cuddle from a happy family man. I was working all hours to support my Lisa and baby Chris.

My first big darts prize. I got £1,000 for winning the Burslem Open but had to split it with my sponsor.

Yvonne was a dab hand at darts. In 1998 we came 9th in the Haywards Pickles Mixed Pairs.

On cloud nine. I'm in the crac[k] Staffordshire county tea[m] alongside Eric Bristow, wh[o] does not tolerate duffer[s.]

Eric liked a pint to celebrate a win. I like black tea and a Chinese meal. We're chalk and cheese, but he became my mentor and my pal.

Yvonne and I got married in April 1988. Then I played darts for the county – and won. Then we had our reception.

Brissy told everybody that his pal Phil would take them to the cleaners. I did. I won the 1990 Embassy World Professional Championship and beat him in the final.

'Blake Street Bloke Done Great' should have been the *Sentinel* headline – the pride on the faces of family and friends says it all.

Playing for England with my idols Eric and Dave Whitcombe was a dream come true. But I am a reality lad – I won Man of the Match on this first outing in 1990

Like the great white shark I never rest; representing England in the Europe Cup I won the singles title with a 95.2 average. Chicken feed, I know, but read on.

I am very proud of this picture. To be in a world-class gallery with Jocky Wilson and Leighton Rees is special.

1992 Mike Gregory and I played
e greatest-ever Embassy final
d the strain shows on both of us.

'Bull's-eye' used to be a national
favourite on telly. Here I am with
the lovely Linda Lusardi and the
one and only Jim Bowen.

Sky brought showbiz glitter to darts
and I got a green Batman cloak. Pity
I played rubbish in it and ended up
giving it to a charity shop.

Sad to say the
Embassy world
trophy is the only
cup my team Port
Vale will ever see.
But the fans cheered
me to the echo.

Rival, pal, gentleman, and family man. For many years Dennis Priestley and I were top of the tree – and often we shared the prize money.

Proud landlord of The Cricketers' Arms with all the family after my fourth world title. Dad had me pulling pints seconds after the photo was taken.

We've just won the long-running bitter dispute with the BDO and Peter Evison, Eric Bristow, Dennis Priestley and I celebrate.

tion of a legend,' said Dave, almost in tears. Sid was on fire: 'What's the melting point of microphone metal?' Whatever that figure is, and I'm sure someone out there will tell us, it was reached again when Eric and I fought out our epic semi-final.

Hardly anybody was sitting down as we made our entrances. Eric was cheered to the rafters. Young lads who had probably still been in nappies when he was Mr Darts in the 1980s were singing. 'London Calling' boomed throughout the club, then the crowd started on 'Walking in a Bristow Wonderland'. Coming through the crowd, 99 per cent of whom wanted me to lose, I felt like Benny Hill's little slaphead sidekick. And slap my head they did; by the time I got on the stage I felt like I'd been amongst the cod in a chip-shop. The shirt was nearly pulled from my back and my hairdo was patted ragged. Paul Aaron Stone and his bouncers did wonders with their flying wedge – I reckon they were the only people with money on me!

Tommy Cox was near the stage when we walked through the crowd. He couldn't stand the tension any more: he went into the Sky scanner, then to the television monitors in the foyer of the club, then he stood biting his nails in the car-park.

Even before we started I was shaking. I had never had a crowd so obviously against me. But at the same time I was pleased and proud for Eric. He had prepared well. He was playing well. And it was great to see the old Crafty Cockney cockiness and arrogance. Later on, though, one flash of this was to gee me up and spur me to give him some pain.

Once we got on the stage I tried very hard, but to no avail, to clear my mind of everything. We were playing for a place in the final and a chance of winning £45,000. It was the most I'd ever played for. The man I was playing was my mentor and former sponsor; I could not assess how much I owed him. I knew how proud he was of my achievements. Some wisecrackers had said in the early days, 'Taylor? He couldn't win a super league match, never mind a world title.' Eric had told them where to go. But my gut feeling was that Eric could not do it under pressure. How wrong can you get?

During the practice darts I was shaking, my eyes were glazed over and I couldn't hold my head straight. I could see before a dart was thrown for real that his self-belief was high. He had been going round telling everybody that he was the only bloke in the tournament who could beat me. I sensed that I might have trouble because Eric came alive on stage; he loved the limelight and entered a new dimension. Getting to the semi-final had made him forget his nerves. He knew how good I was but, just like in the old days, he would offer me not one iota of respect. With all this jumble of thoughts about Eric, no wonder I nearly let the match slip.

As we slugged it out over the first eight sets, with me missing doubles and Eric hanging in, Sid told the viewers all about the massive bet Harry 'the Dog' Findlay, a professional gambler, had on my winning the title. Harry, a former member of the Sky team, had rung Sid that morning to ask if 'Old Brissy' had any chance at all. When Sid said that Eric had every chance, Harry almost choked. 'I stand to lose £18,000 if Eric wins,' he spluttered. He spent the match behind his settee, eyes averted from the television.

The game caught fire near the end of the eighth set. Eric was relaxed and had that 'I'm gonna get you' look in his eyes. He was 4–3 down in sets, and 2–1 down in legs; I wanted double four for the match and he wanted 141 to save the match. On commentary Sid screamed: 'Eric does not look like a man in the form to get this three-darter!' But he did. I felt weak, like a boxer with only the ropes holding him up.

I put up my hand for a high-five and his palm hit mine like a right cross by Mike Tyson. It hurt my hand – and for me it changed the match. His chin was jutting out like Bruce Forsyth's. He was urging himself and the crowd on. It made me focus 100 per cent. Some people might react to a gesture or a word by getting angry and letting their concentration slip; I use such things to sharpen my game. 'Right, you bastard, you're going to get it now!' I thought.

Eric brought the match to 4–4 in sets. He was not letting me play my natural game. He was bullying me when he got the chance. But I could tell by his face that he was feeling the pressure. The crowd were so loud and animated that Sky delayed the start of the ninth set by five minutes and still they were singing

'Walking in a Bristow Wonderland' and 'There's Only One Eric Bristow'.

Off we went in the final set, which had to be won by two clear legs. Eric began snatching the darts and going off balance. The crowd went quiet. I stepped in and took the leg score to 4–3. Then Eric had two darts at double eight to level the match, but he missed. I had double two for the set and the match, and made no mistake.

Eric's face said it all. He was as near to tears as I have ever seen him. Looking back, I think if he had beaten me in that match his career would have changed. He would probably have got his name on the world trophy again. But, as Sid put it, it was 'yet more of the cruel poetry of the game'.

Tommy Cox, as tournament director, was waiting for us both as we came off. Part of his job is to make sure the adrenalin doesn't boil over. There was no chance of that, and there would be no more cracks of 'I hope I get Eric in the draw'. I'd been given the fright of my life and I was white as a sheet. Tommy and I went to the empty office behind the stage. We sat for one hour, occasionally hugging and occasionally weeping.

There was only one hurdle now between myself and Eric's record, Dennis Priestley; pal, pairs partner and the best player I have ever faced. He takes a long time to throw, and this sometimes puts opponents off. This is not a deliberate tactic like that which Alan Evans used to employ, nor like Terry Downes, who once famously beat Jocky by taking three-and-a-half minutes to throw three darts! I regard deliberate slow play as cheating, even though many players do it. With Dennis it is his natural game; he's tried to play faster but it didn't work.

His big downfall when he plays me is that he has always been a close friend of mine. In fact, a couple of years ago I chased some of his family out of the practice room because they were giving him earache; you don't need encouragement five minutes before going on the oche. Dennis said I was right. He cannot bring himself to bully me, whereas I am the opposite. I can be your best buddy, but I'll murder you up there. And you know who taught me that.

The 1997 final between myself and Dennis Priestley was not a classic; I like to think that over the years I have adapted to handle his slow pace, so I did just what I had to. But in the commentary box Sid as usual found plenty to say: 'Here they are, the two best players on the planet . . .' He heralded a bull finish with a classical allusion: 'Hitting the bull as good as Jason and the lads finding the fleece.' Would that be the Fleece in Pudsey or the one in Bradford? And when I really got going – pushing my average up to 101 – Sid reckoned 'Taylor is so hot he could hit the bullseye standing up in a hammock.'

I won the match 6–3 in sets and the emotion swamped me. I could hardly talk through the tears. I had won £45,000. Eric had won three consecutive world titles in 1984, 1985 and 1986 and I had matched that. I had also matched his five world titles. It was all too much for me to take in. In fact, I spent a lot of time on the microphone praising Dennis as the Jimmy White of our game.

On reflection, I think our game goes in eras. Rees was toppled by Lowe who was toppled by Eric. Anderson and Harrington were world number ones, then along came the Power. In 1996 everybody said it would be impossible for anyone to match Eric. Then, as the 2002 Championship came along, they said nobody could win 10 titles. It will be very difficult for anyone to match my achievement. I did it over 12 years. So Mardle and Painter and their generation will have to get their skates on.

How many times do I want to win the world title? I reckon 13. But I may do more, because I think I can play better.

CHAPTER 10

Joining the Legends

It must be clear by now how much I owe to my mentor, Eric Bristow, and how many times I was egged on to achievement by his jibes. Well, one of Eric's cracks was, 'You've won nothing, mate, until you've won the *News of the World*.' Eric had won the title in 1983 and 1984, but in 1990 the great tournament had ended. Then at the end of 1996 we heard that, in conjunction with Big D peanuts, the *News of the World* Championships would be played again, with a prize to the men's winner of £42,000.

The historic event began in 1927 and was for decades the World Championship of darts. In its heyday in the 1940s the tournament involved half a million players. The roll of honour reads like a *Who's Who* of the sport, and seven men have won the title twice; apart from Eric, the heroes are Tommy Gibbons (1952 and 1958), Tom Reddington (1955 and 1960), Tommy Barrett (1964 and 1965), Stefan Lord (1978 and 1980), Bobby George (1979 and 1986) and Mike Gregory (1987 and 1988). Two factors make these achievements special: one, you have to win through from your pub; two, it was always played as the best of three legs! The talent and nerve needed to succeed are massive. Anyone can get lucky over such a short stretch.

The great John Lowe, who won the title in 1981, lost several times at pub level to an old codger called Jack Holmes. And in the run-up to the finals in June 1997 the upsets continued. Lowe went out at pub level. Bristow was beaten by his driver! And Peter Evison went out to his brother-in-law, Robbie Widdows. I am glad to say that I got through to the final stages, which were played at the Aston Villa Leisure Centre.

In setting up the tournament for Sky, Dave Lanning and Sid Waddell spoke passionately of their memories of the tournament. 'I remember Billy Lennard, a Bryl-creemed lorry driver from Manchester, cutting down Leighton Rees in the final. The Welsh fans shed salt tears,' recalled Sid. Dave spoke in hushed tones of Alan Evans giving a Denis Law salute as he won his 1972 semi-final. Dave's assessment: 'This Taff hath skills at the arrows of outrageous proportions.'

Sid was tipping me to win and Bobby George, now a BBC pundit, did the same but in a back-handed way. 'Taylor is the pick of the bunch. Dead boring, but ruthless,' Bobby wrote in the *News of the World*. I ignored the slight as Bobby was firmly within the BDO camp in the long-running dispute that was due to come to court that month.

As if ordered by the hand of fate, Martin Adams and I won through to the semi-final. It was a grudge match. Adams calls himself 'Wolfie', has jet-black hair, lots of gold jewellery and is a cocky player. Just like Bobby, Martin never missed a chance to run down me and the WDC. I was flying the flag for the 'rebels' and I desperately wanted to beat him.

As we started our match my average was 100 to his 91, but this was sudden-death darts. Despite my best efforts, Adams won the first leg, going out on a 71 finish. So I dug extra deep. He threw first in what could have been the winning leg for him. I noticed he was not composed at all; he was sweating, shaking and his flights were trembling. I fired in 100, 100, 100 – and he had, rather stupidly, left 170. This was bad darts; he was trying to show off and it was fatal. I think a better leave would have been 167. He threw three sloppy darts for only 60. Cue the Power: 177 and double 12: a 13-darter that knocked the stuffing out of him. The 177 had the commentators drooling. 'The very middle, the hey-diddle-diddle, of the treble 19!' screamed Sid. He was not exaggerating.

It was time for the deciding leg. I won the bull and went first. I started with 134. Sid was hushed, 'Captain Morgan, Torquemada, you name the torturer. Taylor is dishing out real pain.' Adams was now showing even more signs of stress; he was shaking his head, talking to himself and rubbing his eyes. There was only one big bad wolf on the stage smelling blood, and that was me. I got a bit sloppy in mid-leg but got 140 ahead. Even a maximum in reply did not worry me. I did a steady ton to leave 148. John Gwynne purred, 'The Power eases in a killer 60 to leave a finish.' Adams threw a ton but still needed 196. I could use six darts to win. I didn't need that many. I left myself double four. Game over. The crowd loved it. So did Sid. 'It's like being at a convent the night Mother Superior won the lottery – bad habits coming out all over the place.'

After that the final was almost a formality. My opponent Ian 'Diamond' White told Sky he was happy just to be in the final. I loved it when I heard that. Bad attitude. I took the lad to bits. I won the first leg then did a 12-darter to join the legends. 'Powerus maximus est!' screamed John, a former teacher (not of Classics, I assure you).

Eric was putting his name behind me and I was proud to justify his faith. When he said in interviews just before matches that I was going to annihilate somebody – with the fellow himself standing in the wings listening – it was as good as two 180s for a start.

When I think back, the hardest *News of the World* matches for me were the pub rounds at the Huntsman in Stoke years before. The area finals attracted a galaxy of super league and county players. In that 1997 campaign the man who came nearest to beating me was

Steve 'Adonis' Beaton, who had a dart at double to dump me out. I ought also to make the point that I could never have won the *News of the World* title from the old throwing mark of eight feet. In the revived tournament of 1997 the mark was at the world standard range of seven feet nine-and-a-quarter inches. We are all precision machines throwing precision missiles. Messing around with the oche throws us out completely.

My victory was also good news for the WDC as the day of reckoning in the long dispute approached.

Despite the fact that the dispute between the WDC and the BDO was now reaching the final stages of litigation and the feeling that eventually we would win, it was still good to see that the tide of events in darts generally was going our way. In April 1997 the WDC and Sky Sports announced a million-dollar deal which secured television coverage and guaranteed our financial future for several years. Part of this expansion was a special 'Battle of the Champions' to be held at the Circus Tavern on Saturday 29 June. There was a lip-smacking line-up that was a heady mix of current form and pure nostalgia. Eric Bristow would renew rivalries with Welsh genius Alan Evans; Rod Harrington would take on the 1994 Embassy Champion John Part of Canada; my opponent would be the current pride of the Valleys, former boxer Richie Burnett, the 1995 Embassy Champion.

What was most encouraging about Richie's participation was that in May he had come out openly and joined the WDC ranks. 'When I played in the Antwerp Open I was embraced by all the WDC players and it felt like I'd come home,' said Richie. 'I am looking forward to some challenging matches against the true darts professionals. I think coverage on Sky Sports helps increase the public's awareness of the game, generates interest among the young and people who have not touched their darts for years and means potential sponsors can come to view darts in a positive light.'

As usual Sky gave the event the full glitzy treatment. The 1,300 crowd was swelled by two coachloads of Alan Evans' fans, just like the old days at the *News of the World* finals. As Martin Turner of Sky put it, 'Put these genuine working-class heroes together with high-tech presentation and you're on to a winner. It's a simple game played by ordinary-looking people but at a pitch of excellence. What better combination for a sport. I don't think we'll get pop-star types, but in darts you don't need to be pretty – you need to be a good character.' Sid Waddell was more vivid: 'The atmosphere here is a cross between the Munich Beer Festival and the Olympic Games. This is working-men's archery.'

The Alan Evans who took on Eric was a pale shadow of the mercurial figure who had dazzled the crowd at Jollees. Alan was ill with kidney problems, but showed some of his brilliance in the early legs. The commentators recalled the vitriolic quarter-final match at the Embassy in 1979. In that game there were harsh words between the players and Evans made threatening gestures. It was great television, produced a massive viewer response and Evans won the match in the final leg. Sad to say, at Purfleet the spark soon died and Eric coasted the match by 3–0 in sets.

It was Alan's last appearance in the darting limelight. His health deteriorated and he died in Barry, south Glamorgan, in April 1999 at the age of 49. He will always be remembered for his talent and his pride. In 1976 he walked off the 'Johnny Carson Show' after being asked to throw darts backwards through his legs using a mirror. 'I'm a darts player, not a bloody clown,' he hissed. Good for him.

In the match with John Part, Dennis Priestley had an easy victory by another 3–0 scoreline. I practised near Richie Burnett for our encounter and could sense that he was very nervous. He played well, but opened the door for me a couple of times. In the end I blew him off the board in a 4–1 victory with an average of 114. Like a typical Welsh competitor of the Evans, Leighton Rees and Ceri Morgan school, he was a tough opponent, fuelled on personal and national pride.

As Eric, Dennis and I posed for triumphant pictures there were two reasons to be happy. One, on the playing front the WDC had won the honours. But the second reason was the most significant in the long run. Three weeks before the 'Battle of the Champions' the battle of the darts organizations had been settled at the High Court and we had won. The full story will be told in the next chapter.

The big major tournament coming up was the World Matchplay at Blackpool, which the *Independent* called, with a lot of truth, 'the spiritual home of the game'. Now I don't know what got into me that week but it produced the best sustained darts of my career to date. It could not have been the beer – I don't take more than the odd half or a port-and-brandy before practice – so maybe it was the sea air. Above all, the end of the dispute lifted a weight off all our shoulders. I went to Blackpool to show the world I was the best player in the game and to start the push for my record-breaking sixth World Championship title.

Sky now had 12 cameras trained on the action and was giving us 40 hours of live coverage. John Part and Richie Burnett were in the very strong field, and so was Eric Bristow. Sadly Eric went out early on to Dennis Smith by 8–2 in legs and the press asked me to comment on it. 'It's sad because he's been playing well again,' I said. 'He brought me and a lot of players through and probably wishes he hadn't now.' A lot of people see only the arrogant side of Eric, but he has passed on a great deal of knowledge. As usual he took no prisoners when asked how he had played. 'Played crap. Stevie Wonder would have beaten me.'

I was also pleased to see Dennis Priestley beating BDO player Andy Jenkins to keep the WDC banner high – or PDC (Professional Darts Corporation) as we were now known.

The first player to feel the rampant Power was

Canada's Gary Mawson, who looks like Bluto's hand-
some younger brother. I blitzed him 8–0 in legs with a
112 average; I did an 11-darter and two 10-darters. At
the mercifully quick end Gary dropped to his knees and
prostrated himself like a Christian at the true Cross. In
the commentary box Sid once again made reference to
things that happen to bad guys in Saudi Arabia.

From then on it was a parade to the final. I beat Mick
Manning 8–2; Bob Anderson 11–2; and Rod Harrington
13–9. Rod, I admit, did give me a fright at 12–4 when
he won five successive legs. In the final Alan Warriner
played brilliantly up to 8–8, but in the end had no
answer to a 106.3 average. The final score was 16–11.
On the winning throw a shower of green and gold glitter
drowned the pair of us and Sid gave me the ultimate
accolade. 'That's Blackpool dazzle greeting the greatest
player of all time.' In the *Daily Telegraph*, Giles Smith
made the first of a torrent of serious points on which
the press were soon to agree. 'Let no one say darts isn't
a physically complex sport. Like athletics, really, only
it draws a bigger crowd.' I think my performance at
Blackpool that week set a new context for the discussion
of darts as a proper sport. Later on Giles was to stir a few
feathers by saying that it was even harder than golf!

Talking about stirring feathers, there was a fine touch
of irony during that week in Blackpool. Before the Matchplay, the BDO staged the British Classic at the Norbreck
Castle Hotel, a couple of miles away from the Winter
Gardens. All their top players were there, including

Ronnie Baxter, Martin Adams and Ray Barneveld, a very classy Dutchman. And there was still a lot of needle in the air: Sid Waddell and Alan Warriner were having a beer in the middle of the hall, and were not made welcome at all. No BDO officials, some of whom they had known for years, would speak to them. This was a forerunner of things to come, since in many ways the court settlement changed nothing.

But on the oche we former rebels took all the honours. Dennis Priestley won the singles competition, and he and I won the pairs. We had our picture taken with Sam Hawkins of the BDO, and his smile is one of the most forced you will ever see in *Darts World* magazine.

The Cricketers flourished in our first few years and I learned never to miss a trick to make a bob or two, although running a pub was not without incident. At the end of 1996 I drove up to the front of the pub and saw my dad leaning precariously off a ladder as he cleaned the windows. I shouted up at him to be careful but he went his own way. Five minutes later I was looking out of the bar window and he came sailing off the ladder like Spiderman on a bad day. He broke his foot and was in plaster for weeks.

Then came a body-blow to our family. After 30-odd years at H. and R. Johnson's without a day off due to sickness, dad began to pass blood. For years he had smoked as many as 30 Park Drive cigarettes a day. We told him to stop but he always said the same thing:

'Don't start on at me. My mother smoked and she lived into her nineties. She never had a day's illness.' But my dad was not so lucky. The doctors told him that he had cancer of the stomach.

In the summer of 1997 I was standing in the pub brooding. I felt helpless to do anything for dad, who was terminally ill. It was a Wednesday night and my good friend Mick Connor was with me. It suddenly came to me that there was something I could do. I could try for a miracle. I looked Mick straight in the face. 'You are going to call me everything under the sun, bud, but you and me are going to Lourdes tomorrow – with my dad.' I thought he would try to talk me out of it but he simply nodded.

I asked my mum if dad had a passport and she said he had. 'I'm taking him to Lourdes tomorrow,' I said. A funny look came over her face. 'You must be psychic; your dad mentioned Lourdes to me just 10 minutes ago in the other room.' That made me even more determined. Next day we all went off to Luton airport and then on to Nice. Mick and I shared the driving to Lourdes. We got there at five in the morning, had a couple of hours' sleep and went to the shrine. I stood quietly with dad and mum in the queue for the baths. We had no idea what to expect and we were all very nervous, especially when the odd scream joined the splashing behind the curtain up front. Soon it was my turn to go behind the curtain, and it amazed me when two heavies gripped with fingers of steel and tried to dip me in the water. I tried telling them I didn't want the treatment and managed to drag myself out still dry. My mum felt she had to have the dip along with dad.

We were back in the Potteries within 36 hours. I had Tommy Cox to thank for the funding of the trip, because at the time I did not possess any credit cards.

Back home dad went into hospital for an operation. He died soon after, but I am glad to say there was no suffering in his last days.

As we laid him to rest a memory came back of freezing days out playing as a little lad. I would race into the house, brush the *Evening Sentinel* to the floor and climb on his knee. Though he'd been working hard out in the cold, his arms and chest would always be warm as toast.

Dad taught me one great lesson in life: you only get back what you put in. Whatever I tried – cricket, boxing or darts – he would scoff at me if I didn't give 100 per cent. I remember missing a night at the gym in my weight-lifting days and him giving me a telling off. What with him nagging at home and Eric Bristow mithering me on the oche, no wonder I became a World Champion.

CHAPTER 11

An End to Strife?

Many people are totally in the dark about the outcome of the legal action our organization, the WDC, took against the British Darts Organisation for what we saw as restraint of trade. So it is worth taking a closer look at just what happened.

Here is the timetable of events. Early in 1994 the WDC writ was issued. A High Court date was set for the autumn of 1995. There were countless delays, and discussions in front of Mr Justice Potts about how the case should proceed did not begin until the last week of June 1997.

In 1994 the policy of the BDO at national level and the hawkish attitude of some officials at local level were making life very difficult for the 'rebels'. The result of their actions meant that we were not able to operate as darts professionals. We heard that Olly Croft was accusing us of being greedy and that he thought we should be happy with any prize money there happened to be in the game. And that was even before the ban was passed by the full BDO council in April 1993.

After the ban we at the WDC obviously had to think of organizing and promoting events. The BDO ignored the fact that darts was our bread and butter; our welfare and our jobs were of no apparent concern to them. It was all getting me down personally. Eric Bristow always seems able to go on the road and smile things off, but I need to be happy. If there are problems at home, phone calls containing threats or bans, then I can't function properly. And take it from me, temperatures continued to rise.

At this point it will be as well to recap on the three-pronged nature of the ban as laid out in the BDO resolution. One: any BDO official or player would be banned if they 'associated' with the activities of the WDC. Two: member counties should refrain from 'attending or assisting' exhibitions by WDC players. Three: member counties should exclude WDC players from their events.

On this basis things happened that still leave a bad taste in the mouth. During a county match in Scotland between Renfrewshire and Ayrshire, Jamie Harvey was asked to leave the pub by a BDO player. Happily, the landlord told the player to mind his own business.

Jamie stayed. A BDO picket tried to stop Cliff Lazarenko going into a pub on the Isle of Wight to play. Dennis Priestley was told he could not play in his own working men's club.

There is no doubt that the BDO directive that no one should 'associate' with 'rebel players' was widely interpreted by some sections of the BDO at local level. In the north-east in particular, people were hounded, and phone calls were definitely made to the media and businesses putting across the BDO party line.

One of the focal points of most unrest was the Northumberland area. There Peter Barron, who had served the county as a teenager, both as a player and an official, was harassed by the local organisation. This was totally due to alleged association with the WDC. What Peter had done was to act as a camera spotter on Tyne Tees coverage of the Samson competition in Newcastle, which involved WDC players. This was felt enough of a sin to get him banned from any further involvement with Northumberland darts. With typical dedication, Peter set up the North-eastern Darts Association, which organised successful events and was widely supported by darts players in the north-east.

For myself, after the shabby treatment by Staffordshire that I described earlier, I did not even attempt to argue the case. In fact, I tried very hard to keep out of the dispute. But exhibition work was down to rock bottom; no county player would dare line up to play against us so the pubs and clubs were not making bookings. By the end of 1994 our very livings were in jeopardy.

The situation became much worse when the BDO, through the World Darts Federation, tried to make the ban worldwide. But there was light in the gloom; Canada and the USA would not impose a ban because they were advised that legally they could face penalties if they did.

Tommy Cox went to Europe to argue the case for the WDC with the Scandinavian countries which were members of the WDF. He got a fair hearing in Helsinki, but still a vote was carried in favour of the ban. Tommy and Dick Allix, WDC events director and agent for Eric Bristow and other players, carried the message to a meeting of the WDF in Las Vegas. After talks with WDF president Peter McMenamen, they got what they thought was a deal; in a handwritten letter the WDC agreed to drop the word 'World' from its name. The next day Olly Croft refused to put the proposed deal to a vote of the BDO membership.

This was the last straw. Europe, apart from some tournaments in Belgium where there was a split between banners and non-banners, was persuaded to cut our players out. So was the rest of the world, with the exception of Canada and the USA. We had no other choice but to take further legal action against the BDO for restraint of trade.

There was sound precedent for such a case. Our argument cited the Tony Greig and John Snow case against the Test and County Cricket Board over World Series cricket in the 1970s, and Article 5 of the Treaty of Rome, which governs trade between European Union countries.

The WDC proceeded reluctantly down the road to the High Court. Dick Allix made the situation clear in *Darts World* in early 1995.

'We cannot ignore, of course, the dark cloud of litigation, but while certain factions of the British Darts Organisation continue on their merry way to destroy both the WDC and the professional players, then we must protect ourselves and the players by all the legal means that are at our disposal. We will continue, however, to try and settle the dispute and it would appear that common sense might well prevail in a few months.

I will state once and for all that the World Darts Council wishes to co-exist with the BDO and the WDF and has no desire, and neither has it ever had, to become involved with super leagues, counties or internationals. It must be remembered that we tried to work within the BDO structure for three years prior to the January 1993 split in order to return our game to television.

When it was apparent that the executive of the BDO would not listen to us, the decision to leave was regrettable but inevitable. With the number of amateur players now trying to qualify for our tournaments, the statement that the WDC is "only 14 over-the-hill players" is plainly ridiculous.

We fervently hope peace will be negotiated without a trip to court, after which the sport will then truly thrive. The WDC offers additional opportunities for the world's top players, not alternatives.'

This appeal fell on deaf ears.

The next step for the WDC was to find out how the suit against the BDO looked in terms of European law. A top European barrister said we had a cast-iron case. So the litigation dragged on, with the BDO asking for confirmations and copies of documents, leading to more delays. If they thought we would become tired of wasting time and money and simply give up, they were nearly right; as the weeks went by the legal fees were costing us a fortune.

Up to the settlement in mid-1997 the WDC spent £300,000 on the case, and it is estimated that the BDO spent £200,000. It was disappointing that only eight of our players contributed, but some of them simply could not afford to. I put in about £15,000 and in return was given shares in the WDC. In effect this was a loan to pay the legal costs. Other contributors were Harrows Darts, McCleod-Holden and Unicorn. Most of us got our money back as cash or shares after the settlement, but some of the agencies and manufacturers are still being paid back. At one time things were so tight that only a

£20,000 loan and a £22,000 guarantee by Tommy Cox kept the WDC afloat.

In October 1996, as the case rumbled towards the High Court, Olly Croft had this to say in *Darts World*.

'Put shortly, it is the players who are the authors of this particular saga. It is they who created the problem and are now continuing it in the form of legal proceedings; yet it appears that they complain that the dispute needs to be settled before it goes to court.

There is only one party who can prevent this case from going to court. It is the players.

They brought the case and they can prevent it from going to court by dropping the proceedings.'

Our position was clear. Not only did we want the actions of the BDO directors reversed, we wanted compensation for the losses suffered because of those actions.

The last act of the drama, after five years of bitter squabbling, happened in just over four days at the end of June 1997. In fact, although the case came to the High Court, an agreement was reached without the proceedings actually starting. The first three-and-a-half days were taken up with barristers for each side debating the legal arguments and evidence involved. Then the barrister for the WDC told our people that we would 'probably' win (so much for 'cast iron' by other legal opinion way back!) but the case could possibly go on for another two weeks. What is more, the judge could easily award us just £1, even if we won.

There was no argument. Neither side seemed to have the will to go further. The two opposing barristers worked out a deal and an agreement was presented to the judge. On 30 June the judge ruled that the Tomlin Order, the joint agreement, would settle the case. The BDO agreed to lift their ban and to give the WDC – now the Professional Darts Corporation – £35,000, which would be used to hire BDO equipment. The WDC dropped the word 'World' from its title. Both sides agreed that the top 16 players in each side's World Championship should not be permitted to enter the other's competition in the immediate following year.

A *Guardian* newspaper report had no doubts about what the outcome meant: 'the BDO lost its case'. *The Times* took a photograph of Peter Evison, myself, Dennis Priestley and Eric Bristow hoisting a celebratory pint of Guinness in a pub near the High Court.

The agreement reached by both sides was that players could participate in all competitions, whoever ran them, and take part in exhibition matches and promote and endorse darts products. It fell to Eric to make the main points. 'The ban has been lifted,' he said. 'The BDO and the WDC have made their peace. For the first time in four years I am free to play darts in competitions all over the world.' Eric added that the lifting of the ban meant that he and other WDC players could now take part in exhibition matches with amateur pub and club players who, as BDO members, had been banned from competing with the professionals. The WDC put out a statement welcoming the agreement.

'Under the terms of the agreement the BDO accepts the role of the WDC, under its new name of the Professional Darts Council, to represent the interests of professional darts players throughout the world, including by organizing and promoting darts tournaments, obtaining sponsorship and television coverage for them, maintaining a ranking system, and administering these tournaments.

The WDC has agreed to recognize the role of the BDO as a nationwide organization, a governing body of the sport of darts, organizing and administering darts tournaments, obtaining sponsorship and television for them, maintaining a ranking system, and administering those tournaments.'

The BDO statement made it clear that the ban was over.

'Both bodies recognize and accept that no organization has the exclusive right to organize darts tournaments, and that the BDO and the PDC are entitled lawfully to compete with each other.

As a result of the agreement reached between the BDO, the 14 players and the PDC, all proceedings have been brought to an end on terms agreed between all parties.'

John Lowe articulated the feelings of all of us when, in his capacity as chairman of the World Professional Darts Players Association, he spoke to *Darts World*.

'What a relief. After four years of waiting for the most ludicrous and unnecessary trial to come to court, common sense prevailed.

Arbitration was to be the answer, an agreement thrashed out behind closed doors, with the impending result, vindication for the 14 players and an open playing field for dart players the world over.

This will not be taken as a personal victory by the 14, although they could claim that by the very nature of the settlement. It will be taken and seen, I hope, as a triumph for darts and the freedom of choice of individual players throughout Great Britain and the world.'

Sid Waddell thought justice had been done: 'Ideologically, emotionally and democratically I sided with the players who split off. I think there was an agenda to stop them earning their living, and that Canada and the USA saw that this was in restraint of trade. I think the BDO put their organization before the valid interests of the people who made the game, the likes of Lowe, Bristow, Priestley and Taylor. I am glad that professional dart players are at last free to earn a living from their sport without having to contend with bureaucracy cramping their style.'

Although I tried to keep out of the bickering as much

as possible, I was behind our campaign all the way. During the dispute many BDO county players privately told me and the other 'rebels' that they admired us for sticking to our guns. On top of the £15,000 I put into the kitty to fight the case, I reckon the dispute cost me £30,000 in lost bookings. Rod Harrington estimated the same. The whispering campaign to breweries, pubs and clubs hit us hard financially.

I would have been happy to lose the £15,000 in our quest for justice. We wanted it established that we had the right to work anywhere we wished. That was the significance of the agreement.

Overall I wish we had taken the issue to its conclusion and tried to get compensation for lost earnings. I appreciate the risk and the extra cost of a longer court case, but we had been given a very hard time for over four years. If the BDO had won the case I think they would have taken us to the cleaners.

What was very sad was the damage to personal relations during the dispute. It was particularly bad for Eric Bristow, who had been a friend of Olly Croft since he was 18. And one has to say that even today there is still bad blood. Bobby George, who has never won a World Championship but who still sets himself up as a guru of the game, never misses a chance to scoff at 'Phil's Dart Club', as he calls the PDC, in his *Darts World* column. Some PDC players have gone back to playing BDO county darts, but Dennis Priestley and I have not. There would certainly be none of the old camaraderie.

Just how deep the bad feelings stirred by the dispute were, and how they lingered long after the agreement, was shown in the BBC2 documentary 'Blood on the Carpet', which was aired on 6 February 2001. In this the PDC argued their side of the dispute carefully and, for my money, effectively. However, Olly Croft gave the impression he thought the BDO owned the game and that he had been stabbed in the back by his 'family'. He was talking about Eric Bristow and the likes, I think. The naivete of this was echoed by the words of the late Lorna Croft – not the holder of any official position with the BDO – who seemed to suggest the players had been ungrateful. I think the programme got over to the general public the attitudes we were fighting against.

It would be nice to say that everything in the darts garden is now rosy. Take it from me, it is not. When I went to Lakeside during the 2002 Embassy World Championships certain BDO elements continued to show their hostility. In the January 2003 issue of *Darts World* Bobby George could not resist a cheap jibe at the 16 players who broke away from the BDO. 'I reckon John Lowe must be pretty unpopular with his PDC pals. Why? Because he describes (in a recent article) the original 16 who did a runner as "infamous". If he had checked his Oxford dictionary he might have thought twice about using this word because it means "notoriously vile, evil, abominable". Perhaps it is right after all.'

John chose to see this as an attack on the serious issues raised by the dispute. 'The 16 players were deprived of their rights as citizens and darts players to perform their rightful profession. They were deemed to have committed a serious crime against the almighty powers-that-be – the BDO. If you care to check with the Tomlin Order you will find that it was the BDO who committed the crime and retracted their original actions.'

Sad to say, in the spring of 2003 there were disturbing signs of a similar dispute erupting again.

Bells began ringing when PDC players Steve Beaton, Dave Askew and Dennis Smith were dropped from the England squad, which is picked by BDO people. This seems to be raking of ashes from the past which could easily burst into flames again. If the BDO ever decide to make county signing-on forms exclude players from taking part in other than BDO events, I reckon over 100 regular county players who are members of our Professional Dart Players Association will leave the county scene.

And, would you believe it, there are signs of a dispute in Holland. It would appear that a similar battle is looming. I gather that players and officials have been warned about any 'connection' with the activities of the PDC.

If anyone is in doubt about who 'won' the dispute in the long term, they should consider the position the BDO and the PDC had reached in April 2003. In that month *Darts World* magazine carried two contrasting pieces. In a report of his correspondence with Sports Minister Richard Caborn, Olly Croft said, 'I couldn't persuade Mr Caborn to give darts parity with Formula One and snooker . . . Obviously, in the case of tobacco sponsorship, he is simply following government legislation . . .' The bottom line is that the Embassy World Professional Darts Championship, as such, is finished. In fact *Darts World* was offering souvenirs of 'the last Embassy programme'. No doubt a new sponsor will be found for a BDO World Championship, but the last jewel has gone from the crown.

In the same issue the PDC announced an enhanced world circuit of events that carried over £1 million in prize money. There was to be a new event in early June, the UK Open at the Reebok Stadium, home of Bolton Wanderers, which has since been dubbed the FA Cup of darts and carries prize money of £230,000. In July came the Las Vegas Desert Classic with $120,000 in the kitty. Later that month, the Stan James World Matchplay with prize money of £80,000. The Paddy Power World Grand Prix would be played in Dublin in the autumn for prize money of £75,000, and the year would end at the Circus Tavern for the Ladbrokes.com World Championship where the prize money was £250,000. All of these competitions, every dart thrown, would go out live on Sky.

Now, I don't want to sound triumphalist, but we risked a lot in defending our right to ply our trade as darts players. I now feel that the hard trek we started out on in 1992 was justified. Not just for our careers, but for the good of the game.

CHAPTER 12

Making More History

Towards the end of 1997 the newspapers suddenly woke up to our sport. I think this was due to a number of things: Sky Sports' imaginative and exciting coverage, the emergence of new characters to replace the stars of the Eric and Jocky era, and the fact that I was look-ing at a new piece of darts history – a sixth World Championship.

'Bristow's protégé on target to upstage the master' ran a banner headline in the *Daily Telegraph*. Giles Smith had visited me at the Cricketers Arms and been measurably impressed – like half a page worth!

'The sport has happened upon a prodigy, a living darting legend. Phil "The Power" Taylor is not a thin player. At 37, he has an ample landlord's waist.

He also has unfashionable hair and a moustache. His forearms are like Popeye's: ham-shaped, tattooed. Yet if darts needs "an ambassador" (the eternal cry) then who better than the Power; World Champion five times over, a feat matched only by Eric Bristow; the winner of some 180 of the 200 worldwide professional tournaments he has entered in his nine-year career; a performer of almost hilarious consistency in a sport that mocks the very idea; the man television's Voice of Darts, Sid Waddell, calls "the greatest darts player that's ever drawn breath"?

The only sounds to be heard were the crackle of the fire and the thud of tungsten on cork – or just occasionally, the clatter of tungsten on pub lino. For even the Power clips the wire every now and then. Nevertheless, "I'm confident," Taylor had said earlier, referring to Purfleet and in a manner which did not incline you to doubt him. "If I get my head right, I'll take a lot of beating."

At one point Taylor looked out at the snow falling thickly across the car park and said meditatively: "If you were an Eskimo, you'd have to go out in that and find something to eat."'

I suppose that is exactly my 'philosophy' about being a professional darts player. Once I did a full day working on a lathe, then I went home and lay in the gutter working on cars. Now my work is made up of hard practice, hard matches, exhibitions and travelling. I do it for the same reason the Eskimo sits by the hole in the ice with a spear.

In the months before the World Championship I tried to build up steadily, taking nothing for granted. At the end of October Bob Anderson and I defended our World Pairs Championship at Butlin's Southcoast World in Bognor Regis. Most of us players stayed on the camp with the fans, and maybe this boded well for my support at the pairs tournament and later. Though Bob and I did not win, the crowd seemed behind us in all our matches. I felt they were cheering me on because they thought I was a British bloke who was doing something great at sport. From this period on, I think I only got people against me because they had bets on my opponents. It was no wonder. The punters were flocking to have daft tenners on players at 6–1 when I was priced at 12–1 on!

Just like Eric, I am now at my best on television. Nothing puts me off. But I work the crowd, encouraging them to support me because it gives me a lift. The only trouble is that life on the oche gets no easier. I am now the Manchester United of the game and the young guns coming up are the Port Vales, Jacks with their minds set on giant killing.

It was at Bognor that one of these hungry young lads made a big impression on me. Ray Barneveld of Holland had dreamed of being a darts World Champion since watching the 1985 Embassy as an 18-year-old. He wanted to be up on that stage where Bristow continued

the legend against Lowe in 1985. By talent and per-
severance Ray got there. His Embassy debut was in
1991 – taking time out from his job as a postman, which
was good subject matter for the commentators – and in
1995 he beat Les Wallace, Dave Askew, Colin Monk and
Martin Adams to get to the final. In that he lost 6–3 in
sets to Richie Burnett.

I had watched him on television, but was even more
impressed by his form at Bognor. He was paired with
another Dutch star, Roland Scholten, and they won
the competition handsomely. Despite the agreement in
the PDC/BDO dispute, there were people who saw this
as 'a BDO triumph'. So you can imagine the interest a
couple of years later when Barney and I went head-to-
head for overall prize money of £100,000. You've got to
deliver a hell of a lot of letters to get amongst that kind
of cash.

I tried not to let the thought of breaking Eric's record
of five world titles prey on my mind as I practised for the
1998 PDC World Championships. In my heart I knew I
could win. Beating Eric the year before in the semi-final
in a bearpit atmosphere with most of the crowd willing
him on had been a test, but I had passed it with flying
colours. I knew I could play under extreme pressure.
And now, after the rapturous crowd reaction to me in
Blackpool and Bognor, I knew they would be on my
side. OK, when Rod Harrington got up there the Essex
lads and lasses would give it big licks, but nobody would
ever again scare me as much as Eric had. I had also

recently lost my father, and I wanted to set the record just for him.

In the first round I had an easy victory over Kevin Spiolek by 3–0 in sets. Then I really got going against former greyhound trainer Dennis Smith. I did my benchmark 97.5 average and almost got the nine-darter twice. It would have been worth £25,000 to me. My next opponent was Shayne Burgess, who is a very good player but for some reason is usually beaten before he plays me. He once said to Jeff Stelling that I always gave him good chances, 'like 170, 161 and 150 – easy stuff like that'. I beat Shayne 4–0.

Poor old Rod Harrington. The Essex fans always cheer him until the Christmas tinsel falls and the Circus bouncers go home, but this time he caught me on a good night. In the first few legs of the game I averaged 118, but even so Rod hung on to make it 2–2 in sets. As so often, Rod brought out the best in me. I think in the form he was in he would have blown any other player away. In the end I won by 5–2 in sets. 'I don't know what I have to do to beat you, Philip,' he said at the end. Later he told Sky viewers how disappointed he was. 'I was gutted to lose to Phil. I had prepared and planned perfectly. I started as strongly as he did and matched him dart for dart. But somewhere along the line I started to slip and in the end I know I didn't do justice to my own game.' Rod did not know it, but he was about to hit the richest vein of his darting life.

I think the fact that Rod was the only bloke in the

tournament who had taken a set from me tells the full story. It might sound bigheaded, but I knew that as far as my potential was concerned, 'you ain't seen nothin' yet'.

So to the final, which was becoming a bit like an Old Firm derby. For Rangers and Celtic, or Liverpool and Everton, read Taylor and Priestley. It was our third final on the trot, and I was out to make it a very unhappy anniversary for the Menace. I think Dennis knew that my form and determination were at an all-time high. Before the opening darts he fell at my feet, hands clasped like one of Chaucer's pilgrims. I wasn't thinking about beating Eric's record, only getting as good a start as I had against Rod. I was as impatient as I had been all those years before, waiting for the Huntsman to open so I could get going.

And get going I did. I took the first four sets without Dennis getting a single leg. I hammered in five 180s and finishes of 105 and 122. Sid Waddell had been predicting a wonder performance and was appreciating it on commentary. 'Sometimes, folks, it's the night of the iguana. Tonight it's the night of the maestro of darts.' I was hitting everything; I got to 5–0 with 11- and 12-dart check-outs. 'He's finding that treble 19 like the Holy Grail.' Sid was incandescent as I prepared to sink Dennis and take my sixth title. 'This man is the closest thing to mechanization since they stopped the hand yakkin' of coal! He's here to fulfil a darting destiny. Yes, nemesis. A devastating, pulverizing, procession to destiny.' I hit my 24th maximum of the tournament. Then I piled in an

11-darter. I clinched victory with a 12-dart leg – 139, 125, 133, game shot 104. My average was 104, and I still had a couple of gears left.

My first thought was of my dad. If only he'd been sitting down there with Yvonne and the kids. I kept the tears back during the presentation ceremony, but only just.

Other people had a better perspective on my achievement at that moment than I did. Dennis was one of the first to sing my praises: 'I didn't play as badly as the scoreline suggested. Phil just played that much better. When he plays that well, us mere mortals don't have a chance.' Sid was much calmer once he came back to planet earth and assessed my record: 'I have just been talking to Dave Lanning about perspective. He and I have been watching and commentating on the greats of darts for nearly 30 years. We never thought we would see somebody master the game. But by dedication, talent and the right mental approach Taylor has taken darts to be a science, never mind a sport. In the Rees era a 93 average could win the world title; in the Bristow era maybe 97; now it will need about a 105 average, spread over a week-long competition, to beat the Power. I reckon he will win the title 15 times.'

So, you see, Sid was looking good as a prophet as well as a wordsmith. Though I may stop at 13, and let the hungry lads fight over the bacon.

There had been speculation that Eric Bristow might have been miffed at my breaking his record. How wrong can you get? Eric was magnanimous: 'Phil Taylor is a special dart player. He is a lovely player who deserves his sixth title.' When asked if he regretted the money, coaching, cajoling and insulting he had invested in me, he grinned. 'Everybody deserves a break in life and I gave him his.'

It took me a while to calm down. I am like a weight-lifter; apparently in control, but inside a boiling cauldron of adrenalin and effort. In a way there had been less pressure to beat Eric's record than to equal it. Like Eric, who had always wanted to match Steve Davis' six world snooker titles, I set myself targets. But with targets comes pressure and sometimes confusion.

I have learned lessons about how to handle pressure. You must never walk into the lights of the arena from the practice room feeling like the World Champ. You must have prepared right. Use the first set to settle down. Then use your head at the right moments. If you are going well and your opponent seems cocky, belt him with heavy scoring. I was acquiring self-knowledge all the time and that made me extra dangerous. Eric once said I had more talent in my little finger than any of the others had in their entire bodies – and from him that is high praise indeed.

To some extent I was the victim of my own success in the next few months. I was constantly on the road for exhibitions and public appearances. This heavy schedule meant I did not attend as many tournaments on the circuit as I could have. Meanwhile, Rod Harrington had bounced back from defeat in Essex to come to Blackpool in the summer for the World Matchplay as world number one. He was hot from victories in Calgary and Saskatoon and had just won the Swiss Open.

Another dangerous player in the line-up was Ronnie 'Babe' Baxter from Church in Lancashire. Ronnie had made his name as a BDO player, and had been runner-up in the 1997 World Masters. He is a fast-throwing, robotic player and, with the 'legs-only' format at Blackpool, would be dangerous if he got going.

As it happened I had plenty of time later in the week to study both, especially Babe Baxter. I opened the campaign with an 8–1 victory over Geordie Graeme Stoddart. Then I beat Robbie Widdows 8–2. Next I was up against Baxter and he was terrific. Cheered on by half the village of Church and his lady Rachel – very animated, very vocal – we had a great scrap. In the end he beat me 13–10. He missed nothing and I had no complaints. I knew he would test Rod if they met in the final.

Ronnie had the crowd going wild in his semi-final against the very talented Chris Mason. Mason has great potential and has studied darts videos of the great games since he was a kid. But one thing you cannot learn by any other means than experience is control. Under pressure the gestures and head shaking come out and the concentration slips. His match against Ronnie was a classic, with 12 legs being done in 16 darts or less. After losing, Chris sat and wept in the hospitality suite, asking, 'What have I got to do to win something?' Answer: work on that temperament, son.

There followed one of the best Blackpool finals ever. In blistering heat, and still wearing his trademark waistcoat, Rod trailed Baxter in the deciding legs. Then Rod hit full throttle and won 18–16.

Now going full throttle against his peers over many legs comes easily to Rod. But he really started sweating when darts fan Johnny Vaughan rang him up and asked if he could come on the 'Big Breakfast' and knock a 20p coin off Sid Waddell's tongue with a piece of tungsten! An old darts party piece had been to knock a cigarette out of somebody's mouth, so this should have been a doddle. But with it being live and with a few million people watching and with Sid twitching and trembling . . .

Come the hour, come the man. Sid stood in front of the dartboard and Rod took position. 'Don't worry,' whispered Rod. 'I'll aim high and the flight will take the coin off.'

Sid nodded and the coin fell off. Nervous laughter. Sid replaced the coin. Roll of drums. Sid closed his eyes. The first dart flew millimetres over the coin. The second made the coin wobble but not drop. People could not bear to look. Rod glared. Sid opened his eyes. The last dart flew and hit flesh and coin. The coin tinkled on the floor. Johnny and the studio audience applauded. Rod asked Sid if he was all right. For once the Geordie Lip was stuck for words. 'Yeth, I think tho – no blood!'

Sid mumbled. 'Sorry mate,' said Rod. 'The flight wasn't doing the business so I had to aim the point.'

The producers of the show were very worried. Johnny hadn't told them about the William Tell act and they were worried sick about insurance.

Next stop on the route of the PDC darts caravan was Rochester, and a new venue for a new tournament. At the Casino Rooms nightclub we gathered for the World Grand Prix. This was to be a double-to-start test and once again you could look a bit of a wally if your doubling was not up to par. One of the favourites was Peter 'One Dart' Manley, whose party piece was going out from 80 with two double tops – despite his throwing bomber darts with barrels as thick as Hamlet cigars.

Thankfully I found the double-to-start rule no problem. In fact a couple of times Rod Harrington and I set off looking for a nine-dart finish. The reason that a nine-dart is possibly easier with a double to start is that 140 and then 180 leaves a 161. And this combination – 60, treble 17, bull – is marginally easier to hit than variations on 141, the usual leave for a nine-dart.

I had a steady progression through the tournament, beating Steve Brown, John Lowe and Shayne Burgess before taking on Rod Harrington in the final. Again he tested me, but again he was found wanting. I won 13–8 in legs with a 95 average, which is equal to 104 on a straight start.

The Sky pundits as usual led with their tongues for the 1999 Skol/PDC World Darts Championships. Doyen of commentators Dave Lanning, who commentated on the first network transmission of darts for ITV in 1972 and was formerly a top speedway commentator and Fleet Street journalist, plumped for Shayne Burgess. 'The battler from Hastings, with the throwing action that looks like he's swallowing goldfish while impaling an eyelid, has been threatening the big breakthrough for the past 18 months or so. His number might come up now he's backed a moneybags Lottery winner, which enables him to globe-trot for experience and ranking points. Shayne is making an impact, too, winning both singles in the recent Witch City Open in Boston. He was in red-hot form at the recent World Grand Prix on Sky, walloping Alan Warriner and Gary Mawson before running into Phil Taylor at his deadliest.'

I knew Shayne had lots of talent, but I thought he respected me a bit too much. I happen to draw him a lot in the big tournaments and that preys on his mind.

Sid Waddell does not always tip me for the big ones, but that year he had been spotting signs in my game that he reckoned made me virtually unbeatable.

'Since that win at Rochester and just missing a nine-dart with a double-to-start rule, I think the Power will take them all to the cleaners. Looking at the draw it should be Taylor against Warriner in the final. I don't think Warriner has the sustained hostility to handle Taylor, who is the most efficient darts machine ever.

He lands the first dart in the bottom of the 60

bed, then he stacks the next two above that, so the incoming dart uses the landed darts as a platform.

Taylor is 10 points a throw better than anyone else in the tournament on averages. But darts, as Sky's coverage constantly shows, has never been about dry statistics. It's about character; performing under stress with light, cameras and an audience going mental. Bristow wrote the dictionary of winning, but Taylor has turned it into the thesaurus.

Phil is the greatest player ever to draw breath, the man who turned darts into a science of mathematical precision.'

Now I know the Geordie Lip tends to exaggerate, but there is a lot in what he says, and he has been studying the ballistics of tungsten for 32 years. So no wonder, with Sid issuing the clarion call, the national press turned up in force at the Circus Tavern. They saw some great darts, and many of them commented that the Embassy competition at Frimley Green was but a pale shadow.

I opened the defence of my title with an easy victory over veteran Reg Harding. I won 3–0 in sets with an average of 105, thus reaffirming most of Sid's points. Next up was John Lowe and I beat him 3–1 in sets with a 102 average. This performance moved Sid to recall the blood-drenched days of the French Revolution, 'I hear the rattle of a tumbrel. They're oiling the guillotine. And Madame Desfarges has put down her knitting.'

The mixture of fun, science, sport and entertainment that Sky cameras bring to the viewer was getting through to the press. Kate Battersby of the *Evening Standard* got the message.

'There's nothing like actually going to an event for having your eyes opened. So prepare to be shocked, because while you might not be terribly surprised by the booze or the fags or the greasy grub, what you don't bargain for at the world darts is what fun it is.

"You'll love it here with the tungsten tossers," promised veteran commentator Dave Lanning, and he was right. I can't quite work out why it was such a surprise – maybe because I expected to feel awkward at being female and middle class. The Royal Ascot snobs sniff out someone who isn't one of their own at 50 paces, and being middle class is especially sneer-worthy.

But at the darts you never met such a friendly crowd, happy to make time for you and answer any questions. They all tell you how glad they are that you've bothered to come along and after a while you twig that unexpectedly you're having a good laugh. After that there doesn't seem much point in smart-arse one-liners.'

Articles like this have set the tone for the rest of my career. Trying to win a seventh world title in an individual sport brought comparison with the feats of

Steve Davis and Stephen Hendry. Gone were the jokes about Fatbelly and Fatterbelly and their treble vodkas and double whiskies and the shadow of the 'Not the Nine O'clock News' sketch.

To see how seriously Sky take the sport you just have to spend an hour in the outside broadcast nerve centre, the scanner truck which houses the production team. I popped in during the week and was amazed at the cathedral-like calm. Andy Finn, the director, caressed the panel of buttons and cut effortlessly between dozens of available shots. Producer Rory Hopkins occasionally growled an idea to the commentators while making sure the statistics and stages of the competition were offered at appropriate moments. Production assistant Lidia Summers is such an expert on the shot-outs after years in the truck that she sometimes calls the shot before the official spotters, Keith Deller and Eric Bristow. Eric occasionally laces his spotting with criticism of players; his mildest phrase being 'You tosser!'

On the championship oche I had an easy 4–0 victory over Bob Anderson and a 102 average. Behind the stage curtain after the match I was just calming down for an interview and I could hear Bob almost shouting behind me. 'That man is a machine. You feel as though you have been physically wounded after you've had a match with him.' I liked the sound of that, and I bet Eric would too. I could just imagine him sitting in the scanner yelling at the screen, 'Wound him, my son, wound him!'

Next target for my arrows was Alan Warriner, the

number-two seed. Alan was in good form after victories in Holland, Eastbourne and Germany and making the final of the World Masters. I won the match 5–3 with a 98.7 average. At one stage Alan was 2–1 up in sets but I levelled the set score with a 12-darter and went to 3–2 in 14, 13 and 13 darts. That is what is meant by bullying an opponent. It certainly rattled Wozzer, who missed doubles which would have kept him in the match. Alan averaged 95, his best of the week, so it was no surprise that his frustrations over matches against me spilled over further down the line.

The other semi-final was a belter. Shayne Burgess more than lived up to Dave Lanning's confidence in his ability and Peter Manley let the darts do the talking. With an 11-, 12- and 13-dart leg Manley went 2–0 up in sets. Shayne replied with 14, 14 and 11 to take the third. It was nip and tuck all the way to the deciding set. The crowd was totally involved in the unfolding drama. 'They are like two gladiators of old in the Colosseum at Rome at a Saturday matinee,' enthused Sid Waddell. 'There's less noise here than when Pompeii was swamped with lava.' He was right; the crowd went from crescendo to absolute quiet in seconds. Then Manley fired in a 14-darter and a 15 to put Shayne on the edge of the abyss. 'The darts echo like soil on a coffin,' was Sid's epitaph for a brave display by Shayne.

So to the final. With Peter missing doubles, I went into a 3–0 lead in sets. He pegged back to 4–1, but then a 10-dart leg in the sixth set – 180, 140, 165, double eight – set me up for victory. I did an 11-dart leg in the next set and won the match 6–2. My average for the match was 97.1 and my tournament average was 99.99!

I had won my seventh title. And when the press swarmed round I found it hard to keep things in perspective. No, I did not think I was now an unknown multiple World Champion like George Digweed, of clay-pigeon shooting, and Tony Allcock, of indoor bowls. And no, I did not think I was the greatest darts player ever; I told the press that I thought Eric was the greatest in his own time.

I had been sad to see Eric being thrashed 3–0 in sets by Peter Manley earlier in the tournament. He had not won a leg and had hit only five three-figure scores. People were saying he should pack it in. I knew he wouldn't; darts is his life – that's why he passed on the flame to me.

CHAPTER 13

A Right Barney

While I was winning my seventh world title, the Embassy World Professional Championships were coming to a climax at Frimley Green. I say 'climax', but Giles Smith in the *Daily Telegraph* was underwhelmed by what he saw and heard on his screen.

'Purfleet is all smoke and hot colours; the Lakeside has seemed antiseptic by comparison, the stage decorated in strangely uninviting pinks and greens, the crowd kept at a respectable volume in accordance with a traditional BBC sense of decorum. At Purfleet, the crowd scribble messages and slogans on the backs of paper plates that once held chicken and chips and then press them up to the camera for wider scrutiny. At the Lakeside this kind of interaction does not seem to be encouraged.

Ray Stubbs is also intended to form a kind of brotherhood with Bobby George, who sits beside him in the studio. The relationship has yet to bear fruit in any quantity (sample: "Co Stompe's playing really good") but these are early days.

Whatever Stubbs and George get up to, it is the same old story out on the oche: cold light, quiet crowd and a tragic lack of nicknames. No Bulldogs or Bravedarts here. And no Sid screamimg about Pompeii. That's a lot to miss.'

But the Embassy did have two things going for it that interested me. One, there was a great final between Ronnie Baxter and Ray Barneveld which the Flying Dutchman just pipped by 6–5 in sets. Two, Barneveld had successfully defended the Embassy title and was now being touted in some quarters as the best in the world. Though the old BDO/PDC rivalry was still simmering, it meant nothing to me. But people were beginning to ask the question – who would win in a match between Barneveld and the Power?

More immediately, I was headed for Blackpool once again for the World Matchplay. From the kick-off I had to play well. My first-round opponent was Ronnie Baxter, who had put me out in the previous year. I beat him 10–5 in legs. Next, I struggled to beat Reg Harding 13–10; the veteran gave me a really hard time despite my 99.8 average. That'll teach me to go cracking up the young guns. My next game was a cracker against

Chris Mason, who was on fire. In the end it took a 100.2 average to dispose of Mace the Ace 16–11 in legs. Then I had to take on Peter Manley again. I got him on a good night. He was aiming to get the number-one spot in the world rankings and he played out of his skin against me. I tried but could only manage a 95.5 average, which is rubbish for the Power. I lost 17–14.

Though I have nothing against Peter, I was pleased to see Rod Harrington retain the title. Maybe playing away from the demands of his Essex supporters lets Rod breathe that bit easier. Or maybe it's the good northern air he gets on the gusty fairways of the Fylde.

A few weeks later, at Rochester, the World Grand Prix was beckoning and there were one or two hot lads there. Apart from Harrington, Manley and Priestley, the man I thought would do well was Shayne Burgess. He was seeded number four for the competition, which started as a round robin and then became knockout, and he was in good form. Now Shayne is the lad who in recent years has given the lie to those folk who say there are no characters in the game. It's hard to know where to start to describe his lifestyle.

Shayne likes shooting. He likes nothing better than crawling round a field at night with a gun, popping off rats, rabbits or what have you. He performs a service to farmers in getting rid of vermin. Not only that; Shayne makes pies and fry-ups from the field kill. He knows exactly how many squirrels you need for a decent stew. But sometimes things go awry.

A couple of years back Shayne and a pal were down a Sussex field at midnight shooting vermin. Suddenly they heard a breathy snuffling behind a haystack. They prowled towards the noise, guns at the ready. 'I reckon that's a badger,' whispered Shayne. 'Sounds like a big'un,' said his pal. Wrong. A wild boar leapt out at them and chased them down the field!

When word got round the darting lads about Shayne's collection of game, there was a bit of concern. He often turned up for tournaments in Europe with a holdall full of sandwiches to save money on meals. He used to offer them round but usually got no takers: he insisted they were chicken, but how could you be sure?

But the funniest Shayne story is the time he turned up at the posh reception of Sky Sports in Osterley a day early for a darts promotion trailer. He drove his old white van up to the door at about six the night before the shoot, parked it and went in. He looks like a tame football fan and has a cheery smile, but the commissionaire looked a bit askance, especially at the tatty van in amongst the executive motors. ''Ere mate,' said Shayne. 'I've got to go filming from here at eight in the morning. Here's me letter to prove it. All right if I park up and kip down for the night?' It most certainly was not! Shayne spent the night in a side street further down the business park.

He fought his way through one half of the draw at Rochester and I progressed in the other. In the round robin I disposed of Dennis Priestley and Alan Warriner without too much trouble, then gave Peter Evison a real hammering. He didn't win a single leg of the nine played. In the semi-final against Rod Harrington I did 14 180s and had an average of 93.8, this with a double to start.

Now I don't know how many bunnies went into Shayne's pre-final pie but it did him no good. I had him on the hop from the very start and won the final 6–1 in sets. He played very well against the others but once he met me he lost the mental battle. In essence he went in with negative thoughts; he did not think he could beat me. My tournament average was 95, which on a straight start would be about 104.

While I was plying my trade in Blackpool and Rochester, hectic negotiations had been going on behind the scenes to set up a head-to-head against the BDO champion, Ray Barneveld. It was being billed as the 'Match of the Century' and I was delighted to discover that it was planned for Wembley Conference Centre.

There had been classic head-to-heads before. John Lowe and Brian Langworth of Sheffield had travelled to the Valleys to take on Leighton Rees and Alan Evans, with side-betting reaching thousands. In the early 1970s Evans played George Walsh of Stockport at the Poco a Poco nightclub and the crowd threw fivers in appreciation. In 1995 I played Dennis Priestley at Uttoxeter in front of the Sky cameras for £2,000. Over the years Eric had played Jocky and Keith Deller. I had taken on Rod Harrington and John Lowe in this format.

The deal to play Barneveld was arranged thanks to hard work by Tommy Cox and Barry Hearn, who had been involved with the WDC/PDC since early 1995. At first it seemed that there was no point in Ray playing the match. Despite the massive money win or lose, given my form he was odds on to take a beating. In Holland hardly anyone knew who I was. To the Dutch public, who watched the Embassy, Barney was the best player on the planet. They had twice seen him beat 'the best players in the world'. He was a national hero: he had his own television show and his picture was hanging in pubs next to Ruud Gullit's. So why risk a dent in the image?

Another big minus in the equation was that the BDO did not want the match to take place. They put pressure on Ray and his manager, Ad Schoofs, to pull out of the negotiations. Schoofs said to the papers: 'We were under pressure not to play.' Though the dispute had been 'settled', the BDO knew a victory by me would be a feather in the cap of the PDC. Ray said as much: 'They were scared that if I lost, the PDC would be able to claim they're the best. But that just gave me an extra incentive. This is my chance to show the world I'm somebody. I have had a stack of e-mails saying I will beat him easily.'

Over the months before the match Tommy Cox tried to persuade Ad Schoofs to agree a deal. He seemed to be getting nowhere until Gerry Walters, of Benelux Business, who are distributors of darts, including Barney's, stepped in. He lobbied for the match to go ahead, and eventually Ad Schoofs confirmed the deal to Tommy.

So I began the final countdown to the head-to-head scheduled for 7 November at the Wembley Conference Centre. The deal was that the prize fund would be £100,000. The winner would take £60,000 and the loser £40,000 – a lot of money, whether you use it to buy Staffordshire oatcakes or a tonne or two of best Edam. But the money didn't matter to me; I wanted to show that I was the best in the world.

There was doubt in the air right up to the last minute. A couple of days before the match there was a London press conference on HMS Belfast and Tommy and I did not know if Barney would show up. Then we saw him walking up the gangplank. Tommy heaved a sigh of relief and I made a crack about sending him to walk the plank. Ray had just had a plaster cast taken off a broken ankle, so maybe that was an advantage to me. But I had spent a week at Barnard Castle practising and playing locals lined up by my friends Colin Winley and Malcolm Nixon, landlord of the Cricketers Arms, and this had put me right on my mettle.

As usual Sid Waddell was blowing my trumpet in the programme for the event.

'Two weeks ago I sat in a Chinese restaurant in Rochester with Phil "the Power" Taylor and his bosom honcho, Sean Rutter. Only minutes earlier Phil had destroyed Peter Evison by 9–0 in legs in 21 minutes at average of 101.7. This was with a double to start and was equivalent to 110 with a straight start. As the seven times World Champion sucked in crispy duck and crinkly seaweed, Sean whispered, "That was just for Barney!"

Meanwhile, Barney, otherwise known as 32-year-old Ray Barneveld, twice Embassy World Champion, was in South Africa beating top amateurs to take the World Cup singles title.

But, believe you me, at four o'clock at Wembley Conference Centre, where the pair clash today for one hour precisely and a £60,000 first prize, titles will not count a toss. Taylor, for me and many pundits the best darter of all time, wants to prove that the Dutchman is not even in his league. Phil has had to play the top professionals to gain his status – guys like Dennis Priestley and Rod Harrington – but Barney, it can be argued, has never been really tested.

But, stout Potteries lad that he is, it is brass that bugs Taylor. In a good year he makes around £100,000. Barney, by contrast, in winning the Embassy world title in 1998 and 1999 and wowing the Dutch television audience, is raking in £300,000 a year from tournaments, sponsorships and exhibitions. In just under one year, sales of his personalized darts have reached 40,000, at £20 a throw.

If we judge the two men on pure talent, Barney comes off a long way second best. Since he lost to Richie Burnett in the 1995 Embassy final, he has developed into a good but not a great player. He is a fine 180 scorer and rarely misses doubles, but has never looked the absolute hammer of all opponents. He cannot yet be spoken of in the same breath as Lowe, Bristow and Taylor.

Taylor, however, is the player of the decade, if not of all time. I expect him to lift his average to 112 at points in this game and turn Barney to rubble. I reckon Taylor, now 38, is at the peak of his career. Just over a year ago he was jaded from too much travelling to exhibitions but now his pub in Stoke is going well and he is more relaxed than I have ever seen him.

I expect Phil to win, but a couple of factors will make it tight. In the 1930s professional darters would have wanted a two-hour match for big money, so that pure class would tell. Barney is always a good starter, so Phil cannot hang about in the early legs. Finally, hundreds of Dutch fans could make Wembley sound like Amsterdam when the fleet is in town.'

I think Sid said it all there. I was worried about the hour-long format. I would have preferred a race to 25 legs. But I have never practised harder, or been as nervous before a match. The dispute was not in my thoughts. This was England versus Holland, and I wanted old St George to be proud of me.

Barry Hearn's company, Matchroom Sport, were the promoters and they had a giant clock put on the stage to count down the hour. It stopped during the commercial breaks. Whoever was ahead when the time ran out would be the winner. There was a new rule in force; should a player get well ahead, he must not deliberately slow the match down. If he did the referee could award the leg to the opponent.

I don't think I have ever been in an atmosphere like it. There were about 3,500 fans going mad. The English ones were singing 'There's Only One Phil Taylor', and hundreds of orange scarves, hats and T-shirts were bobbing for Barney. It was like a scene from 'Gladiator', with the seating stepped up away from the stage. The match was going out live on ITV with Eric Bristow and John Gwynne commentating, and on Talksport with lively chat from Dave Lanning and Sid Waddell.

Even before a dart was chucked, I was loving it. I bounced around the stage like Bambi's dad. Ray, on the other hand, looked as sick as a parrot. I think all the argy-bargy with the BDO had got through to him. The first five legs went with the throw. Despite Tommy advising me to take the early legs steady, I played quickly. I was on form and he soon knew it.

At 5–3 to me I won four legs on the trot, a series that included a 12 and two 14-dart legs. He pegged back to 9–4 by the halfway interval. His fans had already gone pretty quiet.

Ray then pulled back to 9–5 and I could sense he was in rhythm. Then I clobbered him with a 144 shot-out and even the Dutch fans applauded. He'd had tickertape receptions and honours from his queen, but they were getting to know the Power now. I pushed on to 13–6. There was clear blue water between us now and, I reckoned, £20,000 in prize money! I was enjoying myself and really wishing the game was a two-hour job. I took it to 15–6 and I was finishing clinically.

He was now undoubtedly sickened, and was just slapping his darts at the board. Instead of fighting to make it 15–7 he gave up. Funnily enough this put me off my game; knowing I could not be caught, I got sloppy. Still, I ran out the winner 21–10; my average was 103.4 and his was 93. It was my greatest win in darts.

Barney spoke up about the pressure he had been under: 'Neither the BDO nor my own organization in Holland wanted me to play. I obviously had this in my mind in the build-up to the game. I did not want to be banned by playing against their wishes. There was a lot of pressure on my shoulders but it did not work out.'

Ray was so upset he did not go for an interview with presenter Eamonn Holmes; instead he left by a side door. I thought he owed it to the fans to put on a braver face. So when I saw a corporate function going on downstairs for loads of people in orange, I went in and shook hands all round. 'Go back and tell all the people in Holland who is the best player in the world,' I told them.

I would now like to play head-to-head against any BDO champion – Ted Hankey, John Walton or Tony David. The format is a great plug for the game.

I have one confession to make about that night's celebrations at the Wembley Hilton: I drank champagne rather than black tea. Lottery winner Mark Gardner bought a bottle for £300 and presented it to me. As I sipped I thought about how many league subs that could have paid in 1987 when I was on four quid a week pocket money.

Interest in my career in general, and in the head-to-head in particular, was growing. A man from *The Times* went to May Bank and watched the action with the regulars at the Cricketers. My daughters had put up a giant poster reading: 'Win or lose, to us you are the best.' Lose?

And it was not only a special night for me; Vince Sturt helped out behind the bar and told everybody who would listen how he once beat me in a darts match. You can probably guess who my next head-to-head was against!

Over the last few years I have got to know Steve Davis very well. Obviously you all know him as an expert on snooker but take it from me and Sid Waddell, he does not just watch darts on television, he analyses the finer points of the game.

Some years ago Sid was at the Crucible during World Championship week and he was watching Steve practise. Suddenly the great man frowned and made a beeline for Sid, who thought his presence was a problem. Not a bit of it; Steve wanted to talk darts to Sid: 'I am a big Eric Bristow fan, and I want you to tell him that I have worked out why he is not putting his big pressure

shots in.' Steve drew back his right arm and demon-
strated. 'The Crafty Cockney is taking his throwing arm
about one foot too far back. So he is leaving much more
chance for error. It's like playing a golf shot with too big
a back swing; the shot wobbles. In essence Eric is not
properly cocked like Phil Taylor or Dennis Priestley.'

Now that is genuine wisdom, and it is not the only
bit of advice Steve has had for a member of the darting
fraternity. He gave me his view of what made a great
sportsman: 'You have to be good all the time and
brilliant some of the time.' It is a good philosophy and
in my case I strive to make the balance favour 'brilliant'.
I could not go to the local pub and play bad darts. It is
not me and it is certainly not what people expect from
me. In my exhibitions I still play to hammer people.

From 1987 I could do 14-darters and better and 95-
plus averages. By hard work and practice you raise your
benchmark. Also, if you have money in the bank and
there are no problems like the infamous BDO dispute
around, then you can flourish. I reckon my destruction
of Barney was the final plank in my springboard to
the 2000 PDC/Skol World Championships. I played out
of my skin in the tournament, ending with an overall
average of 102.5.

As I have frequently said, I constantly set myself
targets. Early on it was a few hundred pounds to buy
a video or a shower or a new coat for my mum. Now I
wanted the darts Grand Slam: the World Grand Prix, the
World Championship and the World Matchplay all in

one season. When I got to Purfleet I already had the Grand Prix in the kitty.

The men to beat were the number-one seed Peter Manley, Shayne Burgess, Rod Harrington and, of course, Dennis Priestley. I reckon I set the alarm bells ringing amongst this lot with my first-round performance against Mick Manning. Mick never had a shot at a double as I hammered out finishes of 113, 102, 116, 144 and 155 on the way to a 3–0 in sets victory. My average was 103.3. Next up – or down – was Graeme Stoddart, who again never took a set. My average went up to 103.8.

As Bob Marley used to say, 'and then we'll take it higher'. On the receiving end in my next match – a very short one at 46 minutes – was Alan Warriner. I did six 180s and a 105.9 average, won 5–0 in sets and Alan won only one single leg. Then he was totally out of order. He stormed off the stage without shaking hands with me or the officials. He was to behave even worse than this in the 2003 championships.

Dennis Priestley was back to his slow, grinding best in his semi-final against Peter Manley. In a match that lasted 102 minutes, Dennis slammed in six 180s and finishes of 108, 116 twice, and 133 to win 5–2 in sets. He had been troubled with his eyes, and later even had surgery on them, so it was good to see him in form and rewarding his loyal and very vocal family with consistent high-quality darts

Blocking my way to a final spot was the very talented

Dennis Smith. He was groomed for top darts by Bob
Anderson, just the way Eric Bristow worked on me. But
he could not handle me in the form I was in, and I won
5–0 in sets with an average of 105.9. At the end of the
match I agreed when Dennis sent hard words across
Warriner's bows: 'I set out to enjoy myself. You have got
to learn to lose before you can win and become a champion.' I have to admit that some of the resentment and
jealousy aimed at me and the publicity I was getting
made me seethe.

In the final Dennis could not hold me early on, but
suddenly he checked out on 122 and 96 to level the sets
at 1–1. It was the first set I had dropped all week. A
series of six legs on the trot and a 119 finish took me to
6–2 in sets. But Dennis hit back to make it 6–3. In the
end I rapped in a 177 followed by my seventh 180 to
win 7–3. My match average was 105.2. It was my eighth
World Championship win, and I felt in that game I had
worked hard to earn the £31,000 first prize.

Dennis was more than gracious in defeat. Twelve
months before, his problems with his sight had nearly
made him pack the game in. But now he was the old
honest, chirpy Menace: 'Phil left doors open and if I
cannot take advantage then I will never win. I would
happily play the winner of next week's Embassy. Coming here is daft; happen we can find somebody from
another planet to play Phil. There is no doubt in my
mind, Phil is not only the greatest darts player but the
greatest sportsman ever.'

Now I am not going to sound like a bighead and pronounce on this statement. But people like Steve Davis and Stephen Hendry were drawing attention to my unique achievement. Sid Waddell, John Gwynne and Dave Lanning were putting me up there with Stanley Matthews, Geoff Boycott and Len Hutton as a British sporting great, and the newspapers were not scoffing. In fact, soon they would be slotting me into a world context of sporting excellence. It made me happy just to put our sport on the map.

CHAPTER 14

On the Shamrock Oche

Later on I will be telling you all about the unique atmosphere of Las Vegas and the excitement generated by top darts in the Desert Classic. But for now I want to take you to a magic land just over the water where they love their drop of black stuff and their singing and they go barmy for darts. Ask any player his favourite darting venue and he will answer 'Ireland'.

Whenever I have played exhibitions there I have been treated brilliantly. They always appreciate your efforts and I have been known to give them a rendition of 'My Way' late at night. The only trouble is getting to your bed. In England most exhibitions get going around 7.30pm and you are finished by 11.30. In Ireland you can be playing number eight out of 14 punters as midnight approaches. The Irish will tell you that they don't come out until late because they work harder and longer than us softies.

Given this enthusiasm for the game, Tommy Cox's company World of Darts, with full PDC blessing, organized the Irish Masters tournament at Rosslare, near the town of Wexford, in February 2000. The tournament was set up in conjunction with publican Mick O'Donoghue, businessman Tom Crosbie and several sponsors. It was to feature the top players as well as locals, and was the biggest darts event Ireland had ever seen.

Stena Line were one of the main sponsors and all the PDC players were given a free ferry-ride over. I took my camper and was in the same party as Bob Anderson, Chris Mason and Sid Waddell, who was looking decidely green around the gills as we sailed out into a calm sea from Fishguard. Sid had been told horrific stories about sudden storms and insisted he sit near the door as we tucked into complimentary steak and chips.

The crossing was no trouble. Eamonn Hewitt of Stena Line took us on to the bridge and we were filmed chatting to the captain and his officers. It took us about four hours to get to Rosslare harbour and soon we were in the Crosbie Cedars Hotel where the tournament was going to be staged – in the disco! I was having a laugh at this when Sid came out of a side room looking worried. He and Cliff Lazarenko were going to commentate on the stage live on radio for Talksport and he had just seen the 'studio'. It was about the size of a phonebox and he had to share it with a presenter and Cliff, who is a big lad. 'Cosy,' I said. 'Sure is,' said Sid, 'We can't see the stage.' I frowned. 'Now that is a problem.'

Within the next 24 hours the broadcasting facilities turned out to be the least of the Geordie Lip's problems.

The PDC party had a very busy publicity schedule the day before the event began. Eric Bristow, Jamie Harvey and I were filmed going for a look at Wexford town and quayside. We stood watching a trawler which we assumed was unloading the night's catch. But something did not seem right; there was a lorry parked by the boat and two men were shovelling fish from the lorry on to the boat! Eric scratched his head: 'Seen it all now – should we tell the Paddies they're doing it the wrong way round?'

We were sauntering round, but the other PDC group of Peter Manley, his girlfriend Chrissie Howat, Trina Gulliver, favourite to take the ladies' title, and Sid Waddell were being whizzed around by car at breakneck speed. They went to a castle and a folk museum, where Sid found a tinker's cart just like the one his Irish forebears use to knock around in. Then they were touted round the local radio station to take part in a radio phone-in before going to St Mary's Golf Club.

Now the idea here was to show off the skills of the darters on the links. From about noon the good darting golfers like Anderson, Lowe and Harrington had gone out in a proper pro-am tournament. Local businessmen had paid £150 a time to charity for the privilege of having a darts star in their foursome. By 1 o'clock even hackers like Shayne Burgess were out on the rolling hills by the sea.

Sid showed up thinking all he had to do was to go out on the putting green and be filmed having an amateur bash. Things turned out a lot different. As Sid swished the putter the club pro came out, and behind him were three gentlemen with state-of-the-art golf gear, covers on clubs and even an electric cart. They did not seem impressed by Sid. Suddenly the pro took Sid aside and explained that these men had paid their cash and needed a 'star' to join them for a round. Sid was in a total panic. He had never played a round of golf in his life. Pitch-and-putt at Criccieth with the kids was his limit, and he had lost there as well. The pro pleaded. Sid gave in. He was given a bag of clubs, didn't have the savvy to ask for wheels, and headed to the first tee.

The next four hours have entered Wexford golfing legend. I was having a cup of tea and a sandwich in the clubhouse when I heard whispers of this Geordie in tracksuit and trainers causing chaos and comedy out on the course. Apparently Sid had never used a driver before and, after a couple of lucky strikes off the tee, his play had become erratic. He could not get the hang of the wedge, either; balls flew off at angles into ploughed fields and even the garden of a convent. At first his partners thought he was kidding. But by hole 12 and the long fairways near the sea, they could hardly play for laughing. John Lowe, a very good golfer, sent a messenger to the clubhouse for us to get on the balcony and watch Swiping Sid: it was funny to see him so red-faced and dripping with sweat, but he would not give up.

When he finally came back to the clubhouse – four hours after he'd started – Bob Anderson led the applause and half the members bought him a pint of Guinness. We all thought Sid was rubbish at darts until we saw him play golf!

The darts competition was a roaring success. The Irish lads who entered did well; they were in no way over-awed by the big names in the competition. John Lowe was put out by Dennis McCarthy of the Waterford Showboat Club; John Browne of Cullenstown beat England international Andy Nye; Brendan Dunne of Tipperary produced one of the shocks of the tourna-ment by dispensing of Eric Bristow. Wexford man Jack Murphy put out Bob Anderson, and I, too, was elimi-nated in the early rounds.

When it got down to the last 16, Jack Murphy, Peter Waters and Dubliner Frank Kelly were still in the hunt. All three made their entrances through a packed arena to the strains of 'The Purple and Gold', the Wexford hurling anthem. I remember thinking that with all this interest and enthusiasm, this would be a great place to host a PDC world event. Just like in our exhibitions, we had taken darts to the public. In what other sport can Joe Public meet and even beat world-standard players, then have a drink and a chat with them?

Trina Gulliver was a convincing winner of the ladies' event and Shayne Burgess and Chris Mason fought out the men's final. Mason won, and went off to play exhibitions all over Ireland. We had a last singsong and listened to stories of how folk had come miles on donkeys, and how there were disguised priests among the merry throng. It was not too long before we were back.

A few weeks later and it was Blackpool time again. There was a lot to play for. I was after the Grand Slam and Rod Harrington was after a hat-trick of Matchplay titles. And we had our own darting fairy-tale. Alex Roy, a 25-year-old rising star from Hertfordshire, worked as a builder for his dad. Now Alex is no slouch at telling you how good he is, and he finally got his chance. He did not qualify for the Matchplay but was called on as a last-minute substitute. His dad let him ditch his hod and Alex beat Peter Evison and Shayne Burgess before going out to Alan Warriner.

I started my campaign against the totally unpredictable Jamie Harvey. He is known as 'Bravedart' and, just like his hero, Jamie is either up in the clouds or deep in a burr-infested burn. As if to illustrate this he led 2–1 in legs with a 13-darter and an 11. But then he got the look of a puzzled professor, shaking his head and blinking. Apparently his pal Eric Bristow went to the bar at that stage, muttering, '10–2 coming up, sure as eggs!' He was not wrong. My average was 101.

In the second round I took out Nigel Justice 13–3.

My next opponent was 'El Lobo' himself, John Lowe, who had just had a brilliant 13–11 win over Chris Mason. I won without too much trouble by a 16–4 scoreline. I had rarely done myself justice at Blackpool, and careful preparation was paying off.

In the semi-final I took on Richie Burnett, the 1995 Embassy champion, and he hit me like a ton of bricks in the opening legs. He shot to a 4–1 lead before I levelled at 5–5. I got to 8–7 but I was averaging only a miserable 88. That was not Grand Slam darts. I kicked in and lifted my average to 102. Richie lifted his to 97, but it was not enough: I won 17–9.

I hoped Alan Warriner would make it a good final for the wonderful crowd. The 'Tarts for Darts' from Essex were here again in force, along with bunch called the 'Maltby Marauders'.

Two lads from *Loaded* magazine asked me if I thought darts should be in the Olympics.

Answer: 'Yes. And I would win the gold medal.'

Was it true darts players now drink wine?

Answer: 'Yes, the practice room is like Ernst and Julio Gallo's warehouse.'

How will you celebrate if you win the final?

Answer: 'Not much. But I'm going to see my ultimate hero.'

Who's that?

Answer: 'Joe Longthorne.' They looked at me very strangely.

The final turned out to be a true classic. I began with

an 11-dart leg and got to 5–4 in 10, 14, 10 and 13 darts. Alan was playing brilliantly but he was still trailing. I hit him even harder with legs in 15, 12, 15 and 11 arrows. I was by now averaging 111. Alan had been averaging over 100, but it was not enough. In the end I won 18–12 with a 100.3 average and nine 180s to his 10.

I was overcome with pride at achieving yet another first in darts: the first ever Grand Slam of world titles. I handed my darts to a little lad from the audience and tried to talk to the press. I told them I would probably pack up in four years' time and go to Spain and put my feet up. Chris Mason was on hand to make something of this remark: 'I wish the Power would go and sit on a beach in Spain now, then maybe one of us lot could nick a title or two.'

I was particularly pleased that Giles Smith in the *Daily Telegraph* was appreciative of what we players, the PDC and Sky Sports and their commentary team were trying to achieve. This is what he made of the Blackpool event.

'"Verily, Dave, this is a good contest," said John Gwynne on Saturday night, talking to us during the final of the World Matchplay Darts. And forsooth the man did speak true words, albeit somewhat antiquated ones – though that's pretty much par for the course during darts commentary where, arguably, language is made to work harder than on any televisual occasion this side of "Call My Bluff".

Take the moment, earlier in the week, during the quarter-finals, when Gwynne had remarked enthusiastically, and with more than a little justification: "This isn't sport – it's pure theatre." To which, quick as a flash, Sid Waddell said, "Old Vic, Young Vic, Queen Vic," tying the whole darts-theatre idea together. And then, being Sid, who is one of broadcasting's most fully liberated free associaters, he went a stage further. "Rub yourself with Vick, it won't get any better than this."

We were watching at the time the shaven-headed Shayne Burgess, who looks a cross between Julian Dicks and Jimmy Somerville and who has one of the most extraordinary throwing actions on the modern darting circuit. In a motion which seems to owe as much to the ballet school as it does to the pub, he seems to be very carefully removing the dart from his eye.

"Shayne isn't exactly built like Brendan Foster," Sid conceded. "He's built like a can of Fosters," observed Gwynne, who later expressed the more recognizably complimentary feeling that Shayne was "as resilient as best Welsh anthracite".

It is handy for Phil "The Power" Taylor that his reign as almost certainly the greatest darts player ever to throw tungsten in anger has coincided with the reigns of Gwynne and Waddell, who are so amply equipped to rise to Taylor's achievements and in whom Taylor gets the chroniclers he deserves.

"They're going to have to redesign the dart board for

this man," Gwynne said as Taylor completed an astonishingly composed and focused victory in the final over Alan "The Ice Man" Warriner. That win secured for Taylor a darting Grand Slam, the Power having already walked away with the World Championship and the World Grand Prix. "He's thinking nine-darter, he's thinking 170 finishes – we are watching a master at work," added Dave Lanning.

The analogy with a certain golfer's recent achievements in Scotland was not lost on Gwynne, who referred to Taylor as "the Tiger Woods of the tungsten kingdom", further assessing his play in the first 15 legs (during which Taylor's three-dart average was a bogglingly consistent 112) as "Donald Bradman darts if ever there were".

"Will the seeds of doubt begin to ferment in Taylor's mind," John wondered. Do seeds ferment? They do now. But not around Taylor, who ploughed on regardless to the big finale, in which two fat bins full of glitter exploded, leaving him the picture of happiness – red-faced and beaming in a shower of desiccated tinsel. Verily, darts knows how to throw a party. And, equally verily, Sid and John know how to talk it up.'

It might have taken years, but it says that the old days of beer-bellies and fags are behind us. And as for those glitter bins, one day I'll remember them and not jump like a kangaroo on a trampoline when they go off.

*

After the great success of the Irish Masters in Rosslare we returned to the Crosbie Cedars Hotel for the World Grand Prix in October 2000.

I was fascinated to look in the programme for the event and find that darts historian Patrick Chaplin had dug up more evidence of the medieval history of the game. Apparently in Ireland in the 15th century fighting men hurled 18-inch iron darts at each other at close quarters. Patrick, whose diligence in researching the history of the game knows no bounds, has also inspected a portrait in the Tate Gallery of Sir Neil O'Neill. This was painted around 1680, and shows the knight handling iron missiles of this type and eyeing up some pheasants. So darts were used in olde Ireland to stock the cooking pot.

Which brings us back to Shayne Burgess. He found the waters around Rosslare teeming with fish called 'dabs', caught a load and got the hotel chef to cook them for his breakfast. Next morning we opened our curtains to see seven big dogfish, neatly gutted and hanging on a clothes line! Shayne the Hook had been cresting the waves since the crack of dawn. When does this lad practise his darts?

The darts this time were not played in the hotel disco, but in a specially erected canvas pavilion that seated 750 enthusiastic fans. And it served its purpose well; despite Force 10 gales sweeping in off the Irish Sea, not so much as a single flight was blown out.

Early in the week we received some sad news: darts

legend Tommy O'Regan had passed away. Tommy left his native Limerick in the 1950s to find fame and fortune as a jockey, but instead became captain of England and Ireland at darts. Dave Lanning tells stories of Tommy going round the board in doubles in four minutes on the 'Indoor League' television programme in Leeds in 1973. Like Alan Evans, Leighton Rees and Alan Glazier, Tommy was a founder of darts as an exciting television spectacle.

I knew that life on the oche would be tough in this competition. The first two rounds were the best of just five sets, so it would only take a flying start by an opponent to cause trouble. And trouble I got in the shape of one of the young guns I have talked about. Kevin Painter of Essex was making his debut in a PDC televised event and I knew he was no mug. In 1997 he'd won the British Open, and he was an established England player.

In my first-round match against Kevin I won the first set. But then he got going and took it to 2–2 in sets. At 2–1 in legs to me in the deciding set he really had me worried. He had a shot-out on 81 to level up the match, and I was still needing 321. I knew he could easily take the leg and pip me in the last leg. But the pressure got to him and he let me peg back to win the leg and the match with a pathetic 21 darts. Kevin shook my hand and gave me the kind of look I don't forget. I knew in future he would be a very tough cookie, and so it turned out.

Next round I met Chris Mason on one of his less consistent nights. He is a great talent, but at times he commits the cardinal error of fretting over missed doubles. This totally breaks his concentration. I beat him 6–1 in sets with a 95 average. Then I had another easy match in the semi-final, putting Dennis Priestley out 6–1.

In the other half of the draw Shayne Burgess was showing what a diet of fresh fish can do for you. He beat Peter Evison and Peter Manley, and then triumphed in a classic match against Alan Warriner. The first set showed the total lack of pity the darts gods have: Alan averaged 106 and lost it.

Shayne had been in Ireland for eight weeks doing exhibitions and had fans in the audience from Sligo to Skibbereen. They made the tent shake with their cheers. Shayne established a 2–1 lead in legs in the deciding set and, with Alan needing 48 to square the match, Shayne did a 147 for victory – 60, treble 17, double 18. Then he put in his plastic Dracula fangs and did a swoop round the stage for his fans.

He got nowhere near my blood system in the final. He had chances at doubles to win three of the sets, but in the end I beat him 6–1 in sets with an average of 91.1.

After the last darts were thrown two young ladies in traditional gear danced a jig on the stage. I tried to copy the steps but had to busk. I gave the crowd a bit of Sneyd Arms' stomp circa 1977 and they adored it. The Irish love to see you doing what comes naturally. They don't judge you by the car you drive or the cut of your suit. Play your guts out on the board and then sing your heart out with them – 'Danny Boy' or 'The Fields of Athenry' – and they'll be your fans forever.

CHAPTER 15

Danger: Athlete at Work

My friend Sid Waddell has had to take some stick over the years for his line describing a match between Jocky Wilson and Cliff Lazarenko as 'a clash of Titans between two finely tuned athletes'. Tongue in cheek? Two blokes swigging lager and one dragging on a fag; both no strangers to a midnight vindaloo?

Sid actually said that in all seriousness. The point is that you have to be 'fit' for your sport. Footballers do not need to build up massive muscles above the waist. Sumo wrestlers need to build up their size to do their sport. Batters and pitchers in baseball need to be athletic enough to do their speciality, not to run marathons. Dart players need to work on the physical side only as much as it means keeping in good shape.

I have very rigid rules for showing up at my peak for

major competitions, and I have been able to implement these with more thoroughness since we moved out of the Cricketers Arms in April 2000. Once my dad died I'm afraid I lost most of my interest in the pub. Also, my travelling increased, and with four children Yvonne could not give the pub the 24-hour attention it needed. We tried having managers in to run it, but this did not work out.

So we moved to our present house in Bradwell and, believe me, Yvonne was delighted not to be living above the job. For me the move meant that late nights, early mornings and convenience eating became things of the past. My new lifestyle centred on the gym: I began a regular routine that I adapt when the big tournaments came round.

When I am not doing the big ones, I still go to the gym most days. I do a couple of hours alternating between the treadmill, the exercise bike and the rowing machine. The daft thing was I had a load of weight-training stuff set up in our conservatory at the new house; some of it is still there and I sometimes trip over a dumbbell when I go to make a cup of tea. But I could not motivate myself in the home atmosphere, whereas at the gym I like the competitive element that is always around.

In the 'close season' I do a bit of darts practice in the afternoon. But in the six-week run-up to a major, I refine the practice. After the gym I do an hour and a half, then I do two hours in the afternoon and finish with a third session in the evening.

For the past few years I have only altered this schedule slightly. I also follow a fat-free diet for most of the year, with lots of porridge, Ryvita, cottage cheese and salads. In the run-up to the World Championship I relax this a bit and have the odd helping of stew or spaghetti bolognaise and, of course, chow mein on successful nights!

I reckon this dedicated lifestyle is essential for top darts now. The young guns coming through now train harder than me. They see darts as a way of earning a cracking living. Sponsors like Unicorn Products, who I have been with for years, are chucking their money away if I sit boozing every night. If I get beaten, it's for sure I haven't lost the match in the bar the night before. I gave a full day's work for a fair day's pay when I worked in the pottery business and I try to do the same now. Mind, I'm weakening in my old age. On Christmas Day I stop practice long enough to open my presents and I might have one snowball – but only one.

On a humorous note, the attempt by some of us to boost the sporting image of darts seems to be getting through to the public. On a television quiz show shortly before the 2001 PDC/Skol World Championships the question was asked: 'With which sport do you associate Rod Harrington, Phil Taylor and Bob Anderson?' Quick as a flash came the answer: 'Squash.' We're getting there, folks.

I was not the number-one seed for the 2001 world title. I hadn't travelled to as many tournaments as I could have, so was seeded only number four. The number-one seed was Peter Manley. Before we got going Kevin Mitchell of the *Observer* came to interview me at the Lakeside Moat House and later wrote this: 'For those not familiar with the frustrations and the niceties of darts, it might be stretching it to say we are sitting down with someone Sid Waddell describes as "one of the great British sportsmen of all time". But he undoubtedly is.'

This view was echoed by the considerable newspaper interest in the fact that I was going for my ninth World Championship. The tone of the articles seemed to suggest that we were now being taken much more seriously. The only person going on about bellies was Sid. 'Taylor is rumbling like a giant with a belly ulcer,' was his line as I took the first set of my opening match against Nigel Justice. I took the second set by pushing my average up to 93. Nigel was throwing quickly and I got the impression he wanted the match over in as little time as possible. I sewed it up with a 151 finish to win 3–0 in sets in 29 minutes. Sid summed up: 'The Power is making it look as easy as peeling unskinned sausages.' I was feeling much better for having eliminated such delicacies from my diet.

One big highlight of the first round was the appearance of the first lady ever to play in the World Championship. Gayl King, the Canadian National Open Singles Champion, looked very nervous as she stepped up to play Geordie Graeme Stoddart. Stoddy had the toughest task of the tournament; if he lost he would be ribbed rotten until kingdom come. He had a chance to sew up the first set 3–0 but blew it. Gayl pegged back to 2–2 in legs, then she brought the Circus Tavern crowd to its feet by taking the set with 76 check-out. Cue fog, curses and tightly gripped betting slips on the Tyne.

Sadly Gayl went off the boil in set two and let in perspiring Graeme to level up the set score at 1–1. I could not believe it as Graeme played ducks and drakes with 17 darts to get the final double. The third set went to the Geordie and, after a unlucky bounce-out of a double in leg three by Gayl, he won the match 3–1. You have never seen two pints of bitter go down so quickly as Stoddy stood trembling like a leaf in the players' bar, shaking his head in relief. Gayl left the stage to a standing ovation and proudly told the world and the folks back in Canada, 'This was my dream and I lived it.'

Generally, I think the ladies do not take the sport of darts as seriously as the men do. This is partly due to lack of hot competition week in week out, and partly due to family and domestic commitments; also, I think in a way they enjoy the game a bit more than we professionals can afford to. The exception is the highly talented Trina Gulliver, who recently posted a 100 average for England. She could give some of the lads a hard time.

The next man in the way of my progress to my ninth title was Les Fitton, a Lancastrian and known as a very good starter. He didn't play that well in the first set, but I took a while to get into my stride. Sid Waddell reckoned 'A rare piece of television, this – Taylor under the cosh.' He was right, but Les could not sustain the pressure. I ran out winner 3–1 in sets with an average of 97. Now that is not exactly the flowering of the Power, but it was at least a shoot.

The blossoming started against 1983 World Champion Keith Deller. Keith is a tough opponent but sometimes gets a lot of bounce-outs due to using very short-pointed darts. Sadly for him he caught me on a good night. As the matches get longer in sets, I get more settled. After my perfect physical and mental preparation I know somebody has to play out of his skin to beat me. I overcame Keith 4–0 in sets with an average of 103.2. I was nowhere near peaking yet.

Now 'Diamond' Dave Askew is one of the nicest lads on the circuit, but I am afraid that somebody was in for a right pasting – and too bad it had to be him. Dave set off with some brilliant scoring but could not match it with doubles. He virtually let me have the first set. Then I gave him some of the bully treatment that Eric taught me: two 13-darters to take set two. I then took eight legs on the trot and took my set lead to 4–0. In the next leg Dave did a 126 shot-out but I took the next three legs and was poised to take set six. I was on fire now and went to the winning post via an 11-darter. Even I was pleased with the statistics: an average of 102.8 and 14 180s! I had never before got near that many maximums in six sets of darts. I felt disappointed that the nine-dart finish had not come, but I reckoned it would not be long.

There was a magnificent tussle between Rod Harrington and John Part to get the other spot in the final. Rod went down and nearly out to a 5–3 scoreline in sets, then pegged back to 5–5. John then showed his class with shot-outs of 122 and 161 to take the match.

Before the final the Sky commentary team reminded people of Part's excellent darting pedigree. John studied English and commerce at the University of Toronto before going into darts full time. He became Embassy World Champion in 1994 and only lost a single set in that tournament. He beat Ronnie Baxter 3–0, Paul Lim 3–0, 'Meatloaf' McCollum 4–0 and Ronnie Sharp 5–1. Bobby George had a bad back in the final and was swept aside 6–0. John hit 55 per cent of his check-outs in that final, which is top darting.

But John is a realist. Just before we started he paid me a great compliment: 'How do I beat Phil? I guess I try to hit a nine-darter every leg. That's what I'll be aiming for.'

It would be nice to report that the match was a classic. It was not. John averaged 92, but won only three legs out of 24 played. At one stage I took 13 legs in a row. I never let him settle. I did a 167 shot-out and a 10-dart finish, this last with a bull to finish rather than messing about. And the arrow hit the dead centre of the bull. I won 7–0 in sets. It was my ninth World Championship and in 38 matches at the PDC World Championships I had lost only once.

After the match John was once again very kind: 'Playing Phil is completely oppressive; take Tiger Woods and double it. He really killed me with his outshots; his doubles percentage must have been around 80, which is ridiculous. It takes away your hope when a guy never misses a double. It was a special performance, unreal, and I just could not measure up.' Great words; great player; with even greater expectations that were to bear fruit in the future.

The Times agreed with the verdict: 'Every so often somebody comes along in the wide and wonderful world of sport whose domination is total: Tiger Woods, Lennox Lewis, Jonah Lomu. In a nightclub in a rundown corner of Essex Phil Taylor reinforced his membership of the exclusive club.'

I was interviewed alongside Eric Bristow, who I said should be made the England football manager. If he was as big a swine to the football lads as he had been to me, we'd win the World Cup. As usual Eric had the last word: 'Phil is making good players look silly. He just does not think he is going to lose. Phil just seems to be three darts in front of them all.' But he would not be drawn on the question: 'Would the Mugger have beaten the Burglar?' What do I think? No comment. Not within 100 miles of Eric, anyway.

In the summer I went as usual to Blackpool in search of my fourth World Matchplay title. Again Peter Manley was the number-one seed, but he was having trouble living up to his 'One Dart' nickname as he was under-performing in the big televised tournaments. There were whispers going round that 'Umpteen Dart' would be more apt. The lads never miss a trick to stick the needle in. I fancied my old rival Martin Adams to be in the hunt and it was about time Andy Jenkins, one of the young guns, brought his top game to a major event.

My first match was an uncanny repeat of the year before. Once again Jamie Harvey lost the plot and the match. I won 10–2 in legs with a 101 average, exactly the figures from 2000. Has Charlie the ghost of the Cricketers Arms moved to the Winter Gardens in Blackpool? Has he started guiding the flights of my darts instead of wrecking my ornaments? Whatever the answer, I went a fair way down the path of a nine-dart finish in that game; just missing a seventh consecutive 60. I knew in my waters that the nine-dart was on, but it would come in a very close game where I was being tested to the utmost.

Alex Roy was my next opponent and he was hitting his doubles early on, but I ground him down 13–4. John Part was in good form, averaging 94, but it was not good enough. I beat him 16–4 with an average of 101.4.

Martin 'Wolfie' Adams was next for the Power treatment. He was in great form, having disposed of Mick Manning, Alan Warriner and Dennis Smith. He gave me a terrific battle in the first 20 legs, but at 11–9 in my favour I put in a spurt and ran out winner 17–9, with a 103 average and 13 180s just to show Martin how tough it is at the top.

I was pleased that Andy Jenkins had come good. He beat Rod Harrington and Nigel Justice before going out to Richie Burnett. He was delighted to break his television hoodoo.

Richie was my opponent in the final. On his day he is a very heavy scorer but sometimes his doubles let him down. He had a lot of supporters waving leeks and dragon flags. In leg seven I did an 11-darter to establish a 5–2 lead, but Richie pegged back to 5–5. But then the old double trouble kicked in and I swooped to 10–5. Richie rallied to bring the score to 16–9 with a 132 finish of 25, 57 and 50, but at the end it was 18–10 in my favour.

Richie was quick with the compliments: 'Playing Phil Taylor, who is the best there has ever been, is hard enough. But with a big English crowd behind him, it's near impossible.'

The next crowd I wanted on my side was a big Irish one.

The 2001 World Grand Prix tournament moved north from Wexford to the Dublin area. In October we assembled at the City West Hotel at Saggart, where the Irish football team make their camp. The village is very pretty and has the remains of a neolithic settlement and the ruins of an abbey; also some fierce clan battles were fought here between the Coynes and their enemies. Good place to shoot things out with arrows, I reckon.

Now I have mentioned omens and odd supernatural occurrences before in this book, but I must admit I never had Sid Waddell down as a shaman. Before explaining, I'll let you all into a little darts secret: Sid is known in the game as the 'Black Spot', because if he tips you to win a competition you will exit in the first round. But this time Sid was not being positive and forecasting a success. Quite the opposite. Just before the competition started he said: 'Taylor has again drawn Painter, who nearly beat him one year ago. It is very short-course darts and I think the Power will go out in round one.'

Hearing this, I laughed. What does Sid know? Answer: plenty.

Kevin Painter was lucky to be in the tournament at all. He was just outside the 24 players who had qualified by right and had to book his place through the play-offs. I knew he would be up for the match, which was only the best of three sets, five legs per set. So I got what was meant to be an early night. I was off nicely when my room-mate Sean Rutter staggered in full of Guinness at 3 o'clock in the morning and woke me up. I could not get back to sleep. This is not an excuse for what followed, but it didn't help.

I took the first set and Kevin took the second. Then he got inspired. 'Are we about to see the perishing of the Power?' Sid asked Dave in tones used by news-readers to describe the fall of the Berlin Wall. As Kevin lined up the winning double, Dave spelled out the significance of what was about to happen. 'Not since Peter Manley beat him at Blackpool over two years ago has Phil Taylor lost a major PDC televised tournament.' Sid wound it up. 'The artist known as Painter giving distemper to the Power.'

Bad night; short-course darts; I have no excuses. On the night I was beaten by the better man. I think Kevin symbolized the attitude of the new lads. It was the old Bristow motto: 'Respect nobody.' It terrified the life out of me. I knew my physical and mental preparation would just have to get better. It was one more bit of motivation to get up in the morning and practise like hell.

The atmosphere after my defeat was amazing. There was a carnival spirit around the hotel, merry Dubliners' ballads like 'The Irish Rover' echoed round the bars. The other players strutted about like farmyard cocks because the Power was out.

That mood was reflected in the standard of play. The quarter-final match between John Lowe and Martin Adams was a belter. At first the legions of Lowe fans had little to shout about. Adams went into the lead 3–1 in sets. But Lowe pegged back to 3–3. His fans began the famous anthem:

'Johnny Lowe, Johnny Lowe,
Johnny, Johnny Lowe
He's got no hair but we don't care
Johnny, Johnny Lowe.'

How about that? World Champion three times in three separate decades. Now an icon to kids who were not even born when he won the Embassy in 1979.

Adams showed his class by ignoring the hysteria of John's fans and taking the set score to 4–3. Lowe pegged back to 4–4. Adams won the first two legs of set nine,

210

and wanted tops for the match. He missed with the first dart, hit 20 with the second and then missed double 10. Lowe made it 5–5 in sets. With the crowd going nuts, it got to 2–2 in legs in the last set. John kept the advantage of throwing first and finished clinically on double 18. Game shot it was, and we nearly lost the roof. As I passed the bar later John was leading a chorus of 'Seven Drunken Nights'. I was off to bed early because I had a new job – co-commentator with Sid Waddell. Now that was going to be an experience.

Sadly, for all his old and new fans, John Lowe could not keep Roland Scholten at bay in the semi-final and the Dutch star went through. Alan Warriner, who had earlier had a 106.5 average against Andy Jenkins, booked his place in the final by beating Dennis Smith.

I took my place in the commentary box with some trepidation. There are stories of Sid breaking the door by kicking his chair backwards and soaking his partner in mineral water by getting the wires all tangled up. But I got a pleasant surprise. Sid was as calm as a surgeon telling an apprentice how to use the tools. He explained the buttons on the panel and the signals for 'keep talking', 'give the stats' and 'shut up as soon as you can'. No problems.

The match was not a classic. Alan was on a massive high and Roland seemed to have played himself out against Lowe. Alan raced to a lead of 3–1 in sets. Sid was as cool as a 'Come Dancing' commentator admiring a slow foxtrot. 'Alan the Iceman has really got his skates on now,' he murmured. Roland's body language was that of a beaten man as Alan went to 7–1 in the eighth set. Then he got a bit of a grip and pulled out a crucial 180. Sid leapt in the air, yelling 'At last he stems the icy tide!', and he landed down hard on my left foot. I hoped Alan would sew it up soon because I didn't fancy spending the night in casualty.

In fact that was Roland's last rally. Alan won the match and the title 8–2. As I limped out of the commentary box Sid asked me if I had enjoyed myself. 'Yes, apart from the GBH.' He looked baffled. Obviously he hadn't been aware of what he had done. The crowd were singing 'The Purple and Gold' and I wondered if they had anything appropriate for my left foot. How about 'The Black and the Blue'?

CHAPTER 16

My Darkest Hour

Life has a strange way of sometimes hitting you hard when you are least expecting it.

In October 1999 I was booked to do a Sunday afternoon exhibition at the Station Hotel, Leslie, in Fife. My driver Mick Connor and I got there the night before and parked our camper van in the car-park. We had a quiet night chatting to the locals and looking forward to a good turn-out next day. We were not disappointed. By 1.00 pm there were about 300 people in the audience as I toed the oche against 14 local players. The crowd appreciated every throw and I had a couple of halves of beer. At 4.30 I played the last challenger and started signing autographs. Two women who I reckon were in their early twenties began talking to me. They said they were darts players and suggested I might like to do an exhibition at their local in Rosyth in the future. I said it would be fine and they should tell their landlord to set it up. At about 5.00 we were asked to move into a smaller bar so the function room could be tidied.

In the bar I played pool against some of the locals and signed more autographs. Again the two women, who'd had quite a lot to drink by this time, began talking to Mick and I. They said that their pub was only a few miles away and wondered if I would care to drop in on the way back to Stoke. It would be, they said, 'a feather in our caps'. We agreed that since Rosyth was on the north side of the Forth Road Bridge and was on our way, we would give them a lift and call in to the pub for a sandwich and a drink. This chat happened as I was standing at the bar signing more autographs. I was sipping a pint of beer. Then the karaoke started and I did a couple of numbers with locals, and sang one with one of the women.

At around 6.40 Mick and I decided to make a move. We went to the camper van and gave the two women a lift. Little could we have imagined that the events which unfolded that evening would be the subject of court proceedings and lead me to one of the darkest periods of my life, and to the edge of despair.

A few days later I was sitting at home when I got a phone call from Dunfermline Police Station. I was told that the two women had called the police and claimed

Hold your body like a rock
and the dart like a scalpel,
and think 180.

That's what it's all about.

John Lowe has won world titles in three
separate decades. We always have ding
dongs – I won this one in Blackpool.

Ray Barneveld of Holland is a great
player but I beat him 21–10 in legs
to win the Match of the Century.

Peter Manley looks as sick as a chip. He refused to shake my hand but who cares
I'm world champion for the tenth time.

One of the world's greatest exhibition players, Cliff Lazarenko, celebrates.

n the shamrock oche. Here I n on my way to victory in osslare, County Wexford in 00. Later, I sang 'Danny oy' for the fans.

The 2001 World Grand Prix in Dublin. Kevin Painter beat me fair and square. So I practised harder – and won in 2002.

Baseball has community singing. American football has cheerleaders.
Mix in wrestling . . . and you've got darts.

Power on multi megawatts. I'm very aggressive up there but I channel it into the performance.

Ten world titles – maybe I'll pack it in when I get 13, or 15, or 17 . . .

Paddy Power World Grand Prix champion again – and time for an Irish-Chinese takeaway.

I have just completed the first-ever live nine-dart finish on British television. The bookies were sick but, bless them, they handed me £100,000 in cash.

The moment you know all the travelling and practice are worthwhile – the Taylor family are happy at yet another win.

Sorry lads. If you want to beat The Power go to bed early, practice and get your head right.

Saluting the lovely, lovely crowd at the Winter Gardens in Blackpool – my favourite venue.

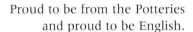

Proud to be from the Potteries and proud to be English.

In my early days they thought I was an arrogant bully like Bristow. I am soft away from the oche but a stone-killer up there.

Puppy fat. As a kid I put weight on easil So the gym and I are good pals.

Dennis Smith is a great player and a great lad; a joking clout round the ear says, 'I'll beat you some day'.

m-line Power. I lost four ones in three months before e 2003 World Championship.

The crowd can only gee you up a bit. It's up to you to get the focus.

When I lived in Blake Street in Stoke I never thought I'd see Hadrian's Wall, never mind the Great Wall of China.

The Chinese gave me a great reception in 2000 – so I sang 'My Way' and 'Mack the Knife'.

Ricky Hatton and I show Sky commentator John Gwynne what we think of his velvet words.

Viva Las Vegas. To see my face on big screens alongside the likes of Cher, Bruce Springsteen and Tom Jones was a complete gas.

As Sid Waddell said, 'John Part has done the unthinkable – he has short-circuited The Power.' But not for long, pal.

I had indecently assaulted them in my camper van whilst travelling from Leslie to Edinburgh. The police officer tried to calm my fears. He said there was no need to panic and that I should go up to Dunfermline and report to the police when I was ready.

I was shocked to the core and, in my turmoil, I made my first mistake: I didn't mention the matter to Yvonne or my close friends. This proved to be a disaster as events unfolded over the next eighteen months.

I contacted my manager Tommy Cox, and told him the situation. He said that first of all I must tell Yvonne and the family and that the truth would come out. Secondly he said I must get a solicitor immediately. When I reminded him that the police had said I had nothing to worry about, Tommy said, 'If the police are asking you to report to a police station, then you have got something to worry about.'

I was in a quandary. I thought all I had to do was go to Scotland, tell the police what has happened and the whole thing would go away. Tommy had warned me that it might come down to my word against the word of the two women. I now realize I should have had a lawyer with me when I went to the police station.

About two weeks after the phone call, Mick Connor and I travelled up to Scotland. At Dunfermline Police Station, they made me take my shoes off and I was put in a cell. I was in there for about an hour and a half. I then gave a statement. I was subsequently cautioned and charged with indecent assault, before being released and informed that I was to be reported for summons at a later date.

At that stage I contacted an Edinburgh solicitor and asked Tommy Cox to handle things with him, as I didn't want any phone calls coming to the house. It wasn't until about a year after my going to the police station that I was told the case was going to court in early 2001.

Before going into details of the case, I must say something about the web of deceit I had constructed in an effort to keep knowledge of these events from my family. For over a year I kept taking the dog out for sudden walks and making calls from phoneboxes. My tension showed at times: I'd sit brooding, and Yvonne remarked on my moods. The kids thought I was having an affair. The only thing that kept me sane was my darts. In the eighteen months of hell before the court case I won my eighth and ninth World Championships with my best-ever averages. I think it was just about all that kept me going.

I maintained the deceit as regards my family right up to the bitter end – I went to Scotland for the court case with Yvonne simply believing I was going to work up there. But any thoughts I had about keeping the story out of the papers vanished as we drove up to the court at the beginning of March 2001: the road was full of photographers.

The two women gave their evidence that afternoon and evening as I sat there in court. One of the women said, 'He challenged me to a drinking competition, saying I could not down vodka and Irn Bru faster than him. I accepted and won four times.'

She said she got into my camper van and was sick. She then said, 'I was lying down in the back and Phil tried to kiss me. I told him to stop and pushed him away. But he kept coming back and undid my trouser zip several times. I kept pushing him off. Eventually, he undid my bra and fondled my breasts. Immediately afterwards I was sick again and he left me alone.'

The other woman backed her up. She said, 'I heard my friend tell Phil to get off her and leave her alone several times. We were under the influence of drink but not drunk. My friend was sick. Then Phil leaned over the front seat, put his hands inside my shirt and fondled my breasts under my bra before I could push his hands out. I was distressed and in tears.'

I agreed that one of the women had been sick in the van but I denied assaulting either of them. I said I had too high a profile in darts to do what was alleged. I also said how deeply hurt I was by the allegations and that the case could well split up my family.

A few days later Sheriff Isabella McColl returned a verdict of guilty. She said to me in court: 'Both girls were credible. I did not find you direct in your answers.' I was told I had to report back at the end of

March for sentencing, but later this was put back to May.

I was in a state of shock when I walked out of the court, but I knew the time for deceit was over. I sat in the car for over an hour building up courage, then called Yvonne. 'You are going to have to sit down, because there is trouble. Something terrible has happened.'

She just kept gasping as I told about the crime of which I had been found guilty. When I got back home and was face to face with her and the kids, things were terrible. My friend Sean Rutter and Yvonne tore strips off me for even giving the women a lift. 'You madman!' they shouted. 'A bloke in your position!' They were right. Yvonne screamed and shouted at me for an hour, then gradually calmed down – at least on the surface.

The next day was a nightmare. The *Daily Mirror* had my picture and the story plastered all over the front page. The street outside our door was full of press people. For three or four nights I got no sleep. I just sat downstairs in a chair, filled with remorse for what I was putting my loved ones through. I had let down my family, my closest friends, my fans and my sponsors.

I had set myself up as a special kind of person, but now was afraid to go out of the house. I had put at risk my reputation, and indeed the wonderful life in darts that my career had given me. It might sound over-dramatic, but if I had been alone I would have killed myself. They could call me what they like, but I'm no coward and I could have done it.

During those horrendous eighteen months Tommy Cox had ceased to be my manager and Barry Hearn had taken over that role. There was no problem in the change; I just thought Barry could develop my career more positively than Tommy. Both men gave me massive support in the crisis, but it was my old pal Sean Rutter and the Stoke public who got me back on my feet. One night when I was sitting moping and thinking the whole world was against me, Sean dragged me out by the shoulders. He took me to play snooker at a club in Newcastle-under-Lyme. When we walked in there were about 200 people in the place, and I felt they were all looking at me thinking awful thoughts. I was wrong. As I stood by the snooker table, looking at the floor and shaking like a leaf, half the people in the club approached me and said they had read the papers and offered their support. The boost was massive – I nearly burst into tears there and then. Over the next few weeks I had many more demonstrations of support from the public. In fact, the only stick I have had away from home has been the odd sarcastic reference to the case from 'fellow' darts players.

On 1 May 2001 I returned to Scotland for sentencing, this time with Yvonne by my side.

Sheriff McColl chose to say this: 'I have been made aware that some people and some sections of the tabloid press consider that drunken young women who get into a camper van deserve all they get. That is a moral judgement. It is not my job to make moral judgements. I am here to apply the law. In our law it is recognized that personal integrity should be protected, even that of drunken young women. However brazen the attitude of the complainers may appear now, they were very upset by it at the time.'

She went on to say that she was persuaded that the offence was at the lower end of the scale and did not consider a jail sentence appropriate. She fined me £1,000 for each offence.

I felt relieved. I think a fine of £2,000 puts the case in perspective. It seemed to me like being convicted of drunken driving and not being banned, not having your licence endorsed nor any other penalty.

I think I also noticed a change in attitude by the Sheriff between my two court appearances. The first time she was very harsh in addressing me, but the second time she seemed more reasonable.

Sad to say though, the story does not stop there.

In November 2000 a letter had come through my door that made me the proudest man in England. It was from Buckingham Palace and it said I had been awarded the MBE for my achievements in the world of darts. It was a great feeling. Yvonne and the family were over the moon.

A month later I broke off practising for the World Championship at Purfleet to go with Sid Waddell and a Sky film crew to stand outside Buckingham Palace and talk about the honour. I recalled all my years standing by a machine in the Potteries making handles for beer pumps and toilet chains. I shed tears when I thought how proud my dad would have been. It meant more to me than any darts title I had won – it was the greatest honour I could think of, to go in those gates, meet the Queen and get the medal. Sky had lettered 'MBE' on my darts' flights and I held them proudly to camera.

I wondered what tales of the ceremony I would be able to take back to Stoke to tell Eric Bristow. He had received the only other darts MBE in 1989 and it had not gone smoothly. 'It was a bit nerve-wracking,' Eric told me. 'There was this lovely room and they tell you to walk up and reverse back. You must not turn your back on the Queen. So, what did I do? Made a right ricket, didn't I. I half turned away and she had bit of a laugh.'

As the months of 2001 ticked away, Yvonne planned her outfit for the visit to the Palace and I wondered what I would look like in a top hat. Around September I saw in the paper that Alan Shearer had just gone for his medal. My understanding was that the awards were given out alphabetically, so I reckoned our invitation would come soon. But it didn't.

After a while Tommy Cox contacted a woman at the

Department of Culture, Media and Sport. She said that, in the light of the court case and the conviction, they were discussing whether they were going to retract the award. Despite a long letter on my behalf from Tommy, I was officially notified in May 2002 that I would not be receiving the MBE.

There was pain, sorrow and humiliation. In December 2001 the *Independent* had given me this accolade in a headline: 'Phil Taylor MBE – Britain's greatest living sportsman.' For months the press had been mentioning the honour, and now I had to set them straight. It had been withdrawn.

As I have already said, throughout this dark period I played some of the best darts of my life. The sport is my living, and I was not going to put my livelihood in jeopardy. I went to all the tournaments even at times when I just wanted to sit in a dark room by myself. My heart was set on winning my tenth world title. 'Think positive' was my constant advice to myself.

Generally the saga of the court case made me very distrusting of people. The baggage of celebrity can be very heavy. In fact, if I did a reckoning, I'd say I've had much more unhappiness in my 12 years at the top of the darts tree than I did in all the years before I started climbing it.

At one stage I did think of giving up the game and leaving this country altogether. The way I looked at it, I had missed the growing up of Lisa and Chris due to my darts career. Why not sell up and go and live a happy family life in retirement in the sun?

In the next chapter you'll read why not.

CHAPTER 17

Showing Them How

Looking back over my life and my career in darts it stands out how I have always set myself targets and often even very slight spurs have got me right on my mettle.

In our poor days in Blake Street, Yvonne and I would decide what the darts money would be spent on; this time a video, next time a shower. Later I would aim for a better car, a better holiday, five World Darts Championships, or even more. Besides these planned objectives, I have often found that it takes very little to get me going. I was bollocked once, and once only, for making a mess of a job at Hackney's; I was threatened once, and once only, with being dropped from the Huntsman darts team; it took only one too-vigorous high-five from Eric Bristow to give me a vicious focus in our classic 1997

World Championship semi-final. I can see tiny things as a massive challenge.

In October 2001 I started preparing to win my 10th World Darts Championship. This time I needed no little spurs. For two years I had lived my life under a cloud, and by then I had grave doubts about getting the MBE. So I put everything I had into my darts. They had never let me down in my time of trial and they flew true in what was to be a golden 12 months. I eventually paid the price in sheer exhaustion, but I certainly blasted away a few dark clouds and sickened a few opponents.

To start with, in only a few months I had got my weight down from 20 stone to 15. Yvonne and I were going to the gym just about every day and I was watching my diet carefully. I was having a bit of back trouble with my new slimline posture, but the pain was diminishing.

I wanted my 10th world title desperately, since I knew it would be an achievement that would probably never be beaten. The John Lowe generation are too old to make the figure, and although Wayne Mardle and Kevin Painter are young enough, the competition is red hot. I really can't see any player getting to more than five world titles after me. And I want 13 at least.

Nor was I satisfied with aiming for another world title. I reckoned I was 70 per cent ready to achieve a nine-dart finish. My form over the last two years argued that it was just waiting to come out under the right conditions: pressure to win a leg or set against a rampant opponent like Rod Harrington or Dennis Priestley. Biting off more than I could chew? I don't think so. Proper mental and physical preparation plus the adrenalin rush of a big tournament mean anything can happen.

A big part of my preparation is getting the right amount of practice. All my experience of watching and sensing weaknesses in my opponents means that I now need less practice, but it has to be the right sort. In the run-up to the 2002 World Championship I cut down on exhibitions in October and November and did none at all in December. I went to the back room of the Saggar Makers and to the old oche by the bed at my mum's house. I didn't want tired eyes or arms: I needed to get to the Circus Tavern fresh and alert.

I think I was lucky to avoid the Tiger Woods syndrome, having my every move chronicled in the papers. One way and another my early success in darts was ignored by the media. It might have gone to my head. And I was not at all surprised to see boxer Joe Calzaghe on a documentary explaining why he still trained in the same old shed. 'I've seen lads earn thousands and get lazy and spoilt,' he said. I agree. At the Saggars and at mum's I get no special treatment; when I want a cup of tea I make it myself.

The field for the PDC/Skol World Championship was just about the strongest ever assembled. In addition to the normal PDC qualifiers, five players who had qualified for both the PDC Championship and the Embassy had opted to play at the Circus Tavern rather than in the

Embassy at Frimley Green: Steve Beaton, Ronnie Baxter, Chris Mason, Kevin Painter and Andy Jenkins. Despite my defeat by Painter in Ireland in October, I was odds-on favourite with the bookies.

My first-round opponent was the very experienced Paul Williams of Lancashire. As we threw the practice darts Dave Lanning suggested that I was 'a scalp that would have made Geronimo's mouth water'. Sid Waddell agreed: 'But it will take much more than a patchy performance.' We were up Monument Valley with the cavalry and the Apache and we hadn't even thrown a dart in anger!

It took me a while to get going and the two commentators just about got the reason why right: I was not 'stacking' the darts precisely in my scoring phases and this possibly had something to do with my altered stance after losing a lot of weight. In the end I bumbled through 4–1 in sets with a 98 average. This was pathetic given my form in practice.

But the Power was on full wattage in the next round, and I regret to say that poor Shayne Burgess was on the receiving end. I won the first 15 legs of the match with an average of 115.6, which is out of this world, even if I do say it myself! The run consisted of two 10-darters, two 11-darters, four 12-darters, one 13-darter, one 14-darter, three 15-darters, one 16-darter and one 17-darter.

John Gwynne and Sid Waddell were quick to twig the mood I was in. 'Shayne had to clatter the Power early

doors,' said John. 'But now it's become a walk in the
cemetery for the lad,' sighed Sid. As I piled into the big
scores, Sid piled into the purple prose: 'Taylor is taking
the game into a different achievable time frame. Shayne
is soon going to have to throw a hedgehog at the board
to have any chance at all. To be allegorical – the Bulldog
could well be sitting with a Bonio and a black eye soon.'
Of Shayne's 87 average Sid was contemptuous – 'about
as much use as a shovel at the bottom of Etna'.

Shayne stopped the whitewash but not the volcano:
I eventually ran out winner 6–1 in sets with an overall
average of 111.2. I was happy; that would put salt on
a few tails. Sid for once was nearly lost for words: 'Get
your own thesaurus, folks, they're cheap after Christmas. This is measurable greatness; this is numbers.
Playing out of your skin is going to do you no good, lads.
You will have to play out of your essence.'

Before I played John Part in the quarter-finals I
watched an amazing match between former World
Champion Richie Burnett and local Essex lad Colin
'Jaws' Lloyd. Now I admire Colin because away from
the board he's a grafter. He has mucked out stables
and laid cables to support his life as a darts player, and
it bore fruit in this match. Colin must have thought he
was home and hosed at 5–0 up in sets and looking for
a double to finish proceedings. His family and the Essex
crowd certainly did. But the old Celtic spirit fired up
and Richie got back to 5–4. The crowd nearly lifted the
roof off the Circus when Colin finally took the match.

My next opponent was John Part and I could hardly wait to get at him. To my surprise I whitewashed him 6–0 in sets with an average of 100.2.

I knew there was going to be a cracking semi-final between Colin Lloyd and Peter Manley and I wasn't wrong. At 4–4 in sets and with eight 180s to his credit, your money had to be on Lloyd. But Manley dug in, won set nine and came from two legs down to steal the 10th.

That put Manley in the final, where I had no qualms about meeting him. Against the others he oozes confidence, but against me, as Sid once put it, 'he's about as comfortable as a penguin in a microwave'.

But first I had to take the lustre off 'Diamond' Dave Askew. A year before I had beaten him 6–0 in sets in the semi-final and in 2002 it was the same story. He did give me a few jitters in the first set: he got to 2–0 in legs and then had four darts at a double to take the set. He missed and I cruised into the final with a 100 average.

Everybody, with the exception of Peter Manley and his lady Chrissie Howat, expected me to win my 10th World Championship. But in the practice room before the match I felt really sorry for Peter. We had a television monitor near us and the other players were tipping me to win by a mile. In the Sky studio Sid Waddell was reminding the viewers of the sporting context in which he, John Gwynne and Dave Lanning placed my achievements. He said you had now to look beyond the Steve

Davis, Stephen Hendry, Geoff Boycott and Bobby Charlton dimension, and try to put what I had done up there alongside Don Bradman, Muhammad Ali, Jesse Owens and Tiger Woods. Looking at the newspapers, it seemed they accepted this opinion. I had said that 13 titles would do me – I was born on the 13th of the month and my mum had always liked the number! Sid reckoned I could go to 15 if I wanted. Eric Bristow, who once told me I could win the world title as many times as I wanted, said I would beat Peter 7–0.

He didn't look very happy, practising away with all this going in his ears.

On the stage Phil Jones began his brash, flash build-up and Peter walked out first. To me he looked pale and worried, even when Chrissie planted a big kiss on him. Then the bouncers lined up in front of me like the All Blacks' front row and off we walked. The crowd went mad. On the microphone Phil Jones called me the eighth wonder of the world. In dodging the patting hands of well-wishers, I bumped my head on a poster pronouncing 'Dartmageddon'. Hope they mean for him, I thought.

The gravel tonsils of referee Russ Bray got us going. I hoped Peter was not going to act up. He had decided not to throw first after he'd won the throw for the bull. This was possibly gamesmanship, possibly bravado and possibly an attempt to catch me cold. Whatever, it did not work. I won the opening leg and took the second with a 12-darter.

Dave Lanning described me as 'just like that other Stoke lad Robbie Williams. Taylor is the number-one hit man.' I took the set comfortably and Peter seemed off balance. He throws big bomber darts that can easily block the bed and they were not flying true. As my first 180 rattled in, John Gwynne pointed to another ominous fact: 'Taylor takes his maximum scoring to 27 for the tournament. Peter had only 18 before this match.' It did not seem to be Manley's night.

I gave Peter a few chances but he missed his doubles. With a bit of lick he could have pulled the set score to 2–1. I coasted to 3–0 in sets and a 101 average. John Gwynne called my scoring 'Bradmanesque'. I felt good and just kept reciting the old mantra of my days in the Huntsman team: 'Keep it in the lipstick' (the treble 20). I did an 11-darter to take the score to 4–0.

By the time we started set six, with me now 5–0 up, Peter had won only three legs. Sid pointed out how easy it was for me. 'Taylor is averaging a mere 97.5, and that for him is cruise control. He is nowhere near maximum juice.' He was dead right; I need a hot opponent to hit my best form.

I strolled to 6–0 in sets with a bull finish and Sid and Dave waxing lyrical. 'The Power is a true giant of sport,' said Dave. 'As Cleopatra said about Antony one steamy night in Egypt: "He doth bestride the world like a Colossus,"' agreed Sid. As Peter plodded on Sid reckoned 'Keeping up with the Power is like trying to hang on to the pants of Halley's comet.'

231

At the start of the seventh set of what was becoming a Phil Taylor parade, Sid and Dave agreed that we were present at 'a unique sporting achievement'. Mind you, the crowd was almost silent, waiting, I suppose, for the inevitable. I was almost ashamed to be doing the business with a mere 96 average. Peter rallied a bit and pulled to 1–1 in legs. Then I banged in some lovely treble 19s. I got to 2–1 in legs. Peter rallied again and made it 2–2. The crowd went delirious; you'd almost think Peter had levelled the match. 'Destiny on the back burner – for the moment,' hissed Sid.

I approached the board to try and take my 10th title. I had no nerves whatsoever. Some say the last leg is the hardest. Not for me. I had kicked at Manley every time he'd had a decent score. My mind was not on £50,000, 10 titles, Bradman or Ali. It was on getting my job done and having a nice Chinese tea. I banged in two 140s and he needed 180 just to hang in. That's bullying and I knew my uncle Eric would be pleased. Suddenly I was looking at double eight to win, and I got it.

'Tell your children to tell their children to tell their children that you were there when Phil the Power Taylor did what no man has done before, or ever will again: take 10 world darts titles!' Dave Lanning summed up proceedings.

I raised my arms in salutation to the crowd then offered my hand to Peter. He refused to shake it and rushed off stage. I was disgusted. Here was I at the pinnacle of my career, and at a great moment in darts history, and he was acting childishly. It was not my fault that I whitewashed him with an average of only 98.4. I remembered the protocol of the game, the handshake, and he ignored it. I think for the rest of his career he will regret what he did. At my exhibitions one of the first questions is always: 'Why did Manley not shake your hand?' I answer what I told the crowd that night. He had to go to the toilet.

Later on, with the crowd still booing him, he did come on stage and shake my hand. I calmed the crowd down by saying how gutted he was at his performance but that was pure diplomacy on my part. There was absolutely no excuse for his behaviour.

After the on-stage presentations and speeches I departed from my usual ritual. Normally I call up a young lad from the audience and give him my winning darts. It is great having a lad of six foot come up to you and say 'Remember me? I'm the kid in short pants you gave your arrows to eight years ago!' That night I called on to the stage three fellows who I admire for spreading the gospel of our game via Sky Sports. Dave Lanning got the first dart, John Gwynne the second and Sid Waddell the third. The crowd showed their appreciation in fine style. Then I reverted to my normal routine and had chow mein and crispy duck in my room with the family.

The newspapers all tried to put perspective on my 10th win. Here's what former county cricketer Simon Hughes of the *Daily Telegraph* made of it: 'Everyone Taylor played wore a look of total resignation. They knew they were confronting an irresistible force. "He makes them sweat like a swamp donkey in a sauna," as one punter put it. To a man they were intimidated by his aura, mesmerized into missing relatively easy doubles, and he didn't give them a second chance. The pressure of the presence of the Power is paralysing. All his opponents resembled men walking to the gallows. At least the execution was swift.'

The *Daily Mirror* picked up on Sid mentioning me in the same breath as Bradman, Woods and Muhammad Ali and printed my picture alongside theirs. I was dead proud to see myself there; proud for myself, my family and for the sport.

Mel Webb, who has regularly featured darts in *The Times*, went a step further. 'Nobody, not even Tiger Woods or Don Bradman, has dominated his sport as overwhelmingly as Taylor has.' But my greatest compliment came from Dave Lanning, who has commentated on darts for 32 years. During the final he said solemnly, 'In all my years of commentating I never thought I would see the game of darts mastered. But take good note, folks, you are looking at the master of the game.'

I went to Blackpool in the summer of 2002 on an all-time high. I had just had a dizzying and highly successful trip to Las Vegas, which I will tell you about later, and I was ranked world number one.

First to feel the Power was Shayne 'Not Phil Again!' Burgess. Poor lad. He was out in a boat fishing for mackerel on day two. I did seven 180s in the match and won by 10–0 in legs with an average of 100.9. Not brilliant, but it would do for starters.

The gods of darts kept pitching me against Kevin Painter and he was next on the menu. He averaged a creditable 98.4 but went down 13–6 in legs. My average was 104.

I have already made reference to what happened in my historic match with Chris Mason, and I will set my nine-dart finish in context in the next chapter.

To get to the final I had to beat John Lowe, and what a match it turned out to be. John started the game with an 11-darter, and it took a 12 and an 11-dart leg by me to get to 6–4. Then John played the kind of darts that won him three world titles and established a lead of 8–7. I have to admit that the pressure of my successful year and the press interest in the nine-dart had drained me. I was missing doubles. Also, John had at that stage a check-out percentage of 62, which is magic.

He really had me worried as he took his lead to 11–9, then he missed two darts at double top to extend his lead and that opened the door. I took that leg and the next to level the game at 11–11. Still Lobo would not lie down. He led at 13–12. But I got a second wind from somewhere and won 17–15, with two 174 shots in the final leg.

On the bald statistics I had to be favourite to take the final against John Part. My tournament average was 102 to his 92.7. But I was shattered and my doubles had let me down against Lowe. I knew John could lift his game. He wanted to banish the memory of my thrashing him 7–0 in sets in the 2001 world final.

John walked out to the 'Star Wars' theme and the crowd were buzzing. I got a great ovation and for once my hair was immaculate as I got on stage; the patters and rufflers were kept well back. Dave Lanning compared the atmosphere to 'the pulsing of a hydro-electric plant' and Sid Waddell predicted an easy win for me by 18–7 in legs. Neither the commentators nor the punters knew what a mammoth job it had been to get out of bed and practise. I felt like a fighter who had taken one punch too many.

Looking back at the tape I can only marvel at how tight on the 60 bed the Sky cameras get. The darts look as thick as Cuban cigars, and the head-on shots show the exact weight of every throw. I was missing the bottom of the 60 with my early stacking. My doubles were not bad at the start, though I did mess up a chance at double four to take a 4–1 lead.

The match became electric at 11–10 to John. My average had slipped to 97 and he had lifted his to 95. Our faces told the story. He was snarling like Lee Van Cleef sighting down the barrel of a Winchester and I looked like a bloke who had gone to sleep on the beach in blazing sun. John Gwynne said I looked vulnerable, which is exactly what I felt.

John pushed ahead 12–11. I levelled the scores. Then I missed a 106 finish and danced with rage. I chastised myself mercilessly. 'Silly, silly Philly,' said Sid. Good job stronger language is not allowed on telly. Then I missed three darts at a double. More self-cursing. John took it to 13–12.

At 13–13 John had the body language of an athlete and I looked like a tramp searching gutters for fag ends. His back was perfectly arched and he was not sweating. Then I looked down at the front row and saw my pal Ricky Hatton, the WBU World Light Welterweight Champion, throwing mock punches at me. Was it encouragement or what he'd do to me if I lost? Did he have a bet on me? Who knows? I bashed in a 161 finish to take the lead. Some people might get distracted, not me. Turn a little spur into a big one, but stay tall in the saddle.

John Gwynne reminded the viewers that against Lowe I really kicked when trailing 13–12; I put in two 177 shots to go to 14–13. But John responded brilliantly. He bashed in a 160 finish to level the game and I led the applause. I remember feeling exactly like I sometimes did in my armchair at home when I'd be halfway through a great Bruce Willis movie and struggling to keep my eyes open.

John pushed his average to 96 and his double scoring to 50 per cent. My double-hitting percentage was only 28. He got to 16–15 and I was almost dead on my feet. But I heard Ricky screaming me on and I dug in. I made it 16–16, then just missed a 167 shot-out. I got to 17–16. One leg needed now. I started with 180 and the crowd sensed my new mood. Last legs are never so hard for me: I just let experience and technique take over. Double two won me the match. 'The greatest dart machine who will ever exist!' screamed Sid. I went off the stage looking for spare parts.

The next stop on the darts circuit was Dublin again for the Paddy Power World Grand Prix. The venue is the City West Hotel and I was one of the first to try out the excellent gym. I was feeling much better than I had in the closing stages of the Blackpool tournament. And there was a touch of blarney in the air about the draw. If I disposed of Keith Deller in the first round I would take on an Irish legend in the second, 60-year-old Jack McKenna from County Kildare. There were sure to be 1,200 'Dublin Jacks' cheering him on.

I had no trouble disposing of Keith 2–0 in sets.

Jack McKenna has the look about him of a priest who has found the public bar and the oche by accident. He was first capped by Ireland in 1974, and was Paul Lim's opponent when Paul did a nine-darter on the BBC in 1990. In his first-round match he had beaten Cliff Lazarenko and sent his supporters wild. Too wild? 'I'd sooner have them a bit calmer for my match against Phil,' said Jack. Only in Ireland . . .

I took the first two legs of the match with the crowd heeding Jack's plea for decorum. Then Jack got a leg back and you could hear the roar in Tralee, I'll bet. Despite getting to a potential 13-darter in the final leg, Jack could not handle me. He shook my hand at the end of the game and thanked me for a wonderful experience. It made me proud to be in a sport that boasted senior citizens at one end and hungry lads in their teens at the other, all competing every inch of the way.

It was now time to tussle with a larger-than-life character who calls himself 'Top Banana'. Mark Holden is a Manchester lad who looks as though he could hold his own against The Rock and Kurt Angle at the grappling game. And he is some dart thrower. But he could not get going as I lifted my average to 94 (this with a double to start). He had a purple patch in the middle of the third leg of the third set and Sid Waddell called it 'tungsten tickling of terpsichorean proportions', though I would think Dumbo would be more graceful on a dance floor than Mark. I waltzed the match 4–0 in sets.

Next up for me was Peter Evison, who like myself spends a lot of time on the treadmill. Sky talked to him as he pounded out the miles and he was focused: 'I want Taylor. I want Taylor. Bring him on.' That sounded fine to me; if half his mind is on me, that's less on his game. I beat him 6–0 in sets with a steady 94 average.

My opponent in the final was John Part. Now I know he's a great player, but in my heart I never thought he would ever beat me on television. At my peak I feel I always have the edge on him, but maintaining that peak, as you will no doubt have guessed, is not a precise science.

The crowd went daft as we came out for the final. It was our second year at the City West and the event now had an identity, just like the World Championship at the Circus Tavern or the Matchplay at Blackpool.

John had just got over a heavy cold and was in good form. I took the first set but he hammered in a 12-darter during it. I went to 2–0 in sets before John struck back to make it 2–1. But then I put in the old kick and won nine legs on the trot, taking the set score to 5–1. I was now averaging 101.6 with a double start; equivalent to 111 on a straight start. Now, two years earlier John might have wilted, but by now he was by miles my biggest rival. His style never falters and his counting skill is second only to Bristow's. He won the next two sets. In fact, so strong was his response that he beat me in set eight by 3–0 in legs, with me averaging over 100! In the final leg he finished from 132 with bull, bull, double 16. That is class. It was the sort of match I have always relished.

I gave him some pain in the next set. I took it 3–0 and did two 177s in the last leg. In the 10th set shots of 154, 152 and another 177 got me to 2–0 in legs. Then John missed double 18 to save the game.

In the end I won 7–3 in sets with a 100.2 average. On the microphone I gave John the ultimate compliment: 'You know you are in a proper game when you realize that you are up against an opponent who will not let you relax for a moment.' I knew that next time we met I would be in for another tough test.

I had now done something that had never before been achieved in darts, and in fact had not been possible prior to 2002: I had won the Grand Slam of the World Championship, the World Matchplay and the World Grand Prix, plus I had won the Las Vegas Desert Classic, making it the Super Slam. And the icing on the cake was the £100,000 for my nine-darter in Blackpool.

Giles Smith in the *Daily Telegraph* reckoned their was only one way of stopping me. 'If this were Formula One, of course, the authorities would even now be working out some way to pin the Power back: by attaching bags of sugar to his darts, perhaps.'

Now that would give the boffins at my sponsors Unicorn something to work on!

CHAPTER 18

The Appliance of Science

Audiences at a darts exhibition are intelligent folk who want more for their money than 180s and bull finishes. They want entertainment and, you might be surprised to know, a bit of erudition. Here are some of the most frequently asked questions.

How much does Cliff Lazarenko drink? I never exactly specify but leave it to their imagination after saying that a few pints of lager is how Cliff warms up.

What is Eric Bristow really like? I think that throughout this book you will have realized what I think of my mate and mentor. Love him or hate him, Eric is a one-off.

Is Sid Waddell mad? Again, you must make up your own mind. I think the 'Geordie Lip' has used his university education and wild imagination to enhance the game. When the press started really listening to Sid I think they twigged that we were genuine high-calibre sportsmen. Mind, he does get very excited – usually at the right times!

What happened to Jocky Wilson? I have already explained that money and health problems led the wee man to retire back to his native Kirkcaldy. Like Eric he is an icon of the sport. Their sometimes fiery clashes, always laced with wit, got the sport noticed in the early 1980s.

What do you think of Bobby George? Well, from what has gone before you will have worked out that Bobby and I are not top of each other's list for birthday or Christmas cards. When I talk about him at exhibitions, I call him 'Marmite': you either love him or hate him. Now if I played him, I would certainly have him on hot-buttered toast! I admire the fact that, like myself, Bobby can grab a shovel or a bag of cement and do hard graft. His Essex mansion, George Hall, was built from the foundations up to the roof tiles by Bobby himself, whose first line of work was laying concrete floors.

Sid Waddell has a load of Bobby stories that illustrate what a great sense of humour Mr Glitter has. In the early 1980s the players were staying at a hotel in Newcastle-under-Lyme during the Embassy World Championships. A lot of the usual spoofing went on; putting drinks on other people's bills and ordering several dozen copies of the *Financial Times* to be delivered to a certain player's room without his knowledge. So Bobby thought it was a joke when hotel reception called his room to say two gentlemen from the local CID would like to talk to him in the bar.

With a huge grin Bobby approached the two men in the bar, where they were sitting with Sid. They explained to Bobby that a local lady had seen his collection of gold rings on television and thought they looked like some stolen from her house.

Bobby's grin got bigger. He rolled back his shirtsleeves to show more gold on his wrists. ' It's a fair cop, mates,' said Bobby. 'I did that lady's house just as I did a lot of houses round Barking to collect this lot.'

Despite furious gestures from Sid, Bobby continued the 'confession'. This patter did not go down well with the CID. They pulled out cards to show that they were really serious. And Bobby's florid face turned purple! But the cops went away happy after Bobby apologised for joking.

A few years later, during a tournament at Middlesbrough, Bobby drove Sid across the Tyne to the village of Lynemouth in Northumberland, home of Sid's parents. Bobby parked his white Rolls Royce outside the Waddell house, told Sid to hide in the car, and went up the path. He knocked firmly on the door. Sid's dad, Bob, answered.

'I am with the local police,' said Bobby, 'We are anxious to interview Sidney Waddell about impersonating a darts commentator . . .'

'Come in and stop talking daft, Bobby,' said Bob.

There followed a dialogue in pure Essex and broad Geordie between the two Bobs which lasted around an hour and covered darts, horses and football – and each man understood about 10 per cent of what the other said.

As a darts player and BBC pundit – where his cheerful Cockney patter hides a lack of analytical depth – Bobby has used what talent he has to its best advantage. If you look at the tape of the 1980 Embassy final, you will see clearly what Eric Bristow thought of Bobby. Eric strutted and made the odd comment, and it was clear that he felt Bobby was nowhere near his class. Bobby's body language was that of a victim. When Eric threw the winning darts he gave Bobby a kiss. Bobby went bright red. Eric said during the post-match interview: 'One day Bobby will make a good number two.' Accurate prediction.

But the questions that amazed me were about the history of the game. How did it start? Was it developed from archery? Was it ever illegal? And, just about every night, where did the word 'oche' come from?

I will start with the hot debate about the origin of the phrase 'on the oche'. Go back 30 years or so and you will find that invitations to play darts from league secretaries ended with the words 'Toe the hockey at 7pm'. The hockey, or throwing line, was a wooden or metal mark on the floor, or a tape or stencilled line on the rubber playing mat. Suddenly, however, in the late 1970s the British Darts Organisation began to use the phrase 'Toe the oche'. It appears that an official had gone to the Anglo-Saxon section of the British Museum and after some research found 'oche', a word dating back to around 1100, and meaning 'groove in the ground used as an archery mark'.

Now this is a lovely poetic idea, linking as it does the mists of the days of Ivanhoe with the heroes of the Circus Tavern. But there is another, much more mundane, theory that sets the phrase in a much later time. Apparently a brewery called Hockey's from Ipswich was one of the first to lay plastic mats in front of dartboards. These had the various throwing distances marked and the name 'Hockey' stencilled by them. So the cry went up, 'Here mate, toe the 'ockey.' You tell me who got it right.

Moving on to the history of the sport, there is sound documentary evidence that darts was developed by archers in the 14th century. In Europe at that time the highest-paid mercenaries were Welsh bowmen who could perform amazing feats of accuracy. One such hero, no doubt a forefather of Alan Evans and Leighton Rees, once took a bead on an enemy he did not want to kill, just take prisoner. The target was a knight in full battle armour who was riding a horse covered in chain mail. Our Welsh hero hit a bull: the clothyard shaft went through all the armour and pinned the knight to his horse! There are other tales of the longbow that show it was the 'smart bomb' of medieval warfare.

At close quarters, the bowmen used hand darts weighted with heavy metal in the shafts. Who knows how long England's wars against the French would have lasted if some bright spark had discovered tungsten! There is also evidence from medieval Japan of hand darts like toasting forks which were part of the fighting equipment of samurai warriors.

For centuries competence at archery was compulsory in England, so what more natural a development than to throw or fire arrows or darts at log ends or beer barrels after the serious stuff? Higher up the social scale, darts were an item of fashion. Around the year 1530 Anne Boleyn presented Henry VIII with a set of 'dartes of Biscayan fashion, richly ornamented'. These arrows could well have come from the Bay of Biscay where the practice of harpooning whales by hand was first developed by fishermen.

In 1620 the pilgrims on the *Mayflower* set up a dartboard and whiled away the hours of their Atlantic crossing. Presumably no strong drink was consumed in the way of a warm-up, and I endorse that attitude.

Moving on to the modern history of the game, in 1898 an American patented a folding paper flight and in 1908 a Yorkshireman patented an all-metal barrel.

Now, you'd think that popping into your local after a hard day's work and throwing a few darts would be just about the most law-abiding pastime possible. Think again. Until the historic Foot Anakin decision of 1908, the legality of darts games in pubs was in question.

The law of the time said that games of chance were illegal in pubs. Foot, a Leeds publican, was brought before the magistrates accused of operating a game of chance. But Foot was no mug. He got permission to bring a board into the court and proceeded to put three darts in the 20 segment (this was on a Yorkshire board that had no treble ring). He was asked to do it again, and duly obliged. The historic judgment rang out: 'This is no game of chance!'

In the days before the tungsten revolution of the 1970s – when slimmer darts that could achieve more spectacular scoring were introduced – a few great names set the trend for the sport as part of show business. Jim Pike and Joe Hitchcock toured the music halls. The great Tommy Barrett of Middlesex won the *News of the World* tournament in 1964 and 1965 and spread the gospel of the game.

So, with this history of a military activity that turned into a pastime, we come to the big question: is darts a sport?

I have had loads of responses, some serious, some flippant. Generally the view is that darts is a pastime rather than a sport. People argue that because it is played in pubs and you don't need to be fit to play, it cannot be ranked with football, cricket, athletics and swimming. They also point to having beer around being a negative factor. This is what caused some newspapers to scoff at the game and its 'beer-belly image' in the early days. However, after attending the 1981 Embassy World Professional Championships at Jollees, Matthew Engel of the *Guardian* said, 'of course it's a sport'.

I can make out a perfectly valid case for darts as a sport, especially as played by professionals like myself, John Lowe, John Part, Dennis Priestley and the lads. For a start, darts involves tremendous hand and eye co-ordination, and in this respect it is very like snooker, cricket and golf. Also, if you practise darts you will become better at it. This seems to be part of the definition of sport: working on a skill to prepare you for another key element – competition. Hitting a tennis ball against a wall is not sport. Playing tennis against an opponent and trying to beat him is.

As for the argument that darts is not physical, I would not agree. I reckon darts demands more physical effort than archery, shooting or golf. Here are a few stories that will open your eyes. Sid Waddell made a television titles sequence for the 1979 Embassy featuring Leighton Rees flinging darts at a cork board. Rees was the holder of the Embassy world title, but for about 10 days over Christmas and New Year had not used his right arm for anything more strenuous than pint lifting. After three hours of hurling tungsten the great man was almost in tears with the pain in his throwing arm. Similarly, at Blackpool in 1998 at the World Matchplay tournament, the eventual winner Rod Harrington was so affected by the heat that he had to keep up a high intake of energy drinks. I myself prepare for six weeks for major championships by a mixture of careful sleep, practice and exercise that would make an Egyptian wrestler take note.

To be absolutely blunt, the old professional way of a few pints before, during and after the match – the way of Rees, Eric Bristow, Cliff Lazarenko and many others – is coming to an end. Life on the road is hard, but sitting up late drinking is certainly not for me. If I socialized and drank alcohol after matches or exhibitions I would be shattered. There is a breed of player banging on the door who look after themselves well – lads like Wayne Mardle and Kevin Painter – and they want to kick your butt and take your bread and butter. If I draw these lads in a tournament I practise hard, since as well as being talented and dedicated they are constantly gaining experience and self-belief.

The more I talk to my boxing friend Ricky Hatton, the more I am convinced that future darts champions will have to train like boxers. And I think one major change in the game is a must: we have to get rid of alcohol altogether. By this I mean that it should not even be allowed in the practice room. For years we have not had it on the oche, but we will never be classed as a true sport until we get rid of booze entirely. Our prize money from blue-chip sponsors would go up. The Sports Council would be more likely to recognize us. We might even take darts to the Olympics.

Why do darts players need drink? I'll tell you in two words: Dutch courage. All right, the game started in the pubs, but now we are a professional world business. The argument about being used to having a drink before or during playing does not impress me. I know players who once swore by lager, or a couple of nips, who now sip wine. Why not change to water or a cuppa? I sometimes have the odd brandy-and-port three hours before I play, because I eat nothing more than breakfast on a match day. Take it from me, Eric, Cliff and Bob Anderson would adapt in no time.

The analogy with boxing hit me hard in the summer of 2002. After my successful trip to Las Vegas, I felt as though I was paying for a few years of massive success. I had won all the major championships and I was exhausted. With a boxer there are months between fights, and you can win some fights with a quick knock-out. Not so with darts. You have to go a certain gruelling distance day by day in a tournament, and then it's only a few weeks to the next one. You could go out and dig the garden after some matches, but the mental pressure is the real killer.

Again, like a boxer, I try to prepare in just the right way. About six weeks before a big tournament I begin the routine. I get up around 8am. I have breakfast and then go to the old house in Blake Street or the Saggar Makers for one-hour's practice. I am grateful to Dave Lewis, a Middlesbrough lad and landlord of the Saggars. He has built a stage set for me just like you see on Sky, give or take a few decibels of sound and the Power theme tune. Here I get the complete isolation that I could not get in another pub; no phones, no mithering, no spectators. Just pure concentration. Tommy Cox used to marvel at this routine. He said I was the most dedicated man on a practice board he had ever seen. I do a bit of swimming, because exercise helps me sleep better. All it needs is one look from Yvonne after a few weeks of this to tell me to 'go get 'em'.

I do not like to leave the venue of a big championship. Some players slip home on days when they are not playing. I like to keep my routine; to me I am at work. And it would not be wise for me to pop back to Stoke from the World Championship in Essex; we play just after Christmas, so I could get snowed in.

I like discussing my sport with other sportsmen. I am not a clever person, and in fact it may be no big fault in a darts player. How can your mind wander if you haven't got much mind in the first place? I never plan ahead or have a theory on how to beat somebody. I read them on their performance against me and capitalize on weaknesses. So what do I tell the likes of snooker star Peter Ebdon when he asks about my winning psychology? All I said was that I enjoy playing and most of all I enjoy winning. I could not play a sport and not be a winner. I think that's what Eric Bristow sensed all those years ago. I shared his attitude to darts: 'Winning is the best medicine known to man.' How many times did I get that drummed into me?

Now you may think it hard to equate this 'philosophy' with being a lifelong Port Vale supporter, but I learned a lot about what marks out winners from losers by watching the team. When I was a kid my dad used to lift me over the turnstiles so I didn't have to pay. Later on I either climbed over the wall or ducked under the turnstiles. In the early 1970s Stoke City was the big local team and was usually around the top end of the first division. They were very unpredictable.

Port Vale had stars like 'Jesse' James, Tommy McClaren and Ray Walker over the years, but the team always threw league matches away. Then they would go and beat Tottenham, Manchester City or Everton in the Cup. Once, before a Port Vale versus Tottenham Hotspur Cup tie Jimmy Greaves in his pundit role laughed off our chances. 'The hardest thing about beating Port Vale is finding the ground,' quipped Jimmy. Well, Spurs found the ground and we beat them. To me Spurs are more a crusade than a football team. I go to watch Manchester United a lot, but the buzz is not the same as watching Port Vale run out. One of my proudest moments was taking the Embassy World Championship trophy on to the pitch in 1990.

I have always loved watching self-motivated players like Roy Keane and David Beckham. I have seen both tear strips off team mates for not getting stuck in. Both these stars play like they are on five quid a week and thankful for it. I think football has changed; once some players get a contract and a massive wage they don't give 100 per cent any more. I recently watched Port Vale youth team play Chelsea in the Cup and beat them. Those lads gave everything. And I bet the first team would be motivated against Manchester United, then next week go back to being average against Scunthorpe.

A hint of this cut-throat, dog-eat-dog mentality of the top sporting professionals was given to me by Roy Keane when I made a recent visit to the United training ground. A lad was showing me around the gym and Roy was on an exercise bike in a corner. The lad told him that I was the World Darts Champion. Keane sniffed and said '*Ex*-World Champion.' Good attitude, mate.

Darts has never been simply a matter of tossing a piece of metal at a mat. There has always been the appliance of science to many aspects of the sport.

Take the missile itself. In the early 1960s most people threw a variation of the Tom Barrett dart. This had a short brass barrel and a long wooden stem that was shaved to the thickness of a matchstick. This type of dart was flighted high and the angle of entry was at about 30 degrees above the horizontal. In effect you were throwing the point, and the stem and flight did the steering.

The arrival of tungsten in the early 1970s changed the way of throwing fundamentally. Tungsten is twice the density of brass so the missile could be smaller. It also had to be thrown harder and on a much flatter trajectory than a brass dart. Players still favoured individual barrel shapes and thicknesses with copper-tungsten or nickel-tungsten darts. The great Swede, Stefan Lord, had a medium-length barrel with a bullet-shaped front, and Bill Lennard used a thinner version of the same. The John Lowe dart has a similar bullet front but the length of the barrel is very short. The ultimate bullet dart is that used by Peter Manley, where the front of the barrel is the size of a small pickled onion. The big problem with all of these darts is that the thick barrel prevents 'stacking' – laying a dart on top of the preceding one. Lowe and Manley score 180s by landing the darts along the bed rather than up or down it.

My own darts are 24-gram nickel tungsten with thin 'knitting-needle' barrels that are appreciably longer than most. In fact they are about half as thick as John Lowe darts. When I started I used barrels that were not so long and I constantly tinker with stems and flights. But the key is that my darts are thin enough to get three in the 60 bed on top of each other. This has been called 'stacking' by the Sky Sports commentary team and is based on common sense. I aim at the middle of the bottom of the bed. If my first dart goes there I have no adjustment to make to land the next two on the 'platform' supplied by the first. Hence my average of over 100 in most of the World Championships I have played in. Even if I land just under the 60 bed I am a good bet for a 140 score by simply aiming at the barrel of the first dart.

Other methods of attacking the 60 bed are less efficient. John Lowe, on form, can start with one dart in the middle of the bed, then put one either side. But the flight and the barrel can both become obstacles after dart number one. The Dennis Priestley technique of 'reverse stacking' is again open to hazard. Dennis's dart has a higher trajectory than mine and lands at about 10 degrees above the horizontal. This means that you have great difficulty getting darts two and three under the first without hitting its barrel or flight. In the old days Alan Evans and Jocky Wilson – both, like me, under five feet eight inches – tried to go along the 60 bed to get the 180. But both often lost balance and went into the five or the one bed. My system is much more efficient.

Mention of Jocky and Alan brings me to the question of style. Both players almost dived at the board when trying to throw important shots above the bull. This builds in problems that you do not need. Tom Barrett used to stress the importance of balance. He stood with both toes to the oche and lobbed the dart, and even he 'hoped' to get the odd bounce in off the barrel. Things are much more scientific these days.

I never ever go off balance with my shots. My front foot is locked to the oche and my back foot – the darter's rudder – never leaves the floor. If I miss it is usually down to lack of weight put into the shot, and consequently the dart falls the odd millimetre short. My throwing action is to pull my chin into my shoulder and simply straighten my arm. Having short forearms actually helps me be accurate; my darts rarely hook sideways.

But if you want to see the perfect darts stance, don't look at me, look at John Lowe. The great Barry Twomlow taught John to eliminate all extraneous movement from the act of throwing the dart. John locks the front foot side-on to the oche and his back foot never leaves the floor. With this secure base the right arm merely straightens. The dart is pitched rather than tossed. But because his darts are thick John has to make adjustments to the weight of throw that are sometimes too marked. So on a bad day his darts at the treble 20 fall up to half an inch short. But when he is on song the darts go cleanly past the flights and barrels of the marker dart and he scores 180.

I am sometimes asked at exhibitions why players go for 180 and not three treble 19s. I think the answer is that psychologically there is much more than three points' difference. An opponent will wilt if you smack in a maximum to his steady ton. Also the tungsten revolution made hitting 180s easier with much slimmer-barrelled darts that do not block the bed. In fact it can be argued that without tungsten we would never have had darts on television; there wouldn't have been such high and dramatic scoring if we had still been using brass darts.

Now I did not work all this out 13 years ago and put the theory of throwing darts scientifically into practice. Oh no, I watched the special flight camera that Sky introduced in 1997 – a development that totally gobsmacked the players. Most of us looked at the super-slow-motion shots and scratched our heads, saying, 'Did we do that?'

Basically, darts coverage did not change much from the first World Championship in 1978 to Sky entering the arena in 1994. The two-way split-screen technique was the key shot; it showed the emotion of the player and the precision, or lack of it, in the throw. At the end of legs it was not used, because then you want to see the double inter-cut with a full screen of the thrower. Sky dug much deeper. From the start they used slow-motion to show throwing technique and they replayed doubles. Just like they did when they started covering rugby union, Sky got to the parts of the action that other people missed.

The flight camera added a totally new dimension to the sport. The super-slow-motion showed a trajectory of the dart that was revelatory for everybody. First, the dart goes up, not forward, immediately on leaving the hand. Second, when the dart reaches the apex of its flight, it sometimes dips up and down depending on how much finger spin has been applied – christened the 'wibble' by Sid Waddell (see opposite). Then it 'weeps' – a term used by Swedish scientists to describe the action of gravity on flying objects – into the target. In short, the flight camera showed that we do a hell of a lot more than simply fling metal at a mat.

Now this innovation did two things. It richly enhanced the viewers' appreciation of our skills, and it had us flocking to the Sky scanner to see our individual 'wibbles', a bit like pregnant ladies rushing to get pictures from the womb. Dennis and I were amazed at the flicking up and down of the dart before entry; in his case the track was a half-helix. Both of our flight paths were like that of a drunken bumble-bee compared to that of Cliff

Dennis Priestley

35°

Phil Taylor

10°

Wibble

Lazarenko, though. Cliff throws his tungsten flat and hard in a pure parabola.

Since then Sky have developed a shot from behind the thrower that shows the precise weight of each throw. This shot shows the fundamental difference in throwing between myself and Dennis in particular. I never consciously tried to 'stack' my darts so that they go in the bottom of the 60, thus leaving more room for others on top. It just happened. In 1987 when I had my first competitive games I used 27-gram normal-length darts. They were thicker than those I use now. Then around 1988 Eric Bristow gave me some darts that were a bit lighter but had shorter barrels. Incidentally, Eric told me to chuck my old ones away or I would revert to them in difficult times. I did. In fact, the darts I have used since then are probably a bit light at 24 grams. This, combined with my height of five feet seven inches and my short arms, means the darts dip on entry. So I did not invent stacking because it was more effective, it just happened. By contrast, Dennis Priestley, like Eric, makes the darts enter the board at an upward angle, which sometimes means that the second and third darts have to be forced past the first.

The path taken by a Phil Taylor dart is not as complicated, because I do not spin the dart as much as, for instance, Dennis Priestley does. The weep of my dart starts earlier than that of Dennis's and the wibble is much less pronounced. What is unique, however, is the downward tilt of my darts in the last six inches of flight.

They land at an angle of 10 degrees below the horizontal and thus 'open' the bed. In essence, I have to adjust only the weight of my next darts rather than tinker with the angles of entry. I think that a style of throwing that came to me naturally could be proved by those blokes in Sweden who have studied golf, football and darts to be the most efficient in the game. But I do not suggest you copy me. Rather you should stand like Lowe and pitch the missile like Lazarenko, and persuade Sky to do a slo-mo of your style.

I was going to start this bit by saying that darts is not rocket science . . . but, of course, it is.

CHAPTER 19

The Holy Grail

At my exhibitions one of the top five questions is: 'Did Sid Waddell's screaming make you miss the nine-dart finish at Rochester in 1998?'

Before giving you my answer, let me set the scene.

Rod Harrington and I were dicing out the final of the World Grand Prix at the Casino Rooms. The place was packed, but as usual the crowd went deadly quiet when a big shot was on. Now you might think that a double-to-start rule would make the nine-dart finish less likely than straight in with 180. But once the lads get going on double top to start, it is amazing how often they hit 160. Slap in a maximum and you leave 161.

Scientists have shown that this combination is appreciably easier to hit than 141, which is the usual shot-out for the nine-dart. Getting 60 should be a doddle. Treble 17 next, then a four-inch adjustment to the bull. No problems – unless you have a commentator about who can scream 'like a banshee with piles'.

What happened as I went for the nine-dart – and the small matter of £25,000 – was not all Sid's fault. Sky had placed the commentary box no more than 40 feet to the right of the oche, and on occasions players have heard Sid loud and clear from 300 feet up on a balcony in Blackpool. So the logistics were not perfect. But acoustically, too, Sid was on a hiding to nothing. When I hit 160 to start the crowd gasped. When I followed up with 180 they seethed for a split second, then there was a dead, cathedral-like, expectant silence.

I planted as sweet a 60 as you will ever see. I had two darts to make history: the first ever nine-darter done live on television anywhere in the world. I drew back my arm.

'TAYLOR IS ON THE NINE-DART ... NEEDS TREBLE 17!' Sid could have been heard at Chatham Docks, never mind Rochester. I stopped and turned to glare at the commentary box. Sid had disappeared – on to the floor in shame. John Gwynne shrugged in apology. 'I think he heard you, Sid,' he said. I could have said a lot, but all I did say was 'Thanks, pal,' and smacked in the treble 17. My shot at the bull missed by less than a quarter of an inch.

I didn't see Sid later that night, but I heard that he

was extremely cut up about losing me £25,000. So a couple of days later I phoned him up at home. 'Don't go fretting, bud,' I said. 'After you shouted I hit what I was aiming at – the treble 17. I missed the bull on my own. Now if you'd screamed "Bull!" and I'd missed, I would have bloody strangled you.'

When he did get to call my nine-darter – this time for £100,000 – Sid was well away from the action and did the commentary in the style of 'Whispering' Ted Lowe.

Many sports have a Holy Grail, and the key factors that bring the achievement are varied. At the Olympic Games the 100 metre record can well go when the best are put together in hot competition. In snooker the 147 is often on the cards, but there is always a bit of luck with how the balls break. The nine-dart I think is harder to get than the 147 because you need perfect placement and luck does not come into the equation.

Before I go through my magical nine-dart at Blackpool on 2 August 2002, let's have just a hint of some other magical moments.

On 18 October 1976 56-year-old Albert Gamble of Stockport lined up for the Fingerpost Hotel against the Nicholson Arms in the Robinson's Brewery League. He was sixth man on in a seven-a-side team competition where only one leg was contested by each player.

Albert planted two 180s and then the audience of about 80 people fell into a stunned silence. He hit treble 17, then treble 18 to leave double 18. After a slight pause Albert slotted the double, and he was still shaking with tension an hour later and telling everybody, 'I'd have missed it if I'd been on the telly.'

Now a lot of people say they have done nine-darters in garages, back rooms or down their local, and I do not doubt them. But Albert's witnesses were legion: two teams, two licensees and two club secretaries.

Another 'unsung' nine-darter was achieved by the one and only Jocky Wilson during the 1982 Embassy World Professional Championships at Jollees. Behind the famous stage was a legendary practice area – the Band Room. It was not much bigger than a phonebox but it had a bar and a board and a nude lady looking down from a calendar. It was the tradition that opponents practise separately in those days, so Jocky warmed up for the semi-final in the Band Room while Stefan Lord was along the corridor.

The wee man was on fire, sinking lagers and smoking as though there was no tomorrow. Ten minutes before he was due out of the door he shot 180, 180 and 141 (60, treble 19, double 12). He pulled his darts out of the board like Rob Roy pulling an arrow from a deer: 'What a stupid sod I am; if I'd waited another 10 minutes I'd have won £50,000!'

In 1984 John Lowe really hit the jackpot. In the MFI World Matchplay tournament at Slough he produced deadly accurate darts in a tight match against Keith Deller. Dave Lanning was commentating and gently spotted the potential drama after Lowe's first 180. 'In superb stroke John Lowe, not even a blink,' said Dave.

After the second 180 Dave was still caressing the ears of the viewers rather than assaulting them: 'Lowe looking assured, thinking of £100,000.'

Then John planted treble 17 to leave 90. Dave called the standard shot-out of treble 18 and double 18. The dart went in the treble, but its flight blocked the double on the television screen. Dave had to go by the crowd reaction. It was ecstatic. Dave raised his voice above the din: 'John Lowe wins £100,000!' It was a marvel of control – Dave had a bet that guaranteed him £12,000 if the nine-dart was hit on television that season!

In 1990 in a match at the Embassy, Paul Lim of the USA, famed as a 180 thrower, did a nine-dart finish against Jack McKenna in the standard fashion: 180, 180, 141 (60, treble 18, double 12) and won £50,000.

The Lowe and Lim nine-darters were not transmitted live on television. Both were recorded and shown later. But in the Dutch Open in February 2002 Shaun Greatbatch of England did a nine-dart live on air. He did seven 60s, treble 15, double 18.

Cut to Blackpool and my match against Chris Mason in the World Matchplay of 2002.

As I have already said, the nine-dart, for me anyway, was not going to come in an easy game. It was going to come in a tight match against an opponent giving me no respect and putting me under pressure. Chris Mason filled the bill. He is a great talent, has confidence and before our match had a 100 tournament average to my 103. Like me years before, Chris was hungry. Beat me and he's in with a good chance of taking the title and £15,000 prize money. Chris knew that taking me out would put his entire career on a new level. As I have suggested, this sort of thing is a much more complex mix than the 147 at snooker. Plus there were 2,500 fans screaming at me to do the nine-dart because they sensed I had been building up to it.

Before the practice darts I looked down at Yvonne and the kids. They seemed nervous. Maybe I should not have told my mate who ordered the Chinese to put a tenner for himself and a tenner for me on my getting the Holy Grail. Maybe I had been tempting Providence.

I had no time to philosophize any more; Mace the Ace came out of the blocks like a whippet and took the first leg. Forget the nine-dart, Philip, I told myself, or you'll be going home sharpish. I knew Chris meant business since there was no emotion or theatricals after the double landed. I remember thinking that this lad could be a World Champion if he could always keep as cool as this. It was time to kick arse and I narrowly missed a 107 shot-out. No sweat; I coolly picked off double 10.

Mason was steaming now. He sailed through the next leg to take it with a double nine.

I knew it was time for a supreme effort. I looked down into the front row and saw young Stan, one of my biggest fans, in his wheelchair. Do it for him, I thought. Hit Mace hard. I concentrated on leg four. I won with a 120 shot-out. Just the job: 2–2. Now it was time to hit him really hard and go into the commercial break 3–2 up in legs.

Chris had the advantage of throwing first so I knew I had to dig even deeper. He started with 135 – even more pressure. But just the catalyst for what happened next . . .

I scored 180. He hit only 60. My brain screamed Eric's creed: 'Jump on him!' Another 180. I honestly did not think of the nine-dart then. I had missed the seventh 60 against Shayne Burgess and said to myself, hit the bugger this time. (This may owe nothing to Freud or Jung, but it is my philosophy.) Even though Sid was all of 300 feet away and enclosed by glass, plywood and thick drapes, I could hear him. 'Ooooh my goodness, he's on the nine-darter. Treble 19 . . . And double 12 for history!'

I relaxed and the final dart went into the exact middle of the double 12. 'We have now in darting terms quite literally seen it all,' said Dave Lanning.

I looked down into the crowd. Little Ned Donovan of Cork, a big fan of mine, was flinging his Viking hat in the air. My roadie George Sutherland forgot he had Nathalie on his knee and jumped up in the air. She shot up too, and thankfully George caught her. I looked over to the Stan James betting office where a conga reel of punters were heading to collect their winnings. The manager stopped counting out the tenners and shook his fist at me. As if it wasn't bad enough my taking Stan James' £100,000, half the Winter Gardens had bet on me.

The officials gave me five minutes to chill. I went into the Stan James VIP lounge and was allowed to look at the money, all neatly bundled up and locked in a cage. They would not let me touch it!

I eventually won the match 16–7 and the crowd went wild. I called Stan up on the stage and gave him my darts and the board. Sky wanted to use it for a special film item but they could not prise it out of his hands!

Ricky Hatton's dad Ray rang to congratulate me and said Ricky was furious not to have been at the Winter Gardens. In fact Ricky thought his dad was winding him up. 'Fuck off, dad, he's never done a nine-dart!' It was the first time Ray had heard his son use that kind of language!

Barry Hearn rang me, bubbling with excitement. He said watching me hit the nine-dart was the best 10 minutes of sport he'd ever seen.

Sky kept repeating the feat and it went out to millions round the world. It was the first-ever nine-dart finish done live on British television. But if you think the story stops there you'd be wrong. In May 2003 at the Golden Harvest North American Cup competition in Saskatoon we had *two* nine-darters.

The first was done by Sean Brenneman, the former Canadian champion, and the second by Roland Scholten. Sad to say the lads only got $1,000 each for their efforts, because the shots were done in the pre-liminary rounds before the televised stages. Now if they'd hung about until the cameras started rolling one of them would have been better off by $100,000!

It just goes to show what the PDC circuit, started at Newcastle and Norwich 10 years ago, has produced: the best players on the planet clashing like Galahad and Lancelot in the Camelot super league in days of yore, with the Holy Grail possibly round every corner.

CHAPTER 20

Have Board, Will Travel

I will start with a question. If you cannot get to Blake Street or the Saggar Makers pub in Burslem to find the perfect oche for dedicated practice, how do you go on? Answer: you take a Dart Mate – an oche, stand, board and lights – with you round the world. Now you may get some very funny looks as you cart the gear into the grand lobby of a foreign Hilton or the Imperial Hotel, Blackpool, but take it from me, the feeling of confidence far outweighs anything else. No matter where I put the gear up – in my room, in the basement, anywhere they let me – I can go and prepare in my own secluded way.

Contrary to rumours I did not take my Dart Mate, nor my darts, to Number 10 Downing Street three years ago. I got the invitation and went along unaccompanied. I was shown up the fancy staircase lined with pictures of previous Prime Ministers. I am not much of a Maggie Thatcher fan but I must say her picture was striking; the charisma jumped out at you. Cherie Blair greeted us at the top of the stairs and we were taken into a room for drinks and sandwiches.

There were no other darts players at the gathering, so I chatted to rugby league player Bobby Goulding. Others there were the England rugby union squad, boxer Lennox Lewis and Manchester United manager Alex Ferguson. Suddenly Nick Faldo pointed at the green jacket I was wearing and said, 'Which major golf tournament did you win?' I took it on the chin, not bothering to ask him about his current world ranking.

One place I did happily go to with no darts was China in November 2000. I went for a week with Richard Lowy of Unicorn Products to boost interest in the game. Unicorn have a factory there so I was happy to pick up a set of Phil Taylor darts from them, knowing they would be spot on for my exhibitions. Could David Beckham show up in China and get just the right boots? I doubt it.

What a trip! It was organized by Unicorn in liaison with the China Darts Association and their government representative. And did I get the VIP treatment? At the airport in Beijing there were cameras flashing everywhere and dozens of people waving as we got off the plane. We were whizzed through immigration and customs in no time, and then there were more cameras and more welcoming parties. Outside the airport it was like a scene from 'Men in Black'. We got into a fleet of black limousines and were taken off to Tianjin, a two-hour drive from Beijing.

Over the next five days my feet scarcely hit the ground. I opened a college that had 4,000 students. I saw how noodles were made. I visited the Great Wall, the Forbidden City and the Imperial Palace. I even had a three-hour banquet just like the Emperor would have had. It was great, even the curried grasshoppers. Every-where people mobbed me and wanted my autograph; this was because they regularly see Sky Sports pictures of darts events. Richard and I were made honorary members of quite a few darts clubs.

I played several exhibitions and never lost one match. The venue in Beijing was magnificent. I was applauded loudly on to the stage and spent three hours playing against 20 local players. The crowd were so appreciative that I took the microphone and sang 'My Way' for them. They cheered me to the echo and would not let me off. For another hour I did 'Danny Boy', 'New York' and a host of other standards, finishing with my own rocking version of 'Mack the Knife'.

The next stage of our tour was to the Philippines and Thailand. There I did exhibitions in about 20 different pubs each night, playing only a couple of games in each venue. I was weighed down with presents; garlands of flowers, vases, ties, shirts and suits.

You will be glad to know that I did tote my trusty Dart Mate over the Atlantic to the Las Vegas Desert Classic in July 2002.

I have never been as excited in my life as I was when Yvonne and I, Kelly and Nathalie met Gayle Farmer, the PDC's media and communications manager, at Manchester airport. We were flying out a few days before the event to do publicity and try to 'educate' the American media about our sport. On the plane we tried to compile a list of the stars of sport and show business who have appeared at the MGM Grand, the tournament venue. Here's what we came up with: Madonna, Frank Sinatra, Engelbert Humperdinck, ZZ Top, Bruce Springsteen, Jay Leno, the Rolling Stones, David Copperfield, Cher, Paul Anka, Elton John, Janet Jackson, Phil Collins, Evander Holyfield and Mike Tyson.

'We've missed one out, dad,' said Nathalie.

'Who?' I asked.

'Phil the Power Taylor,' she said. 'Him who sings "My Way" on the karaoke.'

When we landed in Las Vegas I got the shock of my life. The first thing I saw when I walked out of customs was a 20-foot-square screen showing a video of me throwing darts! I remember thinking that maybe Robert Redford or Keanu Reeves or Engelbert Humperdinck could walk through here and see me. Mind, Engelbert is a dab hand at darts and he'd know who I was.

My next shock was when the taxi pulled into the drive of the MGM Grand. There I was again on the hotel's tower – on what they call the 'Jumbotron' – chucking darts, snarling and jumping with joy for half of Nevada to see, and after me was Cher, and after her was Paul

Anka, and after him were the Rolling Stones . . . I was so excited I nearly left my Dart Mate in the car. There was more to come. The hotel reception desk is over 100 yards long and behind it was the Power again on a massive screen, hitting 180s, the crowd going wild.

'And you are, sir?' asked the ultra-polite lass behind the desk.

I pointed behind her. 'I'm him up there.' Naff, I know, but I was dead excited. Starring in Vegas! Who wouldn't be?

Next day we started our campaign to show the American media what world-class darts is all about. We joined the leading American lady player Stacey Bromberg at CD's Lounge, the premier spot for darts in Las Vegas. Ray Carver, a top American player, was there too and we played a team event for a charity called Make a Wish which helps sick children.

CBS News' number-one man in the area, Kendal Tenny, did interviews and I think we impressed him with the skills needed for top darts. We did not have quite as much success with Fox 5 News, who we talked to the following day. Reporter Dave Hall and his team didn't seem impressed by the dozens of boards set out in the Garden Arena for qualifying, but perked up a bit when they saw the magnificent set in the main playing area. I talked to Dave about the seriousness of professional darts and he seemed to take it all in. But then he insisted on finishing the item by sticking a picture of one of his newsroom buddies on the board and peppering it with darts. Gayle Farmer and I were not best pleased. They wouldn't have done such a silly tag to an item about Michael Jordan or Tiger Woods. Still, if we keep teaching, they'll keep learning.

Later that day I went filming with Sky's Jeff Stelling. He told me that on the vox pops they had just done, nobody had guessed what sport I played. The nearest was a lad who thought I was a cricketer.

Jeff and I stopped beside the MGM Grand's lion statue and he filled me in on some amazing facts about the hotel and the city. The lion statue is the biggest bronze statue in the world; it contains 100,000lbs of the stuff. That is also how many slot machines there are in the hotel's casino. The MGM is the biggest hotel in the world with over 5,000 bedrooms and it has corridors you can hardly see the end of. This last feature nearly landed Tommy Cox in the local nick. Tommy had been ill and had been advised by his doctors to walk as much as he could. A few days later he was staying in Las Vegas at the MGM Grand with temperatures outside so high that walking the streets was out of the question. So Tommy had a brainwave; after breakfast why not walk the hotel corridors? So he did, mooching along gazing at nothing in particular. After a few minutes he was approached by security, who had been tracking him on their cameras, and he just about persuaded him that he was 'exercising'.

Everybody concerned with the Desert Classic was hoping to make an impact on the estimated 21 million darts players in America. Even if they just played in their garage, we wanted to show them a world-class sport in action. Then of course the hope is that an American will be good enough to win a world title. If a Yank could follow in the footsteps of Ray Barneveld of Holland, or Tony David of Australia, the game would really catch on. We were in Las Vegas largely due to Barry Hearn bending the ear of top American promoter Frank Belmont. Frank had been involved with Barry and Sky Sports in coverage of boxing and was fascinated by the idea of trying to build our sport as a high-level attraction.

Wayne Mardle, in a shirt that looked like an explosion in a paint factory, and Alan Warriner got the tournament off to a show-biz start. In the middle of their first set both players were averaging 112. Sid Waddell was in his element: 'That's what we came to Las Vegas to see, folks. Entertainment with a capital E. "E" for eat your heart out Tom Jones, eat your heart out Paul McCartney, eat your heart out Sting. These are the lads this stage was built for!' Slightly exaggerated – but that's Sid.

I was still buzzing with excitement watching the tournament get under way. It is special to play in the USA at any time, but to be there for the Fourth of July holiday was amazing. Mind, as you'll find out later, fireworks and darts can be a strange mixture . . .

On stage Wayne was on fire and blitzed Alan by 2–0 in sets. Wayne did a surfing safari dance round the stage – eat your heart out the Beach Boys – and Sid went ecstatic: 'In a shirt painted by Salvador Dali, Wayne gives distemper to Wozza!' Already some of the very well-behaved crowd were politely telling Sid to keep his voice down. Fat chance!

My first opponent was Kevin Painter, who had beaten me in Ireland in 2001 and was keen to repeat the performance. Sad to say a bit of needle crept into the game and Kevin used some very bad language on stage. A red exclusion zone had been marked behind the oche and you were supposed to stay out of it while the opponent threw. I must admit I never consciously shuffled into it, and if I did I'm sorry. But at such a showcase event on television Kevin should have controlled his mouth.

The first two sets were tight and we won one each. 'Painter one set, the Power one set. Is Phil's nemesis about to strike again?' asked Sid. The lad had his chances because I didn't play very well, but he let me in to win 2–1 in sets with a shot-out from 88.

The crowd were being entertained royally but in a way they were far too sedate. At home the punters dress up as Vikings or clowns and they bring placards. They go mad before you throw but give dead silence for the throw. It will take a year or two but I'm sure the American fans will soon loosen up. We all need the lift of an involved crowd.

On stage the results continued to go the way of the form book. John Part beat Richie Burnett 2–0, and Ronnie Baxter beat Andy Jenkins 2–0. But then we had all-star displays from two of those hungry young lads I reckon are the breed of the future. Simon Whatley of Dorset demolished the experienced Dennis Smith 2–0 in sets and never dropped a leg. Then Lee Palfreyman of Merseyside left Colin Lloyd in tears with another 2–0 victory. Look out for these two names in the future.

One of darts biggest under-achievers was next up. Denis Ovens, the reigning Irish Masters Champion, took on Peter Manley and came out victorious thanks to a 164 shot-out. I watched this one with particular interest because the winner was my next opponent. I was on form right away: I did a 122 and an 84, both finishing on the bull. Sid told the viewers, 'Dennis may be hot on Ovens, but the Power is the master baker.'

The next match was between two class acts. If Ronnie Baxter hits his form early he can beat anyone. And John Part is a thoroughbred. The two players produced a brilliant match and, despite finishes of 152 and 146 by John, Ronnie won 2–1.

Cue the Power versus the Young Gun. Taylor against Palfreyman. And by now the crowd were losing some of their inhibitions – maybe because it was the Fourth of July, maybe because they'd had a few Buds, maybe because it was a semi-final featuring a rookie and the World Champion . . . I don't know. I got the action going with a 142 finish. Crowd roar instead of polite clapping. I now felt I was really on stage in Vegas! My scoring was going well but Lee kept pegging back at me. Then suddenly there was a series of explosions and gasps from the crowd. I stood back from the oche and some people ran out. Terrorists? No – festive fireworks Las Vegas style! Colourful and loud, but not as loud as Sid: 'Rockets whooshing out by the pool and rocket science on the stage . . .' I won 3–0 and Lee and I got a standing ovation. Did this happen to Paul McCartney? I wondered.

The other semi-final was a cracker. Ronnie raced to a 2–0 lead in sets, then Roland Scholten pegged a set back. The Ronnie planted a lovely 177 to set up the win.

I will never forget the walk out from the star dressing-rooms on to the stage of the Garden Arena for the final. Here we were, a bloke from the pie-munching land around Blackburn and a lad from the back streets of the Potteries, walking in the footsteps of the great. We passed photographs of Dionne Warwick, Johnny Cash and Bruce Springsteen, then we heard the crowd shouting for us!

Ronnie kicked off the final with a 180, and the crowd lost their last fleck of politeness. They bayed. I turned and saw a placard that read 'Phil Taylor – Number One in the Universe'. The lady holding it looked like an elderly schoolmarm. Keep supporting, duck, I thought.

Ronnie was averaging 99 so I had to give him the old kick. I got the first set under my belt with an average of only 98. Not 'Universe' standard, but it would come. I started set two with a 14-darter and raced through to 2–0 in sets, my average going up to 101. Sid was so impressed he was making up words: 'Taylor in superb form is murderizing Ronnie.' Ronnie did manage an

11-dart leg in set three, but a 167 shot-out by me put him right on the ropes. He needed a 170 shot-out to save the match and missed. I planted double 12 to take the title 3–0 in sets. My final average was 104. Again there was a standing ovation. Forget a couple of years: the Las Vegas crowd had been well and truly educated in darts in five eventful days.

So I didn't gargle, nor did I gamble by way of celebration. Instead the family and I were guests of honour at a show by Siegfried and Roy, a circus act. They were pretty good, but what I really would have liked to top off my Las Vegas jaunt was a couple of hours listening to Joe Longthorne.

There are perks in being a darts star and one of them was being asked to go fishing by Barry Hearn. When he said fishing, I said great because I know a bit about it. Years back I had done bit of fishing with Nicky White, who was an expert and captain of the Momar White's team (a famous fishing outfit in the Stoke area). I used to love relaxing with a rod in my hand and I also did a bit of sea-fishing. Barry said that both might come in handy, but what he had in mind was a bit different – like the World Marlin Fishing Championships in Mauritius!

I had no idea what to expect, other than it would be a far cry from sitting by a pond in the middle of Stafford-shire. We arrived the night before at 9pm and went out for a walk along the harbour – I saw the massive rods, two to a boat, that I would be using the next day. Back at the hotel the old hands told us tales about fish so big they pulled boats for miles. And I don't think they were kidding. I hoped the other three lads in my team were up to it. I must admit I hardly got any sleep; I kept getting up, having a glass of water and flexing my arms like Popeye.

I was on board our boat at 4 o'clock sharp the next morning, with nothing in my stomach but a cup of tea. Once the fun started I didn't want to be hanging over the stern being sick, so I played safe. The boats lined up and a gun went off. There was one team to each boat and each skipper had a different idea of where the big fish were running. As the bow raised and the white water rushed past me, I felt a little queasy but I kept a brave face for the Sky cameras.

I was in a team with three lads from the Isle of Man and they were agog with the idea that we could win $1,000,000 if we caught a record-size fish – 1,500lbs was the target to beat. Suddenly the boat shot off to where a flock of seagulls were bombing the waves over a shoal of bonito. We started catching the bonito, which are about the size of a pillow, as our bait for the marlin and the crew stuck them live on to the ends of our marlin rods. I was told that the flapping and thrashing of our bait would bring marlin – and probably sharks as well!

Once we began fishing my stomach protested. The boat had cut down to dead slow and we had a decided roll on. I was soon throwing up so hard my chest muscles ached. Then at 3 o'clock in the afternoon there started one of the most exciting and frightening episodes of my life. I was assisting Paul, our rod man, when there was an almighty tug on the line. We had hooked a marlin and it was a big one. It was also a game bugger. It shot off jumping, and nearly pulled Paul's arms out. Then it seemed to give up. We whacked at it with baseball bats and hooks and then it shot off again. There was blood in the water and just about dusk we had a 'visitor'.

Now I've always had a phobia about the sea at night – all those creepy-crawly scissor-toothed creatures that could be down there. And at first I thought the shadow in the water a foot from my right leg was my imagination. No way. There was a dorsal fine splitting the waves and a dark body 20 feet long and as wide as a single bed! The camera girl saw it too and nearly fell overboard as she tried to get a shot of it. With the fish twisting Paul's rod this way and that, I felt I could be bumped in at any time. But after sniffing around for 20 minutes the shark sloped off.

It was nearly 6.30 – over three hours since we'd hooked it – when we landed the marlin. It weighed 527lbs. The boat seemed to limp back to the harbour. Our lights had gone on the blink, so the mate leaned out over the bow with a torch. Home are the heroes and all that. I put my feet up at the hotel and had a port-and-brandy to settle my stomach. Every time I nodded off I pinched myself. I didn't want any nightmares featuring giant sharks snapping away at my legs!

*

Early in 2003 I was invited to go to Tokyo for a week with George Sutherland by Mr Masura of the Japanese Darts Organization. He was acting on behalf of Mr Sakamoto, chairman of the Tokyo Darts Organization.

Our first function was the Tokyo Open, where we were guests of honour at the finals. I then played the winners of the ladies' and men's titles. After that I stood by for a rush of autograph seekers. I got a pleasant surprise. The crowd were excited and eager to meet me, but at a word from Mr Sakamoto they bowed and went quiet. Then they filed slowly up for me to sign their programmes. I love this respectful way of doing things.

Later, at the end of the official banquet, Mr Sakamoto asked me if I preferred silver to black. I got the idea that he was going to give me a special shirt, so I said 'Silver', because I've got a lot of black shirts. He ducked down and brought a superb silver camera out from under the table and gave it to me as a welcome gift. He then gave George a black camera, apologizing profusely that it was not silver.

The generosity of the locals was boundless. One night as I left an exhibition I said I felt chilly. Next thing I knew Mr Sakamoto took off his jacket with the Tokyo Darts Organization badge on it and presented it to me. Next day I was sitting in front of a car and pulled down the visor to stop the sun hitting my eyes. Immediately the man behind me made me a present of his RayBan sunglasses!

At a darting pub called the Palms I played 40 locals –

some of them businessmen with their arrows in their briefcases. George had a bit of a job announcing the names of my opponents, but suddenly turned to me with a big smile. 'The next game will be very fast,' he said. I looked at my opponent and wondered how George knew that. 'Phil Taylor's next opponent will be Mr Suzuki!' yelled George.

Mr Sakamoto had the final word on our trip. Before our last appearance George and I were beginning to feel weary and Mr Sakamoto heard George complaining about 'late nights and smoky atmospheres' which had given him a sore throat. As we walked into the venue Mr Sakamoto was on stage ordering the audience not to smoke 'to help the throat of Mr George'. As we finished playing he announced to the crowd that tonight there would be no autographs and Mr Phil and Mr George would be leaving early to get a good night's sleep. Now that's what I call respect!

As you probably have gathered, I don't need to go to exotic foreign locations to have fun at darts. Like the night at Cleethorpes some years ago where an over-excited crowd took some time to realize I was after a world record.

I was working with caller John Gwynne and there were about 100 folk in the place. I was playing legs of 1001 against 14 locals and was going well. Opponent number 10 stepped up in a shirt with thick stripes and John got us going. My first shot was 180. Crowd appreciated. Another 180. Crowd cheered. Another 180. Crowd went wild. Another 180. Crowd stood and cheered. John had to step in and calm them down. He told the people to please sit down and be quiet for the throw. He added that I was possibly going to make history. 'The world record for 1001 is 19 darts, achieved by both Alan Evans and Cliff Inglis. Phil has now seven darts to do 281. A world record is possible.' My next shot was only 140 – and nobody groaned! In the end I did it in 22 darts.

John could not resist a line about my opponent's striped shirt. 'The last time I saw a fellow in a shirt like that, he was standing on the roof of Strangeways prison throwing tiles at the folk in the street.'

CHAPTER 21

Team Taylor

Whenever I play exhibitions or big tournaments there is a dapper fellow near me most of the time. He is always very smartly turned out and speaks with a quiet Scottish lilt. His name is George Sutherland and he makes sure that Team Taylor runs like clockwork.

Early in 2001 I was looking round for somebody to call my exhibition matches and throw in a bit of fun. It had to be somebody with a good darts background and organizational skills. We'd have to hit it off together because we would be living in each other's pockets for days on end. Somebody told me that George could be just the man.

I was working in Newcastle and rang George up. By chance he was driving up from England to his home in Wick in the far north of Scotland and was only a few miles away. I told him that his skills on the microphone had been recommended to me and that I'd like to meet up. A couple of hours later and we were sitting in Newcastle having a cup of tea and a chat.

George told me that he had been capped at darts by Scotland in 1984 and had played in the same team as Jocky Wilson, Rab Smith and George Nichol. Then the dreaded dartitis struck and his playing days were over. George moved behind the scenes, setting up and organizing exhibitions. He made me laugh out loud when he told me how he became a caller. Apparently George was sitting watching a game when the caller, who was mainly a bingo caller, began messing up the scores. 'Being a bingo caller, he was good up to 90 but rubbish at anything higher,' George explained. 'I just dropped in a bit of humour and it seemed to work.'

George said he pulled people's legs if they played badly; he would duck or take evasive action. But he had three firm rules. Never mock fat women, ugly women or the afflicted. We had a long chat and I was impressed. George is a non-smoker and rarely drinks, but he does like sitting in hotel rooms watching John Wayne kill the bad guys and Errol Flynn conquer the world. And take it from me, we do plenty of that.

We agreed to do a few nights together to see how things went.

One of our first jobs was in Holland. George had organized and presented exhibitions there with Scottish darts players, including Les Wallace, a former Embassy winner. There was a festival and funfair on in the town we were playing in and we were walking round the booths. Suddenly this young lad runs up, pointing. 'Mister Darts! You are here Mister Darts!' I went to shake his hand and he ran straight past me and began clapping George on the back and shouting, 'You are back, MC George, Mister Darts!' The lad was a darts fan who had been at an exhibition George called and, because he did not have Sky Sports, he didn't know me from Adam. The Dutch love their darts. On that trip we got to a venue to find I had to play the locals on a bandstand with a canvas roof! There was a howling gale blowing and it was pouring with rain; the darts went all over the place and a bloke kept jabbing the roof with a pole to make the water fall out – on to the crowd. Still, over 200 kept watching and applauding under a forest of umbrellas.

Well, after that baptism of water I asked George to work for me full time. He would be my MC, keep my diary and share the driving. I would have somebody to talk to on long trips; I could bounce ideas off him. George and I have a lot in common. We are about the same age and are both family men. George is steeped in darts and I respect his views. In fact our relationship is a bit like a marriage without the sex.

Soon after we teamed up George stopped doing work with other players. We are a good pairing. Sometimes we have a code to get away from exhibitions that have gone on until the early hours. Folks are lovely, but sometimes you have to leave the socializing and drive a long way home. That's when I say to George, 'I could really do with a sandwich.' It's our code for 'Time to go.'

We have had a lot of fun on our travels. George knows what a practical joker I am and once on a ferry from Ireland he dared me to buy a 'Hey Jimmy' hat with tatty red 'hair' sticking out of it. I went one further; I bought the hat, put it on and frizzed up the 'hair'. Then I went up to two old ladies and said, 'Excuse me, ducks, but is there a barber on this boat?' Similarly, just before Christmas one year we were shopping in southern Ireland. I picked up a Christmas stocking full of sweets and said to the young lass behind the counter, 'Have you got this in size nine?' She looked at me as if I was crackers.

People can't quite believe that George has to travel 600 miles to work for me. But he has been known to come from Wick to Stoke for a single exhibition. He's very dedicated and I owe him a lot.

Apart from my own family, the people I am probably closest to are the family of boxer Ricky Hatton, the WBU World Light Welterweight Champion. Over the past couple of years Ricky and I have become good friends. He comes to watch me play darts and I go to watch him fight. I go in the dressing-room before the fight, then sit as near the front as I can. I watched his last fight against Phillips, who is no mug, and got worried when Ricky got a deep cut over the eye. I thought the referee might stop the fight. Ricky certainly took some hard shots before being declared the winner, and I screamed so much at him during the fight that I couldn't talk for three days.

Ricky is also a fair darts player and turns out in his local league. Apparently he was a fan of mine before we met. He tells a funny story of how he was driving along the M62 years ago in a battered Mini Metro when my camper passed him. So he put his foot down and managed to draw level with us. I gave him a thumbs up and never gave it another thought. Then Ricky told the story to Stuart Pyke of Sky and he told me that Ricky was a fan. So I went over to Hyde, had a game of darts with him and his dad Ray, and we got on like a house on fire. Mind you, I did pull the Hattons' legs a bit. We played on a log-end board and I did not let on that I had done challenges against log-end champions before. I let them believe I had a bit of beginner's luck.

Ricky is a very similar lad to myself. He is very much a family person and lives with his parents and his brother Matthew, who is also a boxer. I have got to know the Hattons well and they are the salt of the earth. As for Ricky, he is one of the most modest people I have ever met. Before I met him I thought boxers had to come from tough places like the Gorbals or the Bronx. But his supportive family, just like mine, was a rock to build on.

Ricky's father Ray plans every move of Ricky's career meticulously. In fact I'm told he probably trains harder than his son. And Ray has been a fountain of good advice to me. In particular he put his finger on the fatigue that hit me at the end of my Super Slam year of

2002 and contributed to me losing the world crown to John Part. I will go into details of the World Championship later, but here I would like to consider Ray Hatton's analysis of my problem.

My winning career has packed a lot into a short span. I have won 10 world titles and countless other titles in no more than 12 years. Eric Bristow's achievements were over a much longer span: he started playing at 17 and got to the semi-final of the World Championship at 39. Ray Hatton said that I lost the 2003 PDC World Championship because I was like a boxer having too many big fights close together. I won the 2002 world title, the Las Vegas Desert Classic, the World Matchplay in Blackpool and the Paddy Power World Grand Prix in Dublin, all in the space of 10 months. 'Far too punishing a schedule,' was Ray's verdict. He said it was like Ricky having six or seven fights that all went the distance. There are no knockouts in darts. When it got to 6–6 in sets against John Part in the world final and I needed just one to win, the tank was empty. I lost 7–6. It may sound like an excuse, but to me it makes a lot of sense.

In July 2001 world darts got a massive boost when Barry Hearn accepted an invitation to become chairman of the Professional Darts Corporation. Barry had been involved with the PDC since 1995 and had been largely responsible for securing over 200 hours of live television coverage per year on Sky Sports, plus coverage of the sport in over 20 other countries.

Since becoming the manager of an up-and-coming young snooker player called Steve Davis in 1976, Barry has used his business skills to change the face of snooker. He has also made a big impact on several other sports. He has been involved in boxing for many years and has managed world champions Chris Eubank, Nigel Benn and Steve Collins. Since 1995 he has been chairman of Leyton Orient football club. He has also worked on the development of fishing and American pool as televised sports.

As you would expect, Barry was full of optimism when he gave his reasons for taking on the new job. 'Darts is the sport of this millennium. My visits to parts of Europe and the Far East have shown me just how much enthusiasm there is for the sport. The current crop of PDC players are genuine sports stars with unique ability. I intend to give them the profile they deserve to turn them into superstars. The PDC are also committed to bringing on the next generation of stars, and several will undoubtedly come from Asia. This will lead to a television boom the likes of which we've not seen since the explosion of snooker!'

Barry is now my manager and my friend. He told me some years ago that, as a sports fan and follower of excellence, he put me in the same bracket as Steve Davis for dedication and ability. 'Every time I watch you play darts you do something amazing that just knocks out the crowd,' he told me. Two years ago he said that if I joined him I could get better rewards and develop my career with blue-chip sponsors. Barry manages me but we have no written contract. He has been similarly involved with Steve Davis for 28 years, only for the first three of which was there a written deal. With Chris Eubank the first three years of the contract were in written form and the next eight were on trust. The theory is that we like, trust and appreciate each other, and our only formal bond is a handshake.

As with Ray Hatton, I see Barry as a father figure. I can ring him up day or night about anything. We get on together socially as well as having a business connection. On the latter front Barry is blunt. 'You make a few quid for me, mate, and I'll make a lot for you.' That's an attitude which suits me down to the ground. Another of Barry's aphorisms comes from the great Labour politician Aneurin Bevan, and says that you should nurture people from cradle to grave. I hope the grave bit is a long way off.

A final word on my pal and ex-manager Tommy Cox. We parted amicably and our friendship is strong. I'll never forget on New Year's Eve a couple of years back when I tried to stop an argument and a drunk went for me. Before I could lift my hand Tommy was into the bloke like a linebacker and bundled him out of the room. With people like Eric Bristow, Tommy Cox, Ray Hatton, George Sutherland and Barry Hearn on my side, Team Taylor should stay in the premiership of darts a long time.

CHAPTER 22

Part Exchange

There are acres of newsprint about why I did not win my 11th world darts title in January 2003. I have already outlined the fatigue element from my Super Slam year, but the papers got hooked on the fact that I had lost four stones in three months. Maybe my balance had been affected. I read something about weight loss possibly 'altering the fluids of your eyes'. It was mostly rubbish, even though my pals Eric Bristow and Sid Waddell thought there was something in it. A year before I had shed over three stones and won the final 7–0 in sets. Nobody talked about balance or eyesight then. In truth I reckon I was jaded, and when I'm tired I miss my doubles. But maybe that's too simple a tale for the pundits.

I worked on a treadmill and watched my diet in the

weeks before the championship. In my long practice sessions, say one a week mixed in with shorter ones, I was not sweating. I reckoned I was in tip-top physical shape. But you never know with mental shape; remember I said halfway through the Blackpool final against John Part in the summer that I was shattered. Well, that rarely affects my will to win but I had been on the brink. So I have to admit I was not at my sharpest in the run-up to Purfleet.

I did, however, have a laugh at a darts clinic for journalists at the George Inn in Southwark a few days before the championships. Colin Lloyd and I spent two hours showing six of the press's finest key elements of darting technique. I wish I could report that I came across a bundle of talent, but I can't. Andy 'Dangerous' Dillon of the *Sun* looked cocky and aggressive but could only manage 14 with three darts. Gideon 'the Grabber' Brooks of the *Daily Express* had the height and style of Eric Bristow but not the aim. He scored a miserable 18. My prize pupil was Giles Smith of the *Daily Telegraph*. His best three-dart shot was 80, but what he wrote later about the skill of the sport was spot on. 'People who don't think darts is a sport should have a word with Taylor about it. Better still they should check in for a one-to-one tutorial with him. Within moments of attending our workshop with him, the Power convinced me that darts was like golf, only a lot more complicated physically and with much harder sums.'

A few days later George and I were pulling into the

car-park of the Hilton at the Dartford crossing to begin the campaign. And right off there was something we did not need: some joker had cancelled our booking. The trouble continued. I got phone calls to the room in the middle of the night. Then somebody scratched a key along the car. I had deliberately chosen to stay at a different hotel to the other players so that I could get on with my little routine. I know the troubles were maybe minor, but they mounted up. I will say again, I am not a winder-up like Eric used to be. He says I'm soft and that I should take things with a pinch of salt. I can't.

Despite the hassles I had a good start in the tournment. Steve Brown, originally from Surrey but now based in the USA, seemed down and out until the third set of our match, but then went haywire. I was leading 2–0 when he clattered three 180s and a 153 shot-out to make the set score 2–1. I eventually won 4–1 in sets with a 103.4 average. No fatigue of muscles or eyes was yet apparent.

My new earring and gold highlights in my hair had attracted a lot of headlines – just like my green glitter cape did years ago – but the game that set the tourna-ment alight was Peter Evison against Wayne Mardle. There was a diamond dartboard worth £125,000 for any man who hit a nine-dart finish, and Peter nearly did it. He got seven 60s, then treble 15 and the Circus Tavern held its breath. He missed the required double 18! My heart went out to him.

To make matters worse, Peter could not hold at bay the flamboyant Wayne Mardle. The lad has looked a thoroughbred since he was winning junior titles in his teens. For seven legs of the match Wayne averaged 108, and this form was good enough to win it. His end average was 97.1. I watched this match carefully because the winner was due to play me in the next round.

Before my match against Wayne, David Bobin of Sky did an in-depth interview with Sid Waddell about my form. I had said that I was determined to trim down and run in the London Marathon and Sid reckoned I was risking my stance and style at darts. He thought I had taken too much weight off too quickly. Sid said I looked tense in my first match and was not murdering the 60 like I normally did. Also, I was missing my doubles. He's entitled to his views, but on one thing he was dead right. My accuracy was not there 100 per cent. Sid wound up the chat by telling Dave that Mardle would beat me.

Well, Wayne did give me one hell of a fright. Early on he did a 152 shot-out but I replied with an 11-darter to take out the first set. I was averaging just under the ton when I got to 2–0 in sets. But then Wayne showed some of his top form. He took three of the next four hard-fought sets to make it a level game. Sid's commentary suggested that I was about to be beaten. 'It's all in the eyes, folks. Taylor does not look a Colossus tonight.' Maybe not. But I won the next set and Wayne started missing doubles. I ran out the winner at 5–3 in sets. I had done eight 180s in the match but my average was only 98.7. So maybe Sid had a point.

My next opponent was a lad who could give me a real

game. Dennis Smith usually has a belter against me, and this match was no exception. After four sets he was holding me to 2–2 despite my average of 101.6. He dominated the next set with legs of 11 and 12 darts and suddenly I was behind 3–2. The key to the scoreline was that Dennis was putting away 60 per cent of his doubles and I was very slack on them.

I was feeling the pace so I dug deep. I maintained my average at 100 and took the next two sets. But Dennis kicked back hard in the next and I had to fight to take it 3–2 in legs. This gave me the match 5–3.

My next opponent was due to be Alan Warriner, who had decided in his own way to make a point about all the publicity I was getting. He went totally over the top in an interview with Sky, saying he would take the microphone off and go and 'sort me out'. Was it a joke? Was it an attempt to put me off before our meeting? Or was it a pathetic attempt to grab a few headlines? It certainly made all the papers. But it does nothing for the image of our sport if players are threatening violence to opponents. There was one way to answer him, and I took it – on the dartboard.

I reckon all the hot air Alan had been using put the mockers on his preparation for our semi-final. I needed only an 86 average to win the first set 3–0. I also took set two. He rallied and hit three 180s in winning set three, but after that it was no contest. As I sailed to a 6–1 in sets victory he managed only two more legs. So much for his Grievous Bodily Darts!

The 2003 World Championship final was a classic.

I went into it jaded, upset by the jealousy apparent in Warriner's outburst and knowing my doubles were letting me down. I also knew my opponent John Part was in cracking form, particularly on the doubles. But I had the gut belief that John would never beat me in a major televised event. False confidence? I don't think so; you can't go into matches thinking you are going to lose.

Just before we got going Eric Bristow was interviewed and he mentioned that he thought Part might have made a tactical error. He won the bull for starting and said he would give the throw to me. Eric thought this could backfire and give me an advantage later in the game. I did have chances to capitalize on the move, but I did not have the push to do it.

The crowd sensed a night of drama was on the cards and gave us perfect order. They were hushed when we threw, and went wild when the big shots went in. Sadly for me, John started like a Scud missile. In the first leg he scored 180 and then did a 121 shot-out.

Sid Waddell and Dave Lanning made the point that John had to hold me early on. If I got 3–1 up in sets there would be no catching me. But my stacking of the darts was off kilter and so were my doubles. Thank God I was hitting treble 19 regularly to get me out of trouble. Mind you, I was not totally out of sorts: I was averaging 110 to his 105. It was not enough. John took the first three sets to nil. As Sid put it, 'John Part is showing more style than a Frank Sinatra hat.'

Then things started to go a bit my way.

I pegged back to 3–1 in sets via a 122 check-out. The crowd reacted wildly. Dave Lanning reckoned: 'There was less excitement when they opened the wooden horse in Troy!' I think John and I were both tired now. He had had a gruelling match against Kevin Painter and Mardle and Dennis Smith had taken a lot out of me. John took the score to 4–1 in sets.

Tired or not, I knew I had to put in the old kick. I won the sixth set with a 12-darter. I won the next set with a 109 check-out. Then I pulled level at 4–4 and I danced round the stage. It got better: I fired in a 167 shot-out to go ahead 5–4 in sets. John Gwynne called it 'a statement of intent'.

But John was by no means finished. My four-set charge brought out the best in him. At the end of a level 10th set he did an 11-darter to steal it. The set score was 5–5 and by now the crowd and the commentators were gasping. It was swings and roundabouts for the next two sets. We got to 6–6.

As Eric had suggested at the start, having the advantage of throwing first in the odd sets should now favour me. But I blew my first chance; I missed tops for the first leg. He smacked in double 16. My stacking was not good; my first dart was too low to bounce the second in. I missed a 105 shot-out and John got double four to go 2–0 up in legs. I was really under the cosh now. One more leg and he's won. In the next leg I got double 12 to save the match and John shook my hand. Nice to know there's a bit of respect in the game. Then I needed 121 to save the match and my title. I missed the bull and he shot 77 to win.

'It could not have been scripted,' was John's comment.

The press lads asked me what happened when I was 5–4 up in sets and apparently powering to title 11. 'I thought I'd got him at that point but it all seemed to catch up with me. I suddenly felt very, very tired. It was not so much physical as mental. For once the cupboard was bare.' There was little more to say.

But I'm glad Roland Scholten opened his mouth and supported me. 'In my eyes Phil is a true ambassador for the sport. He works incredibly hard, doesn't have a bad word for anyone, and he has just shown that he can lose as gracefully as he can win. I also think it's surreal to talk about him in the past tense because I expect him to do a hell of a lot more winning yet.' Good on yer, my old Dutch! You can pop in for an Edam butty anytime you are in Stoke.

I knew it would take a few weeks for the disappointment to wear off, but I was determined to bounce back and get on track to win that world title back.

CHAPTER 23

Staggers into Saggars

The people who use the Saggar Makers pub are just like the folks we used to have at the Cricketers; salt-of-the-earth Stoke people. They like their football, their darts and their dominoes. Many of my trophies and photographs line the walls and I often pop in for a chat with landlord Dave Lewis. My son Chris also goes in with his pals. After my defeat by John Part it was not long before I went on stage at the Saggars to have a bit of a throw and a bit of a think.

But before I go into that I must give the answer to another regular exhibition question. Why is the pub you practise in called the Saggar Makers? Well, many years ago on the television show 'What's My Line?' the posh panel were well and truly stumped by a 'saggar maker's bottom knocker'. So here is the story. Saggars are boxes made of coarse clay inside which pottery was fired during the great days of the bottle kilns in the Potteries. The sides of the box were made by the saggar maker's frame filler, and the bottom of the box was made by the saggar maker's bottom knocker. The saggar maker was the senior man who joined the two parts together. It was thirsty work and so the saggar-making gang needed their own pub!

In the days after my defeat in the final I practised a bit at the Saggars and at the old oche by the bed at Blake Street. I don't mind saying how depressed I was when people started writing me off. There was talk of 'bubbles bursting', as though I had not grafted for my success.

Still, there's no sense in being bitter or brooding, so I got on with the parts of my life that give me a break from darts. Sid Waddell came down to Stoke for a few days and was shocked to see me whacking tiles down in a little house I have bought to renovate. Sean Rutter and I do a bit of work on it any time we can. It takes my mind off darts and the physical work tones up my muscles. Back at my home Sid was amazed to see me working away on a machine called a vinyl plotter. This puts flock lettering on darts shirts and I have a nice little sideline doing them for the darts lads. I import the shirts from India and work away on my machine in a side room. Remember I did three different apprenticeships and can understand machinery, so I don't make many mistakes. I would go daft just sitting round the house all the time, so I turn my hand to various things.

There was no big competition coming along and I suppose I lost my appetite for the game a bit. I did exhibitions for Hasseroder, one of my main sponsors, and for May Gay, who have a game in pubs where you can challenge me. But then the old backbiting and jealousy kicked in. I had a real sickener when I heard that Warriner was up to his publicity-seeking tricks again. After his crack before our semi-final at the World Championships that he would probably have to knock me out on the oche to shift the limelight away from me, he had this to say on his website.

'Phil "the Power" Taylor – the nickname says it all. He is without doubt the greatest darts player there has ever been. Nobody will ever achieve what he has done in the game – apart from keeping his MBE, that is! Does it make him a nice bloke? Well, it has certainly changed him over the years.

I played him in the world semi-final some years back and he beat me easily. As he hit the last double he turned round to me and I was going to shake his hand, albeit begrudgingly. Before I could he started jumping up and down, so I walked off. All of a sudden I'm the bad boy! I can't work that one out.

In front of the TV cameras he is a different person; he comes over as a nice guy. That's one of the reasons most players don't like him. Another one is what he says to players about money. It's either stay around me and you can make a lot of money, or telling everyone which deal he has done and for how much. Can you imagine Tiger Woods telling Ernie Els that?

We now come to this year's World Championship and again it's Phil Taylor this, Phil Taylor that. It really pisses you off. It's as if no other player is playing in the event. Basically the press and the PDC are up his arse.

For me the blue touchpaper was lit while I was playing Les Fitton. We were told to stop by the referee because Phil Taylor was bulling up in the players' room and they wanted to televise it! I was absolutely stunned and could not believe it. After the game I walked straight into the press room and told them what I thought. The following day Sky asked me to do an interview with my professional head on and I said what I thought.'

I will remind Alan that with his 'professional head' on he mentioned punching me. It's all very well to lead with your tongue to try to get publicity, but you should take other people's feelings into account, not to mention the image of our sport.

There is another dimension as well. Mouthing off like that means that he's under pressure at every tournament he goes to now. He has made a rod for his own back. Not only will the other professional players mark his card, but the crowds will show what they think of him. I have been told by some of the lads that I'm taking the whole matter too seriously, that Alan does not mean anything by his remarks. Well, read his cracks again and make your own mind up. One thing is sure, he will get no more publicity from me in any of the newspaper or magazine articles I write.

It was at this point that the trusty George Sutherland came up with a good idea to get me out of the rut and prepare me for big tournaments in Canada and Bolton. He came on the phone and invited me up to Wick for a weekend of social darts. I didn't hesitate. Let's get back to the roots of the game, I thought. Let's forget World Championships and the sniping and relax a bit. You know, it worked a treat.

On the first night George organized what he called the 'Blind Drunk Triples', which is where you put your name in a hat and play with whichever partners come out. Losers mark the board. It was just like being back at the Huntsman in my early days. Myself and two new pals – Rab Townsend and Brian Cassie – won the competition.

All day Saturday I practised with Alex Mackay, a Scottish international, and folk wandered into the room to watch and get autographs. On the Sunday I won the singles. I flew back home feeling invigorated and ready to do my best in Canada. And who was waiting for me there? John Part, of course.

My aim in Canada was to win the Golden Harvest North American Cup for the fourth time. Rod Harrington had won the title three times so my aim had to be to go one better.

As usual in Canada, I shared a room with PDC caller

Russ Bray, who is a non-drinker and we watch lots of movies together, just like Eric Bristow and I did in 1988 when my career as a professional started.

I was looking to hammer out to the other professionals that I was back and I was hungry. It took just one game to do that. I faced John Part in the semi-final, which was the best of seven sets, and right off he gave me trouble. He started the match with a 14-darter. I was going pretty well but he pipped me to take the first set 2–1 in legs.

I was scoring very heavily but John was flying: in the deciding leg of set two he went out on 102 after hitting 140, 125, 134. He was two up in sets: I was averaging 105 and not even in the hunt! Against the darts I took the first leg of set three in 13 darts. But steady tons and deadly finishing took him to 3–0 in sets.

If I'd got into this situation before I took my mini-break in Wick I think I'd have lost the match. But I was bouncing to get back into the fray. I did a 13-darter. John missed a double and I stepped in to start my recovery. It was 3–1 in sets. He then began missing doubles and I could see the worry on his face. I pegged back to 3–2 in sets. John was labouring after a long day of competition, but I was fresh as a daisy.

I was banging in the 180s now. I did three in set number six to level the match. I was loving it. All the memories of the defeat in the World Championship were melting away. I felt like a prophet who had been out in the wilderness for months. And how about all those people sticking in jibes and writing me off? This was just the way to show them.

In the next set I could see that the pressure was working. I did two 140s and it was four visits to the board before he got a ton. And you know me; the nearer the winning post the more confident I get. On 83 I missed the bull for 1–0 in legs, but John failed to go out on 51. I took the leg. Just one more needed for victory. I banged in a 14-darter to win the match. It was hailed as the greatest come-back in the history of the tournament.

England's Andy Jenkins was my opponent in the final. I took the first set and wanted a simple 41 shot-out to take the second. I missed and Andy took the set. He gave me a hard time with some very heavy scoring, but I managed to win the third set with a 15-darter: 2–1 in sets to the Power and I was feeling strong.

Andy gave it everything in the next set. I went a leg up, then he got to 64 after only nine darts. With me looking at 76 he shot out. The he piled in some big scores to level the match 2–2 in sets. The standard continued into set five. At 1–1 in legs I wanted 161 and decided against trying a bull finish, because I didn't think Andy would hit 167. It was a gamble and it worked. I clicked in the double to go 3–2 up in sets. We were level going into leg three of set six, then I let him have it: 137, 174, 100, leaving 90. I went out on double 10.

Shattered? I'll say I was. The next night I was in bed asleep at 6 o'clock. There was an official dinner but I decided to give it a miss. Suddenly Russ Bray came running in, telling me to get dressed. I was wanted at the dinner for a special presentation. So I went down. I was presented with a Lifetime Achievement Award in the form of a special embroidered shirt and a beautiful Wedgwood vase. The vase was in a box about two feet square and I had a sore arm lumping it on three planes home. Back in Stoke Yvonne took one look at it and began to laugh. 'They make those vases at a factory a mile up the road,' she said.

Looking back on the Canada trip, I reckon it is uncanny that I got all my confidence back in the place where I took my first big step on the darts ladder in 1988. Maybe somebody up there likes me, or maybe Charlie the ghost from the Cricketers has moved there.

It is nice to be able to do charity exhibitions for good causes, and nobody does more than darters.

My connection with Ricky Hatton and the boxing fraternity led me to do a very important evening at Denton West End working-men's club in Manchester the night before the UK Open at Bolton. Ricky's trainer Billy Graham had a friend who was the brother of a woman who had been murdered, and Billy was asked to put on a show to raise money for her teenage son. Billy talked to me about it and I put him in touch with John Gwynne of Sky Sports. John is a great darts MC and would host the night. He had the bright idea of inviting John Part along, so the darts and boxing fans would have a bit of real competition to watch.

What a smashing night it turned out to be. We all had the local pies – seven different varieties – and sampled the local ale. Then John and I played pairs with darters and boxers from the audience. I was delighted to partner a great darting character called 'the Duck', alias Dave Owen of Hattersley, who comes to all my exhibitions in the Manchester area. Dave was the 1992 Tameside Individual Champion but got dartitis shortly after and is only now getting back to normal. Before we got going he reminded me of a night at Hattersley when I played some locals until about 10pm and then the whole of the pub team until gone one in the morning. The Denton night was also a bit of a marathon. People paid into the charity box to play with me and John, then George Sutherland took the microphone and John and I played the best of 15 legs. OK, you might say, this was a bit of gentle practice for the big competition at Bolton, but not a bit of it. For one hour we knocked hell out of each other. We each averaged around 100, but John just beat me 8–7. And I was narked. It really hurt.

I was pleased to hear that our efforts and an auction of boxing memorabilia raised £4,000 for a very worthy cause.

That loss to John set me up just right for the first big televised domestic tournament of the season, the new UK Open at Bolton.

It is a new PDC event and is the FA Cup of darts. For nine months thousands of players had been battling it

311

out to get to the last 128 who would play off the final stages at Bolton Wanderers' Reebok Stadium.

I helped publicize the event by showing up at the Royal Oak pub in Manchester to see Bolton manager Sam Allardyce, alias 'the Dudley Destroyer' try to qualify. He did not impress with his accuracy but there was plenty of enthusiasm there. Sam also took part later in a 'Bullseye' darts challenge and quiz and, according to Sid Waddell, who was the MC, he failed to impress again.

What was impressive when the tournament started, however, was the way Sky Sports covered the action on eight separate boards! There were some very good young players there, including Lee Palfreyman and Simon Whatley who had starred in Las Vegas. Sky cut between famous names and upstarts doing well, and kept tabs on every bit of drama. And a 1,000-strong crowd kept the sound levels high. How the commentary team mugged up on 128 biographies I'll never know.

I was in good form when the top 32 in the order of merit got going on day two of the competition, but Dennis Smith, as usual, gave me a hard game. Dennis used to train greyhounds and he went off like one. He took the first leg of our match with a bull finish and then took the second leg as well. Then he just missed a 152 finish that would have made the score 3–0 in legs to him. Remember, at this stage it was only a race to eight legs. I put a kick in and got to 3–2. Despite some of my fellow professionals saying my bubble had burst, the Bolton crowd cheered me to the echo. Mind, I had been wearing a Wanderers football strip out on the pitch most of the morning!

I got to 4–2 with a 14-darter and then sailed away with the match. I ended by getting 90 with two darts, bull and double top. The score was 8–3 in legs, and I was happy with an average of 103.2. I was even happier as my main rivals like John Part and local favourite Ronnie Baxter fell by the wayside.

The renaissance of Shayne Burgess was a highlight of the competition. Two years ago at Blackpool he had been so bad he threw his darts in the sea and nearly followed them. He said he had lost it completely. But on his 39th birthday he played a blinder against Bolton's own Paul Williams in the semi-final.

In his previous two matches Paul had come from behind with the crowd and his wife Joanne yelling him on. But at 5–5 in legs he missed a 161 shot-out and was chasing after that. Shayne looked happy and confident as he got to 9–7 in legs. In the next leg Paul just missed a 142 finish, and Shayne showed the class he had last produced in the 2000 World Grand Prix final. He won the game with a 156 finish. 'Shayney is back!' sang Sid on Sky. And after all these years I have to report that Sid is losing his reputation as the Black Spot. He tipped me and Shayne to be the finalists.

The Bolton final put an end to the worries and doubts of the past five months. There was £30,000 to the winner but I didn't even think about it. There was no seeding for the tournament and there was a new draw after every round. Nobody was 'cushioned' from any-body else. The crowd appreciated Shayne's performance, but they gave me respect and affection too.

It all added up to an ideal atmosphere. First man to 18 legs was the winner, and I got to 8–1. The commenta-tors were now chanting 'The Power is back.' But then Shayne put in a spurt and did a 170 finish on the bull to make it 11–5. Then at 17–7, with the crowd willing me to finish proceedings, Shayne hit an 86 shot-out to keep me at bay.

I won 18–8 and the crowd were smashing. They applauded both of us for several minutes. My mate Ricky Hatton came up on stage and gave me a hug. I looked round the hall at the cheering Boltonians and thought about the next seven months. There is a lot of darts to play in places as far afield as Blackpool and Las Vegas, but Team Taylor have only one goal: the Circus Tavern and world title number 11.

As in all things in life, you pay a price for fame and for-tune. When I was working at the lathe we didn't have much money but I was at home all the time. When I turned professional as a darts player in 1990 and got lots of work, it meant I had to travel all the time and I missed out on the upbringing of Lisa and Chris, who was born in 1983. In fact I was on the road constantly from 1990, so we never had a family holiday until we went to Cyprus for a week in 2002.

I attended the births of all my children except Kelly,

who was born while I was playing darts in Jersey. Yvonne and I were not together at the births on principle or anything; I just went to hold her hand and give her the odd kind word.

I know Yvonne used to miss me terribly when I first started on the road, but she knew it was my job and she soldiered on. As the kids got older I think they got used to it as well. I always bought them the best presents I could afford – like a scrambler motorbike for Chris. If I could not give them the time, I thought, I could give gifts.

Life was very tough for Yvonne when we had the pub. She enjoyed it, but it was hard work. It was particularly tough on her at New Year. People would be in the pub, kissing and hugging as Big Ben struck, and I would be miles away at the World Championships. Now the kids are grown a bit we take them to the darts and they really enjoy themselves. Nathalie is 11 now and I can always hear her when I'm playing. 'Come on, Dad!' is her usual call if I do well. But if I hit a bad shot the tone changes and she shouts 'Come on, Philip' – just like my mother did when she told me off!

We don't really have any plans for the kids. I reckon in this day and age it is hard to plan. You can go to college for years and still have no guarantee of a job. I believe that who you know is very important. Our Lisa worked for a friend of mine who has an insurance business. Chris had a job for a while with a mate of mine in the sheet metal business. Now he's with my cousin Wayne Walker in the meat trade.

I'd really like to live in a better environment, maybe somewhere like Spain where you're not scared to walk down the street at night. At the Cricketers pub I met old people who were frightened to come out at night, and I used to walk one old bloke home regularly.

We have been to Spain a couple of times now, and each time we come back the tug to return gets stronger. I like the way of life. In particular I like the way the dustbins are emptied every day and the streets are kept clean. Old people can walk around late at night. I miss the days of good neighbours here, and it's a shame some people feel the need to lock themselves away.

I'd like to end this book with one or two comments on success in sport, the people I respect and the few people I don't.

One reason I keep my feet firmly on the ground is that in darts we do not make millions of pounds. In a bonanza year I make good money – winning my Super Slam in 2002 I earned over £200,000 – but every year cannot be like that. So you plod on providing for your family as best you can.

I like to think I have gained respect and even admiration from sportsmen outside the world of darts. Steve Davis and Stephen Hendry both rate my 10 world titles very highly, and Davis once said I deserved a knighthood rather than the MBE.

I rate the dedication of winners like David Beckham, Roy Keane, Chris Eubank, Nigel Benn and Ricky Hatton.

I wanted desperately to be a professional darts player. When Eric Bristow put £10,000 behind my ambition I slogged to give him value for money. I do the same with sponsors. They don't want me sitting in bars drinking with the lads; they want a figurehead for our sport.

This brings me to the vexed problem of the pure jealousy that I have come across in our game. I told the papers that Alan Warriner could have a pop at me when he needed two hands to hold up his World Championship trophies. It does the game no good when television viewers see backbiting and bad behaviour. If the game is to prosper in the coming decades we must be professionals and never cowboys.

Finally, a word on how my achievements have affected the game. Taking nothing away from the eras of Eric, John Lowe and others, I think what I have done has helped change the image of the sport. And I hope you now know a lot more about the graft, dedication and pain that it takes to be World Darts Champion 10 times.

Mind you, I'm a long way from being finished.

Career Highlights

1988

Burslem Open
  (Head-to-head challenge against John Weatherall)
Derbyshire Open
Lincolnshire Open
Canadian Open
  (The win that kicked off my professional career. I beat Bob Anderson in the final 5–1 and picked up $5,000)

1990

Embassy World Professional Championship
  (defeated Russell Stewart 3–1, Dennis Hickling 3–0, Ronnie Sharp 4–0, Cliff Lazarenko 5–0, Eric Bristow 6–1 (Final))
Finnish Open
Danish Open

North American Open
British Pentathlon
Europe Cup Singles and Pairs
   (with Bob Anderson)
World Masters

1991

North American Open

1992

Embassy World Professional Championship
   (defeated Magnus Caris 3–1, Per Skau 3–1, Martin Phillips 4–0, John Lowe 5–4, Mike Gregory 6–5 (Final))
Europe Cup Singles

1994

UK Masters

1995

WDC World Professional Championship
   (defeated Gerald Verrier 3–2, Sean Downs 3–1, Bob Anderson 4–1, John Lowe 5–4, Rod Harrington 6–2 (Final))
World Matchplay

1996

WDC World Professional Championship
   (defeated Cliff Lazarenko 3–0, Shayne Burgess 3–0, Keith Deller 4–0, John Lowe 5–1, Dennis Priestley 6–4 (Final))

Durro Challenge
  *(Head-to-head against Dennis Priestley. I averaged 108.7
  and scored eight 180s)*
UK Matchplay
World Pairs
  (with Bob Anderson)

1997

WDC World Professional Championship
  *(defeated Chris Mason 3–0, Gerald Verrier 3–0, Keith Deller
  5–1, Eric Bristow 5–4, Dennis Priestley 6–3 (Final). This
  win equalled Eric Bristow's record of five world
  championships)*
News of the World Championship
  (defeated Ian White in the final and averaged 107.4)
World Matchplay

1998

PDC World Professional Championship
  *(defeated Kevin Spiolek 3–0, Dennis Smith 3–0, Shayne
  Burgess 4–0, Rod Harrington 5–2, Dennis Priestley 6–0
  (Final). This set a new record of six world championships)*
World Grand Prix

1999

PDC World Professional Championship
  *(defeated Reg Harding 3–0, John Lowe 3–1, Bob Anderson
  5–0, Alan Warriner 5–3, Peter Manley 6–2 (Final))*
World Grand Prix

'Match of the Century'
(defeated Ray Barneveld 21–10 in legs, with seven 180s and an average of 103.5. I also won £60,000!)

2000

PDC World Professional Championship
(defeated Mick Manning 3–0, Graeme Stoddart 3–0, Alan Warriner 5–0, Dennis Smith 5–0, Dennis Priestley 7–3 (Final). My best-ever world championship performance. Against Alan Warriner my average was 105.9, and my tournament average was 102.5)
World Matchplay
World Grand Prix
(I completed the PDC Grand Slam)

2001

PDC World Professional Championship
(defeated Nigel Justice 3–0, Les Fitton 3–1, Keith Deller 4–0, Dave Askew 6–0, John Part 7–0 (Final). Again memorable: my average in the final was 107.5)
World Matchplay

2002

PDC World Professional Championship
(defeated Paul Williams 4–1, Shayne Burgess 6–1, John Part 6–0, Dave Askew 6–0, Peter Manley 7–0 (Final). In round two I beat Shayne Burgess with an average of 111.2. My tenth world championship title)
Golden Harvest North American Cup

Las Vegas Desert Classic
Hasseroder UK Open Welsh Regional Final
World Matchplay
(The first-ever nine-dart finish live on British television in my match against Chris Mason. I won £100,000 for the feat.)
Hasseroder UK Open Northern Irish Regional Final
World Grand Prix
(I completed PDC Super Slam)

2003

Golden Harvest North American Cup
(In the semi-final I got revenge on John Part for taking my world title in January 2003. I beat him 4–3 in sets with an average of 105)
UK Open
(I came top of the heap out of 128 players – just to let them know The Power was back in business)

INDEX

Adams, Martin
  British Classic 1997 134
  Embassy World Professional Darts
    Championship 1995 155
  News of the World Championship 1997
    127–128
  playing for England 59
  World Grand Prix 2001 210–211
  World Matchplay 2001 207
Alderman, Dave 73
Ali, Muhammad 230, 232, 234
Allardyce, Sam 312
Allcock, Tony 168
Allix, Dick
  attempts to professionalize darts
    72–73
  BDO meeting 79
  Bristow's agent 41, 49, 140
  comments on WDC/BDO dispute
    141–142
  negotiations with BBC 82
  Samson Darts Classic 83–84
  World Darts Federation negotiations
    140
Anakin, Foot 247–248
Anderson, Andy 64–65
Anderson, Bob
  BDO meeting 79
  Canadian Open 1988 43
  coaching Smith 183
  cowboy walk-on 102–103
  drinking during matches 251

Europe Cup 1990 59–60
Europe Cup 1992 77
Irish Masters 2000 186, 189
PDC World Championship 1999 166
playing for England 59
playing for Surrey 35
pro-am golf 187, 189
Samson Darts Classic 84
WDC policy statement 78–79
WDC World Championship 1994 86
WDC World Championship 1997 118
World Matchplay 1994 97
World Matchplay 1997 133
World Pairs Championship 1997 154
World Pairs Championship 1996 117
Anka, Paul 274–275
Askew, Dave
  dropped from England squad 149
  Embassy World Professional Darts
    Championship 1995 155
  PDC World Championship 2001 204
  PDC World Championship 2002 229
Augustus, Harry 34

Baines, Tony 96
Barnes, Simon 87
Barneveld, Ray
  British Classic 1997 134
  Embassy World Professional Darts
    Championship 1991 155
  Embassy World Professional Darts
    Championship 1995 155, 176

Barneveld, Ray – *cont.*
  Embassy World Professional Darts
    Championship 1999 170
  head-to-head with Taylor 173–179
  sporting icon 277
  World Pairs Championship 1997
    154–155
Barrett, Tommy 126, 248, 254, 256
Barron, Peter 81, 139
Battersby, Kate 165
Battle of the Champions 129–131
Battye, Ray 41, 59
Baxter, Rachel 160
Baxter, Ronnie
  British Classic 1997 134
  Embassy World Professional Darts
    Championship 1994 205
  Embassy World Professional Darts
    Championship 1999 170
  Isle of Man Open 1990 60
  Las Vegas Desert Classic 2002
    278–281
  PDC World Championship 2002 227
  playing for England 59
  UK Open 2003 313
  World Matchplay 1998 160–161
  World Matchplay 1999 170
Beaton, Steve
  dropped from England squad 149
  News of the World Championship 1997
    129
  PDC World Championship 2002 227
  playing for England 59
  playing for West Midlands 35
  Rotterdam drinking incident 69
Beckham, David 253, 272, 316
Belmont, Frank 277
Benn, Nigel 293, 316
Bevan, Aneurin 294
Beveridge, Doctor 11
Blair, Cherie 272
Bloor, Geoff 37
Bobin, David 298
Bostock, John 79
Bourn, Bobby 2
Bowen, Jim 114
Boycott, Geoff 184, 230
Bradman, Don 230, 232, 234
Bray, Russ 230, 308, 309–310

Brenneman, Sean 269
Bridge, Alan 30, 31, 34
Bristow, Eric
  Allix as agent 41, 49, 140
  arrogant attitude 24, 29, 47
  Battle of the Champions 129–131
  captain of England team 59
  charisma 32
  classic matches 104–105
  comments on WDC/BDO dispute 144
  commercial breaks 86
  Crafty Cockney club 28–29, 48
  dartitis 40, 48, 50
  drinking during matches 47,
    249–250, 251
  Embassy World Professional Darts
    Championship 1978 45
  Embassy World Professional Darts
    Championship 1980 45
  Embassy World Professional Darts
    Championship 1983 45
  Embassy World Professional Darts
    Championship 1984 45
  Embassy World Professional Darts
    Championship 1985 28, 45,
    154–155
  Embassy World Professional Darts
    Championship 1986 45
  Embassy World Professional Darts
    Championship 1990 46–48
  Embassy World Professional Darts
    Championship 1991 61
  Europe Cup 1990 59
  exhibition darts 54
  friendship with Crofts 147
  giving darts to Taylor 66, 260
  happy personality 138
  head-to-heads 173
  high-five incident 121, 224–225
  Irish Masters 2000 187, 189
  long career 292
  MBE 221–222
  mentor for Taylor 34, 48–50, 125,
    297
  motivational psychology 32, 34–35,
    43–44, 48–50, 64
  move to Staffordshire 28
  News of the World Championship 125,
    126

INDEX

official spotter 166
PDC World Championship 1999 168
PDC World Championship 2002 230, 232
PDC World Championship 2003 301
picture on plates 54, 114
playing style 42, 66, 112–113, 180–181, 261
practising with Taylor 31, 40, 46, 78
praise for Taylor 107, 128, 159, 206
public recognition 57
rows with Taylor 49
sponsoring Taylor on world circuit 35–36, 38, 41–44
Staffordshire team 28, 30, 34
support for Taylor 294, 317
Taylor breaking record 158–159
Taylor equalling record 123–124
Taylor's head-to-head with Barneveld 178
Taylor's views on 43–44, 48–50, 242
Taylor's weight loss 295
views on George 245
views on rift between WDC and BDO 87–88
Waddell's views on 8
walk-ons 119
WDC logo argument 76
WDC policy statement 78–79
WDC World Championship 1997 118–122
winning psychology 252
World Matchplay 1994 95
World Matchplay 1995 110
World Matchplay 1997 132
World Matchplay 2000 190
Bristow, George 49
British Darts Organisation
banning WDC players 77, 80–81, 138–140
British Classic 1997 133–134
dispute over player management 72–73
dropping PDC players 149
Embassy reception incident 68
Embassy video incident 74
legal costs 142
meeting with WDC 79–80
origin of oche 245–246

resolutions 80
rift with PDC 71
settlement of WDC case 144–145
started by Croft 30
suspending WDC players 79
Taylor's head-to-head with Barneveld 174, 179
WDC legal action 137–144
Bromberg, Stacey 275
Brooks, Gideon 296
Brown, Chubby 95
Brown, Steve
Malta Open 1990 60
PDC World Championship 2003 297
WDC World Championship 1994 86
World Grand Prix 1998 162
Irish Masters 2000 189
Bulger, Andrew 32
Burgess, Shayne
fishing expedition 195
Irish Masters 2000 190
PDC World Championship 1998 156
PDC World Championship 1999 163, 167
PDC World Championship 2000 182
PDC World Championship 2002 227–228
pro-am golf 188
Quadro board 84
shooting skills 171–172
Taylor's nine-darter 2–3, 268
UK Open 2003 313–314
WDC World Championship 1996 115
World Grand Prix 1998 162, 163
World Grand Prix 1999 171–173
World Grand Prix 2000 197
World Matchplay 2000 190, 193
World Matchplay 2002 234–235
Burnett, Richie
Battle of the Champions 129, 131
Embassy World Professional Darts Championship 1995 155, 176
joining WDC 129–130
Las Vegas Desert Classic 2002 278
PDC World Championship 2002 228
World Matchplay 1997 132
World Matchplay 2000 191
World Matchplay 2001 208
Butler, Larry 99

Caborn, Richard 150
Cairns, Brian 41
Cairns, Dap 25–26
Calzaghe, Joe 226
Canadian Open 1988 42–43
Capewell, Les 30, 34
Caris, Magnus 65
Carson, Frank 96
Carver, Ray 275
Cassie, Brian 307
Chaplin, Patrick 195
Charlton, Bobby 230
Cher 274
Circus Tavern
    Battle of the Champions 129–131
    PDC World Championship 1999
        164–168
    PDC World Championship 2002
        226–233
    Stoddart versus King 202–203
    WDC World Championship 1994 84
Coe, Sebastian 71
Colclough, Sharon 44–45
Collins, Steve 293
Connor, Mick 135, 213–216
Cosnett, John 33
Cox, Tommy
    attempts to professionalize darts
        72–73
    BDO ban 139
    BDO meeting 79–80
    becoming Taylor's manager 54–55
    contribution to WDC legal costs 143
    Darts Council 56
    dispute over player management
        72–73
    Embassy reception incident 68
    Embassy video incident 74
    Embassy World Professional Darts
        Championship 1990 55
    friendship with Taylor 294
    indecent assault court case 215–216
    Irish Masters 2000 186
    lack of TV darts coverage 55–56
    managing Wilson 109
    meeting Taylor 54–55
    MGM Grand incident 276
    negotiations with BBC 82
    Rotterdam drinking incident 69–70

Samson Darts Classic 83
stable of players 56
support for Taylor 136
Taylor's change of manager 219
Taylor's head-to-head with Barneveld
    174–175, 178
Taylor's MBE withdrawn 222
Taylor's practice sessions 251
WDC logo argument 76
WDC World Championship 1994
    57–58
WDC World Championship 1997
    119
World Darts Federation negotiations
    140
Crafty Cockney club 28–29, 34, 38, 39,
    48, 52
Cram, Steve 71
Cricketers Arms
    bought by Taylor 89–90
    Charlie the ghost 8, 13, 93–95, 207
    darts teams 91
    plugged by Taylor 111
    renovation 90–91
    sold by Taylor 200
    Taylor's head-to-head with Barneveld
        180
    traditional atmosphere 91
Croft, Olly
    blocking WDC change of name 140
    comments on WDC/BDO dispute
        143
    cost of playing for England 60
    criticisms of WDC players 138
    demise of Embassy World
        Professional Darts Championship
        150
    Embassy reception incident 68
    Embassy World Professional Darts
        Championship 1990 50–51
    England manager 58
    feelings of betrayal 148
    friendship with Bristow 147
    friendship with Taylor 73–74
    refusal to deal with WDC 73
    starting British Darts Organisation 30
    WDC logo argument 76
Croft, Lorna 148
Crosbie, Tom 186

Daniels, Conrad 45
darts
  alcohol at darts matches 47, 201,
    249–251
  dartitis 40
  darts players as athletes 249–252
  eras of champions 124
  Grand Slam 181–182, 192
  history of 246–248
  lack of television coverage 55–57, 72
  legality of 247–248
  low public image 201
  mathematics of nine-darter 262–263
  need for professional organisation
    71–72
  nine-darter history 264–266
  origin of oche 245–246
  perceived as sport 248–249
  playing styles 255–257, 260
  Quadro board 84
  rift between BDO and WDC 71–83
  science of 254–261
  Sky expanding coverage 129
  Super Slam 240–241
darts fans
  American 278
  Boss Pie Bashers 2
  Catford Skins 86
  Dart Vader 2
  John McEnDart 2
  Lee Van Dart 2
  Maltby Marauders 191
  Tarts for Darts 2, 191
  Vikings 2
  Winter Gardens 1–2
David, Tony 179, 277
Davis, Steve
  admiration for Taylor 316
  managed by Hearn 293–294
  sporting legend 159, 166, 229–230
  Taylor as sporting legend 184
  views on darts 180–181
Deller, Keith
  Canadian Open 1988 42
  classic matches 104
  Embassy World Professional Darts
    Championship 1983 45, 56, 72
  head-to-heads 173
  official spotter 166

  PDC World Championship 2001 204
  WDC policy statement 78–79
  WDC World Championship 1996 115
  WDC World Championship 1997 118
  World Grand Prix 2002 238
Denmark Open 1991 63
Digweed, George 168
Dillon, Andy 296
Donovan, Ned 268
Downes, Terry 122
Dunne, Brendan 189
Durrant, Paul 114
Dutton, Alan 113–114
Dyke, Greg 72
Dyke, Peter 76

Ebdon, Peter 252
Eddie the Eagle 75
Ellis, Fitzroy 15
Embassy World Professional Darts
  Championship
  1978 45
  1979 45
  1980 45
  1982 45, 108, 265
  1983 45, 56, 72
  1984 45
  1985 28, 45, 154–155
  1986 45
  1990 45–48
  1991 60–61, 100, 155
  1992 46, 65–68
  1993 75–76, 78
  1994
  1995 155
  1999 169–170
  demise of 88, 150
  Jollees nightclub 8, 28
  Lakeside venue 35, 46
  organized by British Darts
    Organisation 30
Emery, Roy 36
Engel, Matthew 248
England
  capping Taylor 58
  costs for players 60
  dropping PDC players 149
  Europe Cup 1990 59–60
  Europe Cup 1992 77

England – *cont.*
  team in 1990 59
  World Cup 1991 64
Eubank, Chris 293, 294, 316
Europe Cup
  1990 59–60
  1992 77
Evans, Alan
  1001 world record 286
  Battle of the Champions 129–131
  classic matches 104
  death of 131
  exhibition darts 53
  founder of television darts 196
  head-to-heads 173
  News of the World Championship 126
  playing style 256
  slow player 122
Evison, Peter
  managed by Cox 56
  News of the World Championship 126
  PDC World Championship 2003
    297
  playing for England 59
  playing for Surrey 35
  practice sessions 113
  WDC policy statement 78–79
  WDC/BDO dispute 144
  World Grand Prix 1999 173, 175
  World Grand Prix 2000 197
  World Grand Prix 2002 239
  World Matchplay 1996 117
  World Matchplay 2000 190
  World Pairs Championship 1995 111

Faldo, Nick 272
Farmer, Gayle 274, 276
Ferguson, Alex 272
Findlay, Harry 120–121
Finn, Andy 166
Fitton, Les
  PDC World Championship 2001
    203–204
  PDC World Championship 2003
    306
Flowers, Maureen
  Crafty Cockney club 28–29
  support for Taylor 46
  Taylor sponsored by Bristow 35

Taylor's manager 52, 54–55
Furness, Dai 35

Gamble, Albert 264–265
Gardner, Mark 180
Gardner, Richie
  playing for England 59
  playing for Surrey 35
  WDC policy statement 78–79
Gee, Chris 33
George, Bobby
  criticisms of PDC 147, 148
  Embassy World Professional Darts
    Championship 1980 45
  Embassy World Professional Darts
    Championship 1994 205
  News of the World Championship 126
  police impersonation incident
    243–245
  poor-quality TV commentary 170
  Taylor's views on 243–245
Gibbons, Tommy 126
Gibson, Dave 46
Gittings, Steve 33, 41
Glazier, Alan 35, 53, 196
Golden Harvest North American Cup
  2003 307–310
Goulding, Bobby 272
Graham, Billy 310
Greatbatch, Shaun 266
Greaves, Jimmy 253
Green, Tony 68, 76, 116
Gregory, Mike
  Canadian Open 1988 43
  classic matches 105
  Embassy video incident 74, 149
  Embassy World Professional Darts
    Championship 1992 46, 65, 66–68
  managed by Cox 56
  News of the World Championship 126
  pulling out of WDC 82
  UK Masters 1992 76–77
  WDC policy statement 78–79
Greig, Tony 141
Gullit, Ruud 174
Gulliver, Trina 187, 190, 203
Gwynne, John
  charity darts MC 310
  classic matches 104

commentary skills 116
News of the World Championship 1997
128
PDC World Championship 2002
227–229, 231
PDC World Championship 2003
301–302
Taylor as sporting legend 184
Taylor's 10th world title 233
Taylor's attempt at 1001 record
285–286
Taylor's head-to-head with Barneveld
178
UK Masters 1992 76
Waddell screaming about nine-darter
263
WDC World Championship 1994 86
WDC World Championship 1995
105–106
WDC World Championship 1996 116
World Matchplay 1994 96, 98
World Matchplay 2000 192–194
World Matchplay 2002 236–237

Hall, Dave 275
Hancock, Alec 52
Hankey, Ted 179
Harding, Reg 164, 170
Harrington, Rod
  Battle of the Champions 129
  BDO ban 139
  'Big Breakfast' stunt 161–162
  darts players as athletes 249
  Golden Harvest North American Cup
  307
  head-to-heads 173
  loss of earnings through BDO ban 147
  PDC World Championship 1998 155,
  156
  PDC World Championship 2000 182
  PDC World Championship 2001
  204–205
  pro-am golf 187
  Rotterdam drinking incident 69
  Samson Darts Classic 83
  strong competitor 226
  walk-ons 102
  WDC policy statement 78–79
  WDC World Championship 1995 106

WDC World Championship 1996 113
World Grand Prix 1998 162, 262
World Grand Prix 1999 171, 173
World Matchplay 1995 110
World Matchplay 1997 133
World Matchplay 1998 159–161
World Matchplay 1999 171
World Matchplay 2000 190
World Matchplay 2001 20
World Pairs Championship 1995 111
Harvey, Jamie
  BDO ban 138
  Irish Masters 2000 187
  managed by Cox 56
  Samson Darts Classic 83
  WDC policy statement 78–79
  WDC World Championship 1994 86
  World Matchplay 1994 95
  World Matchplay 2000 190
  World Matchplay 2001 207
Hatton, Matthew 291
Hatton, Ray 269
  father figure for Taylor 294
  Taylor suffering from exhaustion
  291–292
Hatton, Ricky
  boxing training 250
  dedication to sport 316
  friendship with Taylor 290–292
  Taylor's charity darts 310
  Taylor's nine-darter 269
  UK Open 2003 314
  World Matchplay 2002 237
Hawkins, Sam 73, 80, 134
Hearn, Barry
  admiration for Taylor 293–294
  becoming Taylor's manager 219
  Las Vegas Desert Classic 2002 277
  managing sports stars 293
  marlin fishing trip 281
  Matchroom Sport company 174
  PDC chairman 292–293
  Taylor's head-to-head with Barneveld
  177
  Taylor's nine-darter 269
Helms, Phil 90
Helms, Steve 90
Hendry, Stephen 166, 184, 230
  admiration for Taylor 316

Hewitt, Eamonn 186
Hickling, Dennis 47, 59
Hitchcock, Joe 248
Hoad, Lew 71
Hoddle, Glenn 83
Holden, Mark 239
Holmes, Eamonn 179
Holmes, Jack 126
Hopkins, Rory 96, 166
Howat, Chrissie 187, 229, 230
Hughes, Simon 233–234
Humperdinck, Engelbert 274
Hurley, Dave 84, 96
Hutton, Len 184

Inglis, Cliff
  1001 world record 286
  exhibition darts 53–54
Irish Masters 2000 186–190

James, Jesse 253
Jenkins, Andy
  Golden Harvest North American Cup
    2003 309
  Las Vegas Desert Classic 2002 278
  PDC World Championship 2002 227
  World Grand Prix 2001 211
  World Matchplay 1997 132
  World Matchplay 2001 207
Johns, Chris
  Canadian Open 1988 43
  Devon darts match against Taylor 25
  pulling out of WDC 82
  Samson Darts Classic 83
  WDC policy statement 78–79
Jollees nightclub 8, 28, 38, 45
Jones, Derek 36
Jones, Phil
  BDO meeting 80
  PDC World Championship 2002 230
  WDC World Championship 1994 86
Jones, Wayne 36
Jordan, Michael 276
Judge, Peter 102
Justice, Nigel
  PDC World Championship 2001 202
  World Matchplay 1995 110
  World Matchplay 2000 191
  World Matchplay 2001 207

Keane, Roy 253–254, 316
Kelly, Frank 189
King, Gayl 202–203
Kirby, Tom 97
Knowles, Tony 51

Langworth, Brian 41, 173
Lanning, Dave
  bet on Taylor's nine-darter 2
  classic matches 104
  Lowe's nine-darter 265–266
  News of the World Championship 1997
    126
  O'Regan stories 196
  PDC World Championship 1998 158
  PDC World Championship 1999 163,
    167
  PDC World Championship 2002 227,
    229, 231–232
  PDC World Championship 2003
    300–301
  Taylor as sporting legend 184
  Taylor's 10th world title 233–234
  Taylor's head-to-head with Barneveld
    178
  Taylor's nine-darter 2, 268
  Taylor's playing style 112
  UK Masters 1992 76
  views on Burgess 163
  WDC World Championship 1994 86
  WDC World Championship 1997
    118–119
  World Grand Prix 2001 209
  World Matchplay 1994 96, 98
  World Matchplay 2000 194
  World Matchplay 2002 236
Las Vegas Desert Classic 2002 273–281
Lazarenko, Cliff
  BDO ban 138
  commercial breaks 86
  drinking during matches 242,
    249–250, 251
  Embassy World Professional Darts
    Championship 1990 47
  finely tuned athlete 199
  playing for England 59
  playing style 258, 261
  running bar at Crown pub 8
  Taylor's admiration for 24

television commentator 186–187
WDC policy statement 78–79
wibbles 258
World Grand Prix 2002 238
World Matchplay 1995 110
Lee, Dave 35
Lennard, Bill 126, 254
Lewis, Dave 251, 303
Lewis, Lennox 206, 272
Lim, Paul
  Embassy World Professional Darts
    Championship 1994 205
  nine-darter 238, 266
  World Matchplay 1995 110
Lloyd, Colin
  darts clinic 296
  Las Vegas Desert Classic 2002 279
  PDC World Championship 2002
    228–229
Locke, Peter 25, 34
Lomu, Jonah 206
Longthorne, Joe 95–96, 191, 281
Lord, Stefan 128, 254, 265
Lowe, John
  BDO ban 77, 82–83
  comments on WDC/BDO dispute 146,
    148–149
  criticized by George 148
  discouragement for Taylor 51
  Embassy World Professional Darts
    Championship 1978 45
  Embassy World Professional Darts
    Championship 1979 45
  Embassy World Professional Darts
    Championship 1982 108
  Embassy World Professional Darts
    Championship 1985 155
  Embassy World Professional Darts
    Championship 1990 47, 51
  Embassy World Professional Darts
    Championship 1992 65
  Europe Cup 1990 59
  Europe Cup 1992 77
  head-to-heads 173
  Irish Masters 2000 189
  News of the World Championship 126
  nine-darter 265–266
  PDC World Championship 1999 164
  picketing Embassy tournament 85

  playing for England 59
  playing style 105–106, 255, 256–257,
    261
  pro-am golf 187, 189
  professionalism 249
  Samson Darts Classic 83
  shape of darts 254
  Taylor's admiration for 24
  WDC policy statement 78–79
  WDC World Championship 1995
    103–106
  WDC World Championship 1996 113
  World Cup 1991 64
  World Grand Prix 1998 162
  World Grand Prix 2001 210–211
  World Matchplay 1984 265–266
  World Matchplay 2000 191
  World Matchplay 2002 235–236
  world title ambitions 225
Lowe, Ted 264
Lowy, Richard 272–273

Mackay, Alex 307
Manley, Peter
  bad behaviour 232–233
  Irish Masters 2000 187
  Las Vegas Desert Classic 2002 279
  PDC World Championship 1999
    167–168
  PDC World Championship 2000 182
  PDC World Championship 2001 202
  PDC World Championship 2002
    229–233
  playing style 255
  shape of darts 254
  World Grand Prix 1998 162
  World Grand Prix 1999 171
  World Grand Prix 2000 197
  World Matchplay 1999 171
  World Matchplay 2001 206–207
Manning, Mick
  PDC World Championship 2000 182
  World Matchplay 1997 133
  World Matchplay 2001 207
Mardle, Wayne
  darts players as athletes 250
  heavy scorer 113
  Las Vegas Desert Classic 2002
    277–278

Mardle, Wayne – *cont.*
  PDC World Championship 2003
    297–298, 301
  world title ambitions 225
Markovic, John 83
Marley, Bob 182
Martin, Jonathan 82
Mason, Chris
  commercial breaks 86
  Irish Masters 2000 186, 190
  PDC World Championship 2002 227
  Quadro board 84
  Taylor's nine-darter 1–4, 266–268
  WDC World Championship 1997
    118
  World Grand Prix 2000 197
  World Matchplay 1998 160–161
  World Matchplay 1999 171
  World Matchplay 2000 191, 192
  World Matchplay 2002 235
  World Pairs Championship 1996 117
Massey, Kenny 20–21
Masson, Peter, 59
Matthews, Stanley 51, 184
Mawson, Gary
  World Grand Prix 1998 163
  World Matchplay 1997 133
McCarthy, Dennis 189
McClaren, Tommy 253
McCoist, Ally 32
McColl, Isabella 218, 220
McCollum, Steve 205
McKenna, Jack
  Lim's nine-darter 266
  World Grand Prix 2002 238–239
McKenzie, Keith 76
McMenamen, Peter 140
Mitchell, Kevin 202
Monk, Colin 155
Moody, Roger 57–8, 96, 82
Morgan, Ceri 34
Murphy, Jack 189

News of the World Championship
  1997 126–129
  history of 125–126
Nichol, George 288
Nixon, Malcolm 175
North American Open 1991 63

North Staffordshire Royal Infirmary 27,
  58
Norvelle, Duncan 75, 95
Nye, Andy 189

O'Donoghue, Mick 186
O'Neill, Sir Neil 195
O'Regan, Tommy 196
O'Shea, John Joe 78
Ovens, Denis
  Canadian Open 1988 42
  Las Vegas Desert Classic 2002 279
Owen, Dave 311
Owens, Jesse 230

Painter, Kevin
  darts players as athletes 250
  heavy scorer 113
  Las Vegas Desert Classic 2002 278
  PDC World Championship 2002
    227
  PDC World Championship 2003 301
  Taylor's nine-darter 3
  World Grand Prix 2000 196
  World Grand Prix 2001 209–210
  World Matchplay 2002 235
  world title ambitions 225
Palfreyman, Lee
  Las Vegas Desert Classic 2002
    279–280
  UK Open 2003 312
Part, John
  Battle of the Champions 129, 131
  charity darts 310–311
  Embassy World Professional Darts
    Championship 1994 205
  Golden Harvest North American Cup
    2003 307–309
  Las Vegas Desert Classic 2002
    278–279
  PDC World Championship 2001
    205–206
  PDC World Championship 2002
    228–229
  PDC World Championship 2003 292,
    300–303
  professionalism 249
  UK Open 2003 313
  World Grand Prix 2002 239–240

World Matchplay 1997 132
World Matchplay 2001 207
World Matchplay 2002 235–238, 296
Payne, Tony 61
PDC see Professional Darts Corporation
Peel, Ronnie 41
Phillips, Martin 61, 65
Pike, Jim 248
Platts, Daniel 12
Potter, Bob 85
Potts, Mr Justice 137
Priestley, Adam 110
Priestley, Dennis
  admiration for Taylor 183
  Battle of the Champions 131
  BDO ban 139
  British Classic 1997 134
  Embassy World Professional Darts
    Championship 1991 61, 100
  eyesight problems 183
  family man 100
  friendship with Taylor 100–101, 123
  head-to-heads 173
  PDC World Championship 1998
    157–158
  PDC World Championship 2000
    182–183
  playing style 66, 122–123, 255–256,
    258, 260
  professionalism 249
  Quadro board 84
  refusal to play BDO county darts 147
  Samson Darts Classic 83
  strong competitor 226
  teaming up with Taylor 61, 100–101
  walk-ons 102
  WDC policy statement 78–79
  WDC World Championship 1994 85,
    87
  WDC World Championship 1995
    103–104
  WDC World Championship 1996 113,
    115
  WDC World Championship 1997
    122–124
  wibbles 258
  World Grand Prix 1999 171, 172
  World Grand Prix 2000 197
  World Matchplay 1994 98–99
World Matchplay 1995 110
World Matchplay 1997 132
Priestley, Jenny 100, 110
Prince, Jimmy 81
Professional Darts Corporation
  BBC documentary 148
  creation of 144
  criticized by George 147, 148
  enhanced world circuit 150
  Hearn appointed chairman 292–293
  PDC World Championship 1998
    155–158
  PDC World Championship 1999
    162–168
  PDC World Championship 2000
    181–183
  PDC World Championship 2001
    201–206
  PDC World Championship 2002
    226–233
  PDC World Championship 2003
    297–302
  players dropped from England squad
    149
  rift with BDO 71
  Taylor's head-to-head with
    Barneveld 174
  UK Open 2003 311–314
Pyke, Stuart 291

Raby, John 81
Ramsey, Sir Alf 30
Raw, Steve 117
Rawlinson, Alf 24, 39
Rawlinson, Dorothy 24, 39
Rawlinson, Yvonne
  see also Taylor, Yvonne
  birth of Lisa 26–27
  Blake Street house 27
  darts-playing skills 24
  Devon darts match 24–25
  marriage to Phil 39
  meeting Phil 22
  oche in bedroom 30
  Phil called up by Staffordshire 33
  Phil turning professional 37
  Phil's first darts 29
  pregnacies 26–27
  working as fettler 24

Reddington, Tom 126
Redford, Robert 274
Rees, Leighton
  absence from WDC World
    Championship 83
  classic matches 104
  darts players as athletes 249
  drinking during matches 249–250
  Embassy World Professional Darts
    Championship 1978 45
  Embassy World Professional Darts
    Championship 1979 45
  founder of television darts 196
  head-to-heads 173
  News of the World Championship
    126
  playing for Glamorgan 34
Reeves, Keanu 274
Reid, Mike 87
Reynolds, Paul 41
Riley Arms 9, 20
Robertson, Marcus 79, 82
Rosewall, Ken 71
Ross, Alex 118
Roy, Alex 190, 207
Rutter, Sean
  friendship with Taylor 175–176
  indecent assault court case 218–219
  Taylor's DIY activities 304
  World Grand Prix 2001 209

Saggar Makers pub
  origin of name 303–304
  stage set for Taylor 251
  Taylor's practice sessions 19, 89, 226,
    303–304
Sakamoto, Mr 284–285
Samson Darts Classic 83–84
Savage, Randy 114
Scholten, Roland 155
  Las Vegas Desert Classic 2002 280
  nine-darter 269
  support for Taylor 302
  World Grand Prix 2001 211–212
Schoofs, Ad 174–175
Shane, Paul 75
Sharp, Ronnie
  Embassy World Professional Darts
    Championship 1990 47

Embassy World Professional Darts
  Championship 1994 205
Shearer, Alan 222
Skau, Per 65
Sky Sports
  Battle of the Champions 129–130
  cameo films 98
  commentary box 97–98
  commentary skills 116
  commercial breaks 86
  enhanced world circuit 150
  expanding coverage of darts 129
  extent of darts coverage 292
  flight camera 257–258
  innovative techniques in darts
    coverage 257–258, 260
  outside broadcast centre 166
  panache in darts coverage 84–85,
    96–99, 152
  support for WDC 82
  Taylor's 10th world title 233
  Taylor's MBE 221
  Taylor's nine-darter 2–3, 269
  UK Open 2003 312
  walk-ons 102–103
  WDC World Championship 1994
    57–58, 84–86
  World Matchplay 1994 96–99
  World Matchplay 1997 132
Smith, Dennis
  dropped from England squad 149
  Las Vegas Desert Classic 2002 279
  PDC World Championship 1998 156
  PDC World Championship 2000
    183
  PDC World Championship 2003
    299, 301
  UK Open 2003 312–313
  World Grand Prix 2001 211
  World Matchplay 1997 132
  World Matchplay 2001 207
Smith, Giles 133, 152, 169, 192, 241,
  296
Smith, Lionel 30
Smith, Rab 288
Snow, John 141
Spiolek, Kevin
  Embassy World Professional Darts
    Championship 1993 78

PDC World Championship 1998 156
WDC policy statement 78–79
Stelling, Jeff 156, 276
Stewart, Russell 47
Stoddart, Graeme
  BDO ban 139
  competing against King 202–203
  PDC World Championship 2000 182
  PDC World Championship 2001
    202–203
  World Matchplay 1998 160
Stone, Paul Aaron 119
Stubbs, Ray 170
Sturt, Vince 180
Summers, Lidia 166
Sutherland, George
  charity darts MC 311
  Mister Darts incident 288–289
  PDC World Championship 2003 296
  recruited by Taylor 287–289
  support for Taylor 289–290, 294
  Taylor's nine-darter 268
  Taylor's trip to Wick 307
  trip to Tokyo 284–285

Taylor, Chris (son) 223, 314, 315
  birth of 26–27
  drinking in Saggar Makers 19, 303
  working as butcher 9
Taylor, Doug (father)
  coconut-shy incident 14
  cricketing skills 13–14
  death of 134–136
  Devon darts match 24–25
  honesty 92
  Mill Hill house 13
  ouija board incident 93
  Phil's marriage to Yvonne 39
  Phil's near-drowning incident 11
  playing darts at Riley Arms 20, 29
  publicans' course 91
  redundancy 89
  running Cricketers Arms 92
  support for Phil 41
  television without electricity 13
  trip to Lourdes 135–136
  Tunstall house 10–11
  work in Potteries 11–12
  love of pubs 19–20

Taylor, John 79, 82
Taylor, Kelly (daughter) 274, 314
  birth of 27
Taylor, Lisa (daughter) 223, 314, 315
  birth of 26–27
  trip to America 63
Taylor, Liz (mother)
  managing family finances 12–13
  Mill Hill house 13
  miscarriages 11
  Ouija board incident 93
  Phil's bad language 42
  Phil's marriage to Yvonne 39
  Phil's near-drowning incident 11
  television without electricity 13
  trip to Lourdes 135–136
  Tunstall house 10–11
  white wool outfit for Phil 14–15
  working life 11
Taylor, Nathalie (daughter) 269, 274,
    315
  birth of 27
Taylor, Peter 35
Taylor, Phil
  10th world title 232–234
  attempt at 1001 record 285–286
  avoiding publicity 226
  bad language on oche 42, 45
  Battle of the Champions 129–131
  BDO ban 77, 80–82
  birth of 10
  births of children 26, 314–315
  Blake Street house 10, 27
  Bradwell house 200
  breaking Bristow's record 158–159
  Bristow as mentor 34, 48–50, 125
  Bristow's motivational psychology 32,
    34–35, 43–44, 48–50, 64
  British Classic 1997 134
  Burslem Central team 29–31
  Burslem knock-out title 41
  butcher's boy 18
  camper van 8, 101
  Canadian Open 1988 42–43
  capped by England 58
  career highlights 319–323
  ceramic turner 23, 36–37
  charity exhibitions 27, 58, 81–82,
    310–311

Taylor, Phil – *cont.*
  childhood 12–17
  church green incident 101
  classic matches 104–105
  cocky attitude 20–21, 47, 66
  college course 22–23
  commentating with Waddell 211–212
  commercial breaks 86
  contribution to WDC legal costs 142, 147
  cost of playing for England 60
  Cox becoming manager 54–55
  Crafty Potter nickname 47, 83
  Cricketers Arms 8, 89–99, 111, 200
  Dart Mate 271, 273, 275
  darts Grand Slam 181–182, 192
  darts players as athletes 199–201, 249–252
  death of father 134–136
  decision to turn professional 36–38
  Denmark Open 1991 63
  depressed by WDC/BDO rift 138
  Derbyshire Open 42
  desire to live in Spain 316
  Devon darts match 24–26
  diet 201
  DIY activities 304
  doing up old cars 38–39
  dropped from Huntsman team 31–32
  dropped from Staffordshire A team 77
  earnings 147, 176, 316
  Embassy reception incident 68
  Embassy video incident 74, 149
  Embassy World Professional Darts Championship 1990 45–48, 50–52, 55
  Embassy World Professional Darts Championship 1991 60–61
  Embassy World Professional Darts Championship 1992 63, 64–68
  Embassy World Professional Darts Championship 1993 78
  equalling Bristow's record 123–124
  Europe Cup 1990 59–60
  Europe Cup 1992 77
  exhibition darts 53–54, 61–62, 113–114, 184–185
  first big-money tournament 33
  first darts 29
  first serious darts playing 20–21
  fitter's mate 18–19
  Flowers as manager 52, 54
  formation of World Darts Council 73
  friendship with Cox 294
  friendship with Croft 73–74
  friendship with Hatton 290–292
  friendship with Priestley 100–101, 123
  ghost incidents 8, 13, 93–95, 207
  given darts by Bristow 66, 260
  giving away winning darts 233
  Golden Harvest North American Cup 2003 307–310
  green glitter cape 15, 114, 115
  handling pressure 159
  head-to-head with Barneveld 173–180
  Hearn as manager 219, 293–294
  hero in Stoke 51–52
  high-five incident 121, 224–225
  Huntsman team 31–32
  impoverished background 10–15, 27, 33–34
  indecent assault court case 4, 213–221
  Irish exhibitions 184–185
  Irish Masters 2000 186–190
  'I've Got the Power' theme tune 2
  Jollees nightclub 8
  journalists' darts clinic 296
  lack of public recognition 56–58, 106
  Las Vegas Desert Classic 2002 273–281
  Lifetime Achievement Award 310
  Lincolnshire Open 41
  love of family 100, 314–315
  Malta Open 1990 60
  marlin fishing trip 281–284
  marriage to Yvonne 39
  MBE withdrawn 4–5, 221–222
  media coverage of achievements 152–153, 164–165, 202, 233–234
  meeting Bristow 29
  meeting Cox 54–55
  meeting Yvonne 22
  Mill Hill house 9, 13
  motivating forces 210, 224–225
  moustache 66

near-drowning incident 11
nerves 42
News of the World Championship 1997
    126–129
nine-darter 1–4, 266–269
North American Open 1992 63
oche in bedroom 10, 30–31
PDC World Championship 1998
    155–158
PDC World Championship 1999
    163–168
PDC World Championship 2000
    181–183
PDC World Championship 2001
    201–206
PDC World Championship 2002
    226–233
PDC World Championship 2003
    296–302
playing at Riley Arms 9
playing for England 59–60
playing style 66, 112–113, 255–256,
    260–261
Port Vale supporter 252–253
Potteries background 7–10
Power nickname 101–102
practising at Saggar Makers 226,
    303–304
practising with Bristow 40, 46, 78
professionalism 153–154, 201,
    248–249
Quadro board 84
question-and-answer sessions 62,
    242–245
recruiting Sutherland 287–289
refusal to play BDO county darts 147
returning home from airports 63–64
Rotterdam drinking incident 69–70
rows with Bristow 49
Samson Darts Classic 83–84
schooldays 15–17
shape of darts 255
Sky commentary box 97–98
Sneyd Arms 21–22
sponsored on world circuit by Bristow
    35–36, 38, 41–44
sponsors 113, 118, 201, 305
sporting legend 184, 229–230
Staffordshire team 30, 33–35

starting to play darts 16
studying shot-outs 32
suffering from exhaustion 236–238,
    291–292, 295–296, 302
suicidal 4, 219
Super Slam 240–241
tattoos 66
tea drinking 62–63
teaming up with Priestley 61,
    100–101
television without electricity 13
tour of China 272–273
training regime 200–201, 251–252,
    295–296
trip to Lourdes 135–136
trip to Tokyo 284–285
trip to Wick 307
UK Masters 1992 76
UK Open 2003 311–314
Unicorn darts 272
unorthodox England outfit 58
Vanroy job 22–23
views on alcohol at darts matches 47,
    201, 249–251
views on Bristow 24, 29, 43–44,
    48–50, 132, 242
views on future darts stars 278–279
views on George 243–245
views on Waddell 242–243
views on Warriner's jealousy
    299–300, 305–307, 317
views on WDC/BDO dispute 146–149
views on women's darts 203
visit to 10 Downing Street 271–272
visiting Wilson 112
Waddell screaming about nine-darter
    262–264
Waddell's tour of Potteries 7–10
walk-ons 119
WDC policy statement 78–79
WDC World Championship 1994
    57–58, 84–87
WDC World Championship 1995
    102–107
WDC World Championship 1996
    113–116
WDC World Championship 1997
    118–124
weight loss 225, 227, 295

Taylor, Phil – *cont.*
  weight training 21
  white wool outfit 14–15
  wibbles 258
  winning psychology 252
  work ethic 11–12
  World Cup 1991 64
  World Grand Prix 1998 162, 262–263
  World Grand Prix 1999 172–173,
    175–176
  World Grand Prix 2000 195–197
  World Grand Prix 2001 208–212
  World Grand Prix 2002 238–240
  World Masters 1990 60
  World Matchplay 1994 95–99
  World Matchplay 1995 102, 110–111
  World Matchplay 1996 116–117
  World Matchplay 1997 132–133
  World Matchplay 1998 160–161
  World Matchplay 1999 170–171
  World Matchplay 2000 190–194
  World Matchplay 2001 206–208
  World Matchplay 2002 234–238
  World Pairs Championship 1997 154
  World Pairs Championship 1995 111
  World Pairs Championship 1996 117
  world title ambitions 124, 225, 314
Taylor, Yvonne
  see also Rawlinson, Yvonne
  births of children 315
  Blake Street house 224
  buying Cricketers Arms 90
  Cox appointed Phil's manager 55
  darts-playing skills 40–41
  Hayward's Pickles tournament 44
  indecent assault court case 4, 215,
    216, 218–219, 220
  Las Vegas Desert Classic 2002 274
  North American Open 1991 63
  PDC World Championship 1998 158
  Phil's Lifetime Achievement Award
    310
  Phil's MBE withdrawn 221–222
  Phil's nine-darter 267
  Phil's training routine 252
  Phil's weight loss 225
  practising with Phil 40–41
  pregnancies 77
  sale of Cricketers Arms 200

support for Phil 315
Waddell's tour of Potteries 7–10
Tenny, Kendal 275
Thatcher, Margaret 272
Thompson, Tommy 79
Townsend, Rab 307
Turner, Martin 84, 96, 130
Twomlow, Barry 105, 256

UK Masters 1992 76
UK Open 2003 311–314
Umberger, Jerry 63, 103

Vaughan, Johnny 161, 162
Verrier, Gerald 102, 118

Waddell, Bob 244–245
Waddell, Sid
  admiration for Sky darts coverage 85
  Battle of the Champions 130
  bet on Taylor's nine-darter 2
  'Big Breakfast' stunt 161–162
  Black Spot reputation 208–209, 313
  British Classic 1997 134
  classic matches 104
  commentary skills 116
  comments on WDC/BDO dispute 146
  Crown pub 8
  darts players as athletes 199, 249
  discussing darts with Davis 180–181
  Embassy World Professional Darts
    Championship 1979 45
  Irish Masters 2000 186–189
  joining Sky Sports 96
  Jollees nightclub 8
  Las Vegas Desert Classic 2002
    277–280
  News of the World Championship 1997
    126–127
  PDC World Championship 1998
    157–158
  PDC World Championship 1999
    163–164, 167
  PDC World Championship 2001
    202–203
  PDC World Championship 2002
    227–232
  PDC World Championship 2003 298,
    300

police impersonation incident
243–245
pro-am charity darts competition 75
pro-am golf incident 188–189
Samson Darts Classic 83–84
screaming about Taylor's nine-darter
262–264
Taylor as sporting legend 184
Taylor's 10th world title 233–234
Taylor's Crafty Potter nickname 47
Taylor's DIY activities 304
Taylor's head-to-head with Barneveld
175–178
Taylor's MBE 221
Taylor's nine-darter 3, 268
Taylor's views on 242–243
Taylor's weight loss 295, 298
tour of Potteries 7–10
UK Open 2003 312, 313
views on Taylor 62, 163–164,
175–177, 202
WDC World Championship 1994 85
WDC World Championship 1995
104–106
WDC World Championship 1996 116
WDC World Championship 1997
118–123
wibbles 258
World Grand Prix 2001 208–209,
211–212
World Grand Prix 2002 239
World Matchplay 1994 96–98
World Matchplay 1997 133
World Matchplay 2000 193–194
World Matchplay 2002 236–238
World Pairs Championship 1996 117
Walker, Ray 253
Walker, Wayne 9–10, 315
Wallace, Les 155, 288
Walsh, George 173
Walters, Gerry 174
Walton, John 179
Warriner, Alan
  BDO ban 82–83
  British Classic 1997 134
  commercial breaks 86
  Europe Cup 1992 77
  jealousy of Taylor 299–300, 305–307,
  317

lack of public recognition 57
Las Vegas Desert Classic 2002
277–278
managed by Cox 56
PDC World Championship 1999
166–167
PDC World Championship 2000 182
PDC World Championship 2003 299
Quadro board 84
WDC policy statement 78–79
WDC World Championship 1997 118
World Grand Prix 1998 163
World Grand Prix 1999 172
World Grand Prix 2000 197
World Grand Prix 2001 211–212
World Matchplay 1997 133
World Matchplay 2000 190–192
World Matchplay 2001 207
Waters, Peter 189
Watkins, Jim 86
WDC see World Darts Council
Weatherall, John 33, 38, 41
Webb, Mel 234
Westlake, Arnold 73
Whatley, Simon 279, 312
Whitcombe, Dave 24, 44
White, Ian 128
White, Nicky 281
Widdows, Robbie 126, 160
Wilkinson, John 32–33, 37, 51–52
Williams, Freddie 81
Williams, Paul 227, 313
Williams, Robbie 9, 15, 16, 231
Wilson, Jocky
  BDO dispute over player
  management 73
  classic matches 104–105
  dentures 108
  drinking 47, 108–109, 111–112
  Embassy World Professional Darts
  Championship 1982 45, 108, 265
  Embassy World Professional Darts
  Championship 1990 55
  exhibition darts 54
  finely tuned athlete 199
  head-to-heads 173
  managed by Cox 54, 56
  nine-darter 265
  picketing Embassy tournament 85

Wilson, Jocky – *cont.*
  playing style 256
  playing with Sutherland 288
  public recognition 56–58
  retirement from darts 112, 243
  Taylor practising darts 31
  Taylor's arrogant attitude 47
  'Top of the Pops' incident 108–109
  walk-ons 98
  waxworks incident 98
  WDC logo argument 76
  WDC policy statement 78–79
  WDC World Championship 1994
    57–58, 85
  World Matchplay 1994 95, 98
  World Matchplay 1995 109–110
  World Pairs Championship 1995
    111
Wilson, Malvina 112
Winley, Colin 175
Winter Gardens
  Charlie the ghost 207
  crowds 1–2, 97, 110
  glamorous venue 96–97
  Taylor's nine-darter 1–4, 266–268
  World Matchplay 2001 207
Wood, Greg 104
Woods, Tiger 205–206, 226, 230, 234,
  276
World Cup 1991 64
World Darts Council
  BDO ban 80–81, 138–140
  BDO meeting 79–80
  change of name 144
  Embassy reception incident 68
  formation of 73
  glitzy event presentation 75
  legal action against BDO 137–144
  legal costs 142–143

  logo argument 75–76
  need for reformation of sport 56
  organizing World Championship
    82–83
  origins as Darts Council 56
  players suspended by BDO 79
  policy statement 78–79
  settlement of BDO case 144–145
  start of circuit 75
  WDC World Championship 1994
    57–58, 84–87
  WDC World Championship 1995
    102–107
  WDC World Championship 1996
    113–116
  WDC World Championship 1997
    118–124
World Grand Prix
  1998 162, 262–263
  1999 171–173
  2000 195–197
  2001 208–212
  2002 238–240
World Masters 1990 60
World Matchplay
  1984 265–266
  1994 95–99
  1995 102, 109–111
  1996 116–117
  1997 132–133
  1998 160–161
  1999 170–171
  2000 190–194
  2001 206–208
  2002 234–238
World Pairs Championship
  1995 111
  1996 117
  1997 154